# Ideas, Ideologies,
# and Social Movements

# Ideas, Ideologies, and Social Movements

## The United States Experience since 1800

Edited by

## Peter A. Coclanis
## and Stuart Bruchey

University of South Carolina Press

Published in Columbia, South Carolina, by the
University of South Carolina Press

03 02 01 00 99   5 4 3 2 1

Manufactured in the United States of America

"Responsibility, Convention, and the Role of Ideas in History" by Thomas
L. Haskell previously appeared in slightly different form in his *Objectivity
Is Not Neutrality: Explanatory Schemes in History* (Baltimore: Johns Hopkins
University Press, 1998) and is used here by permission. "From Child Labor
to Child Work: Changing Cultural Conceptions of Children's Economic
Roles, 1870s–1930s" by Viviana A. Zelizer previously appeared in slightly
different form in her *Pricing the Priceless Child: The Changing Social Value of
Children* (New York: HarperCollins Publishers, 1985) and is used here by
permission.

**Library of Congress Cataloging-in-Publication Data**

Ideas, ideologies, and social movements : the United States experience
   since 1800 / edited by Peter A. Coclanis and Stuart Bruchey.
      p. cm.
   Includes bibliographical references and index.
   ISBN 1-57003-313-7 (cloth : alk. paper)
   1. Social movements—United States—History. 2. Ideology—United
States—History. I. Coclanis, Peter A., 1952– II. Bruchey, Stuart.
HN57.I33 1999
303.48'4'0973—dc21                                          99-6131

# Contents

Contents

# Editors' Introduction

## Peter A. Coclanis and Stuart Bruchey

The theme of this volume—the role of ideas and ideologies in American social movements—is an intriguing one. It grew out of a project sponsored by the International Commission on the History of Social Movements and Social Structures, which in recent years has studied a variety of topics ranging from youth movements to the parts played by small enterprise and by technology in the economic life of member nations.[1] In this case, the commission originally asked member nations, including the United States, to study social movements in relation to nothing less than cultural values. Obviously, this assignment proved not merely challenging, but well-nigh impossible without further specification. The reason for the difficulty, in retrospect, seems clear: the term "culture" is so widely embracive that scholars from the various member nations around the world were bound to define it differently—unless, that is, guidance was provided.

Recognizing this problem, delegates at the commission's meeting in Madrid in the summer of 1990 proposed that member nations focus their investigations by seeking answers to the following question: what part have *ideas,* and the cultural values aligned in supporting or opposing their realization in social change, played in leading social movements of the last two centuries? Once investigations were focused in this way it would be possible to be selective in the identification of cultural values. For every movement makes use of those facets of culture that promise to hold together the participants in the movement and to energize and inspire them. Music (songs and marches), paintings, poetry, history, perhaps uniforms, elicitations of the memory of historical persons or events ("Remember the Alamo")—all these and many other elements of culture (both highbrow and lowbrow) are drawn upon to provide the cement or glue that binds the participants together.[2] To the extent that surviving sources of information allowed we would attempt to identify these cultural elements of social movements and try to estimate their importance in the success or failure of those movements.

But that is not all one should try to do in order better to understand the role of ideas in social change. Every idea or complex of ideas, together with their associated cultural baggage, attracts individuals and groups with a variety of motives or incentives to promote or retard their advance. For some, there are economic incentives; others hope to profit politically. Still others can only be described as moved by idealistic or ethical considerations. Surely there are persons who act in what they regard as the interests of humanity.

In sum, an understanding of any social movement requires that one take into account factors of many kinds—economic, political, demographic, historical (the "timing of the movement"), ideational, and cultural. What we were after in our inquiries were answers to such questions as these: How do we account for the emergence of the idea as a social phenomenon? How did the idea make its way through the various interests of society? What facets of the culture proved useful in its journey? Detailed answers to some of these questions proved elusive. Historians do not have to be reminded of the limitations imposed by the sources. But all of us addressed questions such as these as best we could, making it possible for our general reporters to point up similarities and differences between nations and seek to explain them. These considerations guided the scholars who contributed the essays on which the American report—delivered in preliminary form in Berlin in 1994 and in final form in Montreal in 1995—was based.

The editors of this volume, who also wrote the American report, began their analysis with the most widely embracive constellations of ideas affecting social movements in the United States, viz., those associated with capitalism—about which we shall say more below. Scholars appear widely in agreement on the close connection between capitalism and individualism, between private property, with its associated freedom of the individual in a market economy to decide how, when, and where to invest his or her savings, and freedom of political dissent. This connection was clearly in the minds of the "founding fathers" of American political independence in the late eighteenth century. As everybody knows, they were deeply influenced by the thought of the English philosopher John Locke, who defined "property" broadly to include life and liberty as well as "estate."[3] Americans tended to favor a narrower definition of property as estate but they nevertheless insisted on the close relationship between property so defined and liberty. As Alexander Hamilton put it, "Adieu to the security of property[,] adieu to the security of liberty."[4] John Adams emphasized the same close relationship. "Property must be secured," he wrote, "or liberty . . . [cannot] exist."[5]

Two additional contributions to this underlying philosophy need to be noted to set the stage for the studies on which both the American report and this volume are based. First, James Madison's famous observation: "as a man is said to have a right to his property, he may be equally said to have a property in his rights." And second, the less famous, but no less important extension of the Madisonian position articulated by the U.S. Supreme Court in 1958, when it opined that citizenship in this country essentially meant "the right to have rights."[6]

Although the term capitalism was not coined until the mid-nineteenth century, the economic and social system it describes came into being well before that time. Precisely when is a matter of debate. Whether capitalism arose in the twelfth century, the sixteenth century, or the eighteenth century is not central to our argument, however. Whichever century one prefers for capitalism's birth—a plausible argument can, in fact, be made for each—in essence, what we are witnessing in parts of the West is a progressive loosening of "traditional," non-market or extra-market constraints on land, labor, and capital, and a concomitant individuation, rationalization, and commercialization of economic and social life. With this loosening we see a release of economic energy and the achievement over time of historically high rates of economic growth and expansion. We also witness, partly as a result, the demystification and secularization of many aspects of cultural and intellectual life, as increasingly individualistic, rational, and commercially minded human beings struggled to reconceptualize and recast their spiritual lives.[7] By the nineteenth century, when our story formally begins, these developments were quite advanced in many, but by no means all parts of the United States.

The ideational manifestations of these changes were legion. First and foremost, of course, we find a more explicit appreciation of and fiercer attachment to private property and greater esteem for other Lockean principles—life and liberty most notably—that extended the economic and civil rights of the individual.[8] Moreover, republican notions of virtue, disinterest, and independence were predicated at least in part on reason and science, and, more especially, on new materialist premises in ethics and epistemology, premises that capitalism underpinned and reinforced. Indeed, the relative benignity of the Enlightenment world view was conditioned, if not determined by the economic gains attending the West's emerging capitalist economy. Finally, if Thomas L. Haskell is correct—and we believe that he is—capitalism and the economic and technological efficiencies arising directly and indirectly therefrom led over time to a new sensibility, to a new perceptual and cognitive style, as it were, which in turn led some members of society to drastically different conclusions about both moral responsibility and the efficacy of human actions in the social realm.[9] Just as slavery, in Lincoln's view, was *somehow* the cause of the Civil War, capitalism, perhaps the most important development in the West in the last quincentennium, was *somehow* the animating or at least enabling force behind virtually all important social movements in our nation's past. On this, the authors of the papers included in this volume would generally agree.

Having staked out such vastnesses, let us backtrack a bit. At this late date it hardly needs restating that historical interpretations based on narrow economism, on the old base-superstructure causal sequence, so to speak, have been laid to rest and go largely unmourned which is all to the good. Against such interpretations, our argument, simply stated, is that capitalism, considered in the broadest systemic terms, provided the economic and ideological support necessary for the various movements treated in this volume—some of which, ironically, arose in opposition to capitalism—to become sufficiently important to merit discussion today.

We do not argue that impersonal forces, abstract imperatives and the like determined precisely which movements would shape our history over time. Nor do we believe that the movements that became prominent did so solely because of the conscious or even unconscious will of a particular class. What we are arguing is that: (a) it is impossible to understand America's historical development without recognizing that the core beliefs, cultural disposition, and behavioral characteristics associated with the capitalist project were widely diffused among Americans almost from the start; and that (b) these considerations made some types of movements much more likely to become important than others.

More to the point, in order to make sense of any aspect of American history—intellectual, social, or otherwise—one must give due weight to our cultural commitments to private property and to individual autonomy, to freedom and to competition, to natural rights and to limited government, and to science and, particularly, to technology. So, too, to our cultural tendencies toward moral righteousness, relatively unbounded rationality, and utility maximization. In our view, such commitments and tendencies shaped the movements we will be discussing, and it is to capitalism, more than to anything else, that these commitments and tendencies, considered in toto, are associated, if not attributable. The fact that Americans have often been subjected to parody, even obloquy, not just for possessing such commitments and tendencies but for embracing them so vigorously testifies—albeit in a backhanded way—to the interpretive power of our argument as well.

Capitalism has evolved over time, of course, and the social movements it has spawned have changed too. Therefore, it is not surprising that the social movements that were prominent in the early nineteenth century differ in certain ways from those that are important today. Such differences are even more understandable in light of the fact that such movements are shaped not just by capitalism but by macro-level contextual factors that may be more or less independent of capitalism—demographic factors, for example—and by micro-level factors specific to individual movements themselves. To study any social movement, let alone differences between social movements, we must know something, then, of each movement's ideology and the "constitutive ideas" of the same. We must know how a movement fared in translating its ideology into a program for action, which ipso facto brings us to organizational questions, and to matters of strategy and tactics.[10] Capitalism. Broad historical context. Particulars. Only then can we begin to understand a social movement, which can be defined for our purposes as a collective (and at least somewhat structured) attempt to bring about—or, conversely, to prevent—social and institutional change, whether radical or incremental.

To reiterate, then, without the income gains, technological innovations, and organizational and administrative efficiencies attending the expansion and elaboration of capitalism, it is unlikely, even implausible, that the social movements treated in this volume would have developed as they did. To be sure, in a narrow consequentialist sense, none of the movements covered here owed its existence exclusively to the changes, however profound, that capitalism evoked in the material world. In a broader sense, however, all of these movements were dependent upon the material framework established by capitalism, and capitalism made possible and rendered meaningful the ideational expressions characteristic of these movements. The capitalist road, in other words, extended well beyond the counting house.

It led, among other places, to epistemological innovations that reflected both a new set of moral conventions and a more capacious view of human agency, the instrumental importance of which innovations, in turn, were magnified by the development of more viable means of effecting social action. As a result, some members of society—relatively few at first, but more as time passed—began to act forcefully to right newly discovered wrongs or to protect long-cherished rights. Although much is still unclear about these developments, we know that they were not completely class-specific. With all due respect to Marx and Engels, then, it was not the bourgeoisie alone that played a most revolutionary part in modern history, but also capitalism considered systemically.

Nowhere is this more apparent than in the United States in the first half of the nineteenth century. As Thomas L. Haskell, to whom we referred earlier, and others suggest in essays included in this volume, the most important social movements in the United States during this period—movements espousing political democratization, evangelical religion, abolitionism, women's rights, and other humanitarian and social reforms—were predicated on new conventions regarding moral responsibility and moral worth, inspired by capitalism above all else.

If scholars, in explaining these movements, have often highlighted more limited, middle-range belief sets—republicanism, liberalism, associationism, the Scottish Enlightenment, for example—it is nonetheless true that it was capitalism that allowed such belief sets to take root. Without the material, ethical, and epistemological freedom capitalism inspired, that is to say, social movements calling for such things as the incorporation of all adult white males into the body politic, conversionism, biblicism, activism, and crucicentrism in religion, the abolition of slavery, and the amelioration of various and sundry social ills would have been unsuccessful and perhaps inconceivable. Indeed, even reactionary social movements such as that which grew up in the first half of the nineteenth century not merely to defend slavery but to promote the institution as a positive good, can be seen at least in part as responses to the material and ideational world capitalism beckoned and helped to bring about.[11]

As capitalism progressed further, moreover, and as hitherto unknown and perhaps undreamt economic and technological possibilities opened up, other social movements, of course, grew to prominence in the United States. These movements often appeared in new institutional forms and employed vastly different strategies (and media) to get their messages heard. Until relatively recently, however, such movements reflected further elaboration of, or at most minor departures from beliefs and conventions characteristic of capitalism since the early nineteenth century. Thus, in formal terms, the same ideational concerns that motivated, let us say, abolitionism persisted in the late nineteenth century and into the twentieth century as well, animating and informing American social movements with decidedly different programs and overtones.[12] What we are saying, essentially, is that the basic mental regime ushered in by capitalism remained sturdy for a long time, and despite decades of attack, still has not been undermined completely.

To say that this ideational regime remained basically intact does not mean that the ideas and beliefs contained therein were completely static over time. If liberal ideology and natural rights philosophy—sometimes clothed in republican outer garb—continued to dominate the American scene, from the late nineteenth century on, attempts were made to broaden and extend the universe to which this ideology and philosophy applied.

As a result, constricted and rather formalistic nineteenth-century conceptions of freedom, independence, and justice—concepts which, along with property, are crucial to the capitalist project—broadened considerably, and social movements arose demanding the inclusion of workers, the young and the old, the disabled and the disadvantaged, and racial and sexual minorities into what one might call the "commonwealth of rights." Nor was this all, as movements sharing the same social beliefs and moral conventions emerged in support of "human rights" around the world and, eventually, the rights of both animals and the nonhuman environment generally. Indeed, as the twentieth century draws to a close, it is becoming increasingly difficult to identify other plausible subjects to place on the rights agenda.[13]

Does this mean that we have reached the end of this particular ideational line? And, if so, should we view this development in positive terms, as did Francis Fukuyama a few years back in his best-seller *The End of History and the Last Man*?[14] Or, rather, in negative terms as many Marxists did a generation ago, and as some despairing communitarian thinkers do today?

Although it is still too early to say for sure, the stirring in recent years of capitalist sectors in the former Soviet bloc, and in China, Latin America, and South and Southeast Asia suggests that the economic, technological, epistemological, and, ultimately, moral journey begun by capitalism centuries ago may not be over yet. Moreover, the journey may not lead to precisely the same destination Fukuyama believes. Even if it did, we would still have our moral work cut out for us so long as glaring discrepancies exist, as they do, between rights talk and rights reality in even the most "advanced" capitalist nations in the world.

The principal purpose of social movements, as we have just seen, is to bring about or to prevent social and institutional change. Following the lead of Thomas Haskell, we have argued that economic and technological forces unleashed by or at least associated with capitalism significantly increased mankind's potential to effect such change, and, in so doing, gradually reshaped moral conventions regarding both human agency and social responsibility. Simply put, as capitalism's advance shrank the realm of necessity in the West, the moral distance between what *is* and what *ought*

*to be* seemed to shrink as well, leading to new conventions regarding the efficacy of reform activity. In his fine essay "Responsibility, Convention, and the Role of Ideas in History," Haskell explores the logic and implications of this change in moral conventions, at once historicizing Western conceptions of agency and responsibility, and providing the material and ideational context for the upsurge in reform sentiment and activity in the West beginning in the early nineteenth century.

In no part of the West was the reform spirit heartier or more earnest than in the United States of America in the pre–Civil War era. Indeed, several generations of scholars have busied themselves cataloguing, chronicling, and positioning movements of one type or another under the American reform umbrella. As a result, we now know a great deal about American branches of important trans-Atlantic movements espousing temperance, penal reform, and the abolition of slavery, for example, and a good deal, alas, perhaps too much, about a number of rather bizarre utopian communities and cults.[15] Aspects of three particularly important nineteenth-century movements, namely, those calling for political democratization, religious reform, and women's rights, are treated in essays in this volume. Each sheds new light on the matters at hand.

In his brisk essay on the democratization of American politics and political culture, Lacy K. Ford, Jr., argues that between the time of the adoption of the Constitution and the outbreak of the Civil War, the U.S. political system was transformed from a "quasi-aristocratic" system to one characterized by "vigorous if immature democratic republicanism."[16] A variety of forces, not surprisingly, was responsible for this transformation, but Ford focuses on the way in which American circumstances—most notably, a very favorable man/land ratio—interacted over time with the rather elastic teachings of classical republicanism to produce an increasingly democratic political order both in the North and in the South.

Ford seeks to demonstrate his central point regarding political democratization by looking at four key issues: (1) the right of suffrage; (2) the apportionment of representation in legislative assemblies; (3) the emergence—and acceptance—of extra-constitutional partisan competition as a defining characteristic of American political culture; and (4) the antebellum controversy over the moral compatibility between slavery and republicanism.[17] According to Ford, forces favoring democratization won a number of victories relating to these issues prior to 1861; even so, he is quick (and correct) to point out that even at the very end of the nineteenth century the process of political democratization was far from complete in the United States.

If the American political order was democratized in the nineteenth century, verily, it can be said that the new nation's religious order was evangelicized. In religion as in politics, moreover, ideas associated with the Enlightenment proved indispensable to change. According to Mark Noll, one particular strain of Enlightenment thought, the "supernatural rationalism" characteristic of the Scots, was particularly important to nineteenth-century American evangelicalism.[18] Lacking the anticlerical dimension associated, for example, with the French Enlightenment, the "Didactic Enlightenment" of the Scots allowed peoples steeped in the world of Locke and Newton to link their belief in reason with their belief in God in what Noll, drawing from T. D. Bozeman, calls a "'Baconian' approach to the faith."[19] This linkage was to endure for much of the nineteenth century before being severed, perhaps irreparably, by Darwinism and the rise of objectivist science.

Enlightenment ideas informed the women's movement in nineteenth-century America as well. In her essay, however, Ruth Nadelhaft focuses not on the role of the Scots but on familiar Lockean ideas—liberalism, individualism, and natural rights—particularly as reflected in the writings of Mary Wollstonecraft, whose 1792 work *A Vindication of the Rights of Woman* Nadelhaft views as the urtext of American feminism. Indeed, to Nadelhaft, Wollstonecraft's ideas and insights—her prescient argument against biological essentialism, for example—helped to create the theoretical underpinnings that have supported the American women's movement for two hundred years and in some ways still support it today.

To say that the movements discussed above were ideological expressions of capitalism is not to suggest that this is all that they were. Clearly, democratization, evangelicalism, and feminism each had complex and disparate ideological roots, as we have just seen. The traditions animating American workers were equally diverse. According to Gary Gerstle, a congeries of ideas associated with republicanism, liberalism, socialism, and so-called industrial democracy all found their way into the ideology of American labor. To Gerstle, however, the broad principles arising therefrom—liberty, equality, democracy, and the like—were always grounded in and given structural coherence by another lesser-known "ism": Americanism. Indeed, it was Americanism, a rationalist ideology at once suspicious of governmental power and possessed of an avidly proprietary notion of independence, that has distinguished—some would say distorted—American labor ideology over time.

As capitalism evolved in the United States in the latter part of the nineteenth century, it not only created the conditions necessary for the emergence of a labor *movement* in this country, but those necessary, if not completely sufficient, for the emergence of a variety of other movements as well, including those calling, however faintly at first, for the protection and promotion of the rights of children and the elderly. More to the point, with urbanization and industrialization, the very young and the very old saw their economic roles diminish considerably, and this decline begat movements calling for these groups' social and moral revaluation. As a result of such movements, children, for example, have gradually been "repositioned" in American society, most notably through their removal from our increasingly commercialized economy. Moreover, they were, thus, transformed from economic assets into emotional assets, economically worthless, as it were, but emotionally priceless. This transformation, and the broad movement supporting it, are the subjects of the provocative essay by Viviana Zelizer included here.

The same basic forces that reduced the economic role of children in the late nineteenth century affected the elderly in a similar way, leading by 1900 or so to a significant decline in their status. Over the course of the twentieth century, however, a number of groups have promoted the rights of the aged, often with considerable success, as Eleanor Bruchey points out. Since the 1960s, in fact, advocates for the elderly, espousing liberal, rights-based ideologies for the most part, have succeeded in dramatically redistributing public resources toward older Americans, who have never had it so good, at least in material terms, in our nation's entire history.

Urbanization and industrialization affected others besides children and the elderly, of course. The imperatives of large-scale, assembly-line production—what Marx referred to as machinofacture—led, for example, to a surge in demand for unskilled factory labor in the late nineteenth and early twentieth centuries, which demand was met in large part by immigrants. In his essay, Reed Ueda sheds light on the identity, beliefs, and behavior of these newcomers to American shores. He does so by focusing closely on a single question, that of naturalization.

Over the years, scholars from a variety of disciplines have shown that the initial decision to immigrate generally reflected rational calculation on the part of migrants, most of whom came from southern and eastern Europe during this period. Much less work has been done, however, on the factors that led some migrants, once in this country, to pursue naturalization. Employing his own data relating to Boston immigrants, Ueda demonstrates that the decision to pursue naturalization, like the decision to immigrate, was a rational one, reflecting strategic assessment of individual and family interests. According to Ueda, then, interest, strategy, and calculation explain much about both the naturalized and their worldview. With this in mind, the idea that various and sundry European immigrants would buy into what Gerstle calls "Americanism" seems not merely plausible but entirely understandable.

Just as immigrants flowing into the United States have transformed this country over the years, ideas flowing out of the U.S. have helped to shape, if not to transform the world. This point can clearly be seen by looking at an issue much in the news: human rights. Although today there are other, competing conceptions of human rights, the Anglo-American, "Lockean" version, focusing, as Lewis Henkin puts it, on "the individual as a 'rights-holder,'" laid the foundation for them all.[20] Indeed, the "inalienable" rights to life, liberty, and the pursuit of happiness—"property," in Locke's more straightforward language—are once again seen as fresh and vital in our post-socialist human-rights world.

An American can scarcely write the words "human rights" and "United States" in the same sentence without thinking of the long, hard road endured by African Americans in their drive for equality with the majority white population of this country. In his thought-provoking essay on the role of ideas in the civil rights movement, Hugh Davis Graham utilizes so-called resource-mobilization theory to explain how and why the movement succeeded brilliantly between 1955 and the mid-1960s and how and why the movement's record since that time has been spotty at best. That there are many reasons for the civil rights movement's many failures over the past three decades is obvious. Nonetheless, as Graham points out, one reason is certainly related to the fact that the movement's leadership felt constrained by and, thus, moved away from the individualistic, rights-based notion of nondiscrimination, which notion, ironically, had been indispensable to its earlier success. In embracing group-based policy schemes such as affirmative action, that is to say, the civil rights movement appeared to be rejecting Lockean, liberal individualism, an ideational complex associated with this country almost from the start.

The power of liberal individualism is evident even in movements considered "radical" and/or "extreme" by many Americans. The animal rights movement is a case in point. Whether one focuses on the nineteenth-century promoters of "animal protection" or on contemporary devotees of the animal rights philosopher Tom Regan, it is clear that in the United States "rights talk" has been the preferred discourse of people involved in the movement.[21] To be sure, other discourses have mattered at times—one thinks of antivivisectionism in the nineteenth century and of so-called critical anthropomorphism today—but, as James Jasper suggests, the mainstream animal rights movement in America has always been inspired and in some ways limited by the premises, assumptions, and principles of liberal individualism and natural rights.

One movement that at times has attempted to break loose of liberal premises, assumptions, and principles is the modern environmentalist movement, the rather obscure origins of which are sensitively explored in the essay by Donald Worster included in this volume. According to Worster, modern environmentalism was part of the cultural fallout from the first atomic bomb, the dropping of which led an assortment of scientists and social scientists at once to question Enlightenment ideas, particularly the belief in technological progress, and to push for a sense of limits or restraints on man's science-based power over nature. In the quarter century between 1945 and 1970, from Alamogordo to Earth Day, as it were, the American environmentalist movement came of age, and Worster's essay can by read at least in part as a kind of bildungsroman depicting the movement's hero-ic challenge to consumer culture and to bourgeois values in general.

Whether or not the future is as dark and forbidding as many envi-ronmentalists contend is the subject of Giulio Pontecorvo's essay, the final piece in this collection. Calmly and dispassionately blending economic and scientific analysis, Pontecorvo offers a cautiously optimistic forecast of the long-term future of Gaia, a.k.a. Spaceship Earth, particularly if we can bring world population under control. To Pontecorvo, and, indeed, to the editors of this volume, then, it appears likely that the world created and now overwhelmingly dominated by capitalism will endure. For we are hopeful, if not completely confident, that there will someday be as much sense as sensibility in the moral order that capitalism evoked.

# Ideas, Ideologies,
# and Social Movements

# Responsibility, Convention, and the Role of Ideas in History

## Thomas L. Haskell

> It is commonplace—we are all Marxists to this extent—
> that our own society places unrecognized constraints
> upon our imaginations. It deserves, then, to become a
> commonplace that the historical study of the ideas of
> other societies should be undertaken as the indispensable
> and the irreplaceable means of placing limits on those
> constraints.
>
> Quentin Skinner (1969)

The "unrecognized constraints" upon imagination of which Quentin Skinner wrote were those of convention.[1] History is, indeed, one means of bringing such constraints to light, as many besides Marxists can confidently attest. By reading "between the lines" of a historical text, alert to what is not being said because the author felt able to take it for granted, we become aware of differences between the conventions that shape our own thinking and those that prevailed in other eras.[2] Awareness of such differences cannot liberate us from convention—nothing can—but it can earn us a saving measure of maneuvering room vis-à-vis the seductive illusions of originality, intellectual self-sufficiency, and transparency of communicative intent that the present always holds out to us. An awareness of the role that convention plays in our own lives is no guarantee of wisdom, but without it we have no hope of interpreting the discursive practices of other times and places on their own terms. Denying our own dependence on convention, we mistake our own ways for universal ways and experience the Other as an imperfect approximation of ourselves, always obstinately falling short of the good, as currently and locally understood.

Insofar as the history of ideas[3] succeeds in exposing the operation of convention, it unavoidably highlights the limitations of reason, but it need not do so in a mood either of iconoclasm or despair. Hans-Georg Gadamer's chillingly fatalistic assertion that "the self-awareness of the individual is only a flickering in the closed circuits of historical life" contrasts sharply with Skinner's guarded optimism.[4] A critic of Enlightenment excess who remains loyal to its central traditions, Skinner urges us to explore convention's shadowy domain of unconscious habit, presupposition, prejudgment, and prejudice neither to discredit reason, nor to belabor its shortcomings, but in hopes of strengthening its claims within a more defensible perimeter. When successful, a history that aims at elucidating the operations of convention equips us with some of the elementary cognitive tools we need in order to shape our own destiny. It does this even as it complicates our picture of life and gives us a degree of immunity against the "terrible simplifiers," as numerous in our generation as in any other. The prophylactic value of the history of ideas is perhaps greatest at a time such as the present, when the prevailing currents set strongly in the direction of social history. Insofar as harnessing the past to present politics is taken to be history's paramount virtue, and group interests defined in terms of race, class, and gender are believed to constitute a three-tiered royal road to historical understanding, social historians will not tarry long over convention, finding in it little more than a reflex of interest.

Without suggesting that all historians should be historians of ideas, or even that historians of ideas are always sensitive to the workings of convention, my aim in what follows is to set forth some of the problems and possibilities of such an approach through examination of a single example, the "idea" of responsibility. Far from thinking that the approach exemplified here is the wave of the future or that aspiring young historians will find it an expedient career choice, I believe on the contrary that the history of ideas will continue to be uphill sledding in a discipline whose mainstream members will, in all likelihood, continue to define themselves by their discomfort in the presence of "ideas." Possession of a Ph.D. in history is no guarantee of sensitivity to anachronism, any more than it is proof against parochialism or epistemological naïveté. As long as historians continue to flee from theory, confuse description with explanation, and make a fetish of accumulating redundant empirical detail, the approach set forth here will seem to most members of the profession an unduly abstract and exotic enterprise. That means, however, that those who do adopt such an approach will do so out of conviction, not conformist expediency, and in that lies the principal strength of the history of ideas today.

My debt to Quentin Skinner is already apparent. In the interest of brevity, my plan here is to hoist myself up on the shoulders of two other scholars, neither of them historians, who have had penetrating things to say about the conventions that had to prevail before "responsibility" could take on its present range of meanings. The first is Friedrich Nietzsche, who had no qualms at all about asserting the priority of convention over reason, just so long as he secured recognition that both were subordinate to the "will to power." The second is the philosopher Bernard Williams, whose recent book, *Shame and Necessity,* addresses (among other issues) a classic problem: the puzzling absence from ancient Greek culture, in spite of its undeniable philosophical sophistication, of any conception of responsibility capable of sustaining an attack on slavery. Although the judicious balance Williams strikes between the claims of reason and the force of convention has much to commend it, I shall argue that certain amendments might yield a still more satisfying formulation.

"Responsibility" is a word of surprisingly recent coinage. Like "individualism" and "altruism," French imports that entered the English language only in the 1830s, "responsibility" plays such a central role in the form of life we inhabit today that it is not easy to imagine how our ancestors ever got along without it. Yet the word is as young as the United States, its first recorded usage having occurred in 1788, during the debate over the Constitution. *Federalist* paper 63, written by James Madison, speaks of frequent elections as a means of insuring "a due responsibility in the government to the people," and notes that "responsibility, in order to be reasonable, must be limited to objects within the power of the responsible party."[5] "Responsabilité" first appeared in France at about the same time.

Although born under political auspices, the word's meaning has never been confined to politics. This is not surprising, for although the abstract noun "responsibility" was new in 1788, the adjective "responsible" was not. No counterpart either to the noun or the adjective existed in classical Latin, but "responsible" or its equivalents existed in French as early as the thirteenth century, in English by the end of the sixteenth century, and in German by the middle of the seventeenth century. These dates considerably lengthen the word's lineage, yet even they seem surprisingly recent, given the primal quality of the values and practices to which the word refers. Once coined, "responsibility" was easily assimilated to philosophical controversies that had been begun in other terms, such as "free will," "accountability," "answerability," and "imputability." Richard McKeon found the earliest philosophical treatment of responsibility in 1859, when Alexander Bain mentioned it only to recommend an alternative, "punishability." Bain contended that "a man can never be said to be responsible, if you are not prepared to punish him when he cannot satisfactorily answer the charges against him." John Stuart Mill agreed, declaring in 1865 that "responsibility means punishment." By the 1880s, L. Lévy-Bruhl was using the term in a more ambitious way that made it a touchstone for moral inquiry of all kinds, but precisely because the term could be so easily substituted for older alternatives, McKeon concludes that its introduction did little to alter the course of philosophical debate.[6]

The element of continuity should not be exaggerated, however. What is most intriguing about the comparatively short etymological lineage of "responsible" and "responsibility" is the thought that our conceptions of morality and human agency, in which these terms figure so prominently today, may be less a timeless feature of human nature and more the product of changing historical conditions than is commonly recognized. No one would argue that the consequentiality of human choice only began to be noticed in 1788, but it puts no strain on common sense to suggest that the emergence of a new word signifies something new in the lives of those who use it. At the very least we might say that a relationship between persons and events that had hitherto been a comparatively compartmentalized matter, discussed in other terms by theologians and philosophers, took on in these years a sufficiently novel prominence or centrality in everyday political and civil affairs to prompt the adoption of a new word, one sufficiently attractive that it came into wide use, eventually displacing established alternatives. Praise and blame obviously were not new in 1788, but conventions governing their imputation may well have been changing—possibly in response to rising standards of accountability in government, triggered by democratic revolutions in America and France, or more broadly in response to an escalating sense of human agency, fostered not only by political events, but also by economic development and the accelerating pace of technological innovation in societies increasingly oriented to the market.

Developments of this kind, originating far outside the usual orbit of the history of ideas, alter everyday social practices and expectations and thus are liable to change the tacit conventions by which people live and assign meaning to their lives. It was to just such conventions that

Quentin Skinner called attention, but for reasons that differ from mine in one significant way. He was concerned about the danger of misunderstanding historical texts through failure to grasp the context of social and linguistic conventions in which they were written. "An understanding of conventions, however implicit," he argued, is a "necessary condition for an understanding of all sorts of speech act[s]." Texts written in the past obviously pose special problems of interpretation because the passage of time threatens to disrupt the shared conventions on which both author and reader rely. "The success of any act of communication necessarily depends on at least a mutual intuiting by Speaker and Audience of a whole complex of conventions, social as well as linguistic, about what can and cannot be stated, what sorts of meanings and allusions can be expected to be understood without having to be explicitly stated . . . and in general what criteria for the application of any given concept . . . are conventionally accepted as applying in that given situation and society."[7]

When we shift our attention to the subject of this essay, the history of responsibility, sensitivity to the role of convention can help us avert another kind of misunderstanding, one that concerns not the intended meaning of *texts,* but the ethical import of *actions* (and, equally important, *omissions to act).* If the rules for imputing praise, blame, and responsibility (or, to speak generically, moral liability for the consequences of one's acts and omissions) have indeed varied in time, as few historians will doubt and the recent emergence of the very word "responsibility" strongly suggests, then obviously there is a danger that we historians will unwittingly project into the past our own attributive conventions, supposing them to be universal, when in truth they are of recent vintage and therefore not simply or straightforwardly applicable to people who lived prior to their ascendancy.

Although my argument is addressed to the danger of misunderstanding acts and omissions rather than texts, in other ways it closely parallels Skinner's. Thus Skinner warned that "the historians of our own past still tend [perhaps because our own past looks more familiar than a primitive society] to be much less self-aware than the social anthropologists have become about the danger that an application of familiar concepts and conventions may actually be self-defeating if the project is the understanding of the past. The danger in both types of study is . . . that Audience at time two will 'understand' Speaker at time one to have intended to communicate something which Speaker at time one might not or even could not have been in a position at time one to have had as his intention."[8] The parallel danger concerning action and responsibility is that we will retrospectively condemn past actors for failing to live up to a set of obligations that, although familiar and normative in our era, may not have been in place at the time the actors lived. In ethical acts as in communicative acts, the passage of time breeds misunderstanding by occluding past conventions, creating, as it were, a vacuum into which the conventions of our own day rush with a specious appearance of naturalness.

Skinner focused all of his attention on the single sin of anachronism, the better to catechize his readers on rules suitable for its avoidance. But we would do well to remember that anachronism is the twin of ethnocentrism. These two primordial sins against cosmopolitan understanding mark, respectively, the diachronic and synchronic axes between which the entire universe of human affairs is suspended. It makes little difference whether we describe the sin in question as a failure to acknowledge the force of convention, developing through time, or a failure to acknowledge the force of culture, varying from one human community to another. The temporally varying "social and linguistic conventions" to which Skinner called attention are, after all, seamlessly interwoven with the multiple levels of meaning that anthropologist Clifford Geertz was evoking when he called for "thick description." Geertz said that in order to make sense of human conduct we must pay close attention to "webs of significance," "stratified hierarch[ies] of meaningful structures," "piled-up structures of inference and implication," and "socially established structures of meaning." These are the elements of which culture is comprised, and culture is nothing other than convention, frozen at a moment in its development. To be sure, "culture" has in recent decades become the more familiar term for historians as well as anthropologists; some may even think of it as the more inclusive and interesting category, of which convention is only a particular (and perhaps oppressive) part. But "culture" in this nonevaluative, anthropological sense is a twentieth-century neologism that has not yet displaced "convention" in the vocabulary of philosophers. For both Skinner's purposes and mine, "convention" is the more generic and therefore the more resonant and inclusive category.[9]

All three projects have much in common. Geertz worried about "thin descriptions," culturally myopic and therefore incapable of detecting any difference between involuntary tics and meaningful winks. Skinner worried about an anachronistic way of reading texts, one that highlighted "perennial problems" only to lose sight of the shifting meanings that words acquire as language games change from one generation to the next. Transposing their concerns to the realm of ethics, I worry about a facile moralism that in trying to create a more "usable" past, disregards (usually inadvertently) historical changes in the way humans beings have allocated praise, blame, and responsibility. All three of us preach against complacency and warn that convention's grip is too often underestimated, even by professional historians.

One last caveat is in order. If being oblivious to the role of convention has its dangers, so of course do exaggerations of convention's force. This is true in ethnography and textual criticism as well as ethics, but the danger is especially acute in ethics because the very idea of moral responsibility implies the existence of obligations that overleap narrow boundaries of place and time. Exaggerating the force of convention reduces morality to the will-o-the-wisp of social conformity, depriving it of any legitimate force of its own and allowing it no purchase beyond the borders of a particular community at a moment in time. The classic defense against this danger is to invoke, not mere conventions—things of human creation—but absolute standards that are said to be timeless and universal, having their being outside human history altogether. Denying, as it must, history's first lesson of change, this maneuver gets historians nowhere. But neither will it do to run to the opposite extreme, saying that the rules of human conduct change with every passing breeze and are wholly contingent on time, place, and situation. Between the local and the universal there is much middle ground, well suited to human habitation. The trick in achieving balance is to give the devil of convention his due, without abandoning the claims of reason. Balancing acts are, of course, easier to recommend than to perform, but that is no argument for stepping off the wire into the void.[10]

Although Friedrich Nietzsche cared little for balance, he deserves our attention because no one has explored the conventions and presuppositions underlying modern concepts of responsibility with greater insight. He opened the second essay of *The Genealogy of Morals* with an eloquent tribute to responsibility. "To breed an animal *with the right to make promises*," he asked, "is this not the paradoxical task that nature has set itself in the case of man? is it not the real problem regarding man?" Keeping promises is a habit that can only be formed by a human animal that has developed the capacity to remember what it once willed and then act on that memory rather than immediately felt wants. Memory, argued Nietzsche, is a precondition of responsible conduct, yet it obstructs the fulfillment of this moment's desires and is in that sense diametrically opposed to animal good health. Forgetfulness, he contended (in passages strongly suggestive of Freud on repression), is "a form of *robust* health," without which man can experience "no happiness, no cheerfulness, no hope, no pride, no *present*."[11]

However formidable the obstacles, humans have to a great extent become animals with the right to make promises. This seemed to Nietzsche a "remarkable" achievement, a "tremendous labor" of self-overcoming.

Spelling out the cognitive and psychological elements of responsible conduct to show how much was at stake, he put causal thinking at the center of the drama.[12] Keeping promises presupposes not only memory, linking past to present, but also a causal imagination that construes the present as a staging ground for the construction of the future. Promise keepers must not only suspend present impulse and remember what they once willed, but also know how a desired future state of the world can be produced by action undertaken in the present. Promise keeping, Nietzsche wrote, requires

> a desire for the continuance of something desired once, a real *memory of the will:* so that between the original "I will," "I shall do this" and the actual discharge of the will, its *act,* a world of strange new things, circumstances, even acts of will may be interposed without breaking this long chain of will.
>
> But how many things this presupposes! To ordain the future in advance in this way, man must first have learned to distinguish necessary events from chance ones, to think causally, to see and anticipate distant eventualities as if they belonged to the present, to decide with certainty what is the goal and what [are] the means to it, and in general be able to calculate and compute. Man himself must first of all have become *calculable, regular, necessary,* even in his own image of himself, if he is to be able to stand security for *his own future,* which is what one who promises does!
>
> This precisely is the long story of how *responsibility* originated.[13]

Scornful of asceticism, "bad conscience," and all the other signs of "morbid softening and moralization through which the animal 'man' finally learns to be ashamed of all his instincts," Nietzsche nonetheless had immense respect for the early phase of instinctual renunciation that made responsibility possible. He likened the acquisition of causal thinking and calculability to the evolutionary emergence of amphibians. Just as the first animals to give up the supportive buoyancy of the sea had to fight instinct every step of the way and learn by trial and error how to carry themselves erect on land, so in the development of responsibility human animals who were "well adapted to the wilderness, to war, to prowling, to adventure," suddenly found all their instinctual drives "disvalued" and had to rely on "consciousness," their "weakest and most fallible organ!"

The "ripest fruit" of this stupendous development was what Nietzsche called the "sovereign individual," who, having earned the right to make promises, could not help but be aware of his "mastery over circumstances, over nature, and over all more short-willed and unreliable creatures." "The proud awareness of the extraordinary privilege of *responsibility*, the consciousness of this rare freedom, this power over oneself and over fate, has in his case penetrated to the profoundest depths and become instinct, the dominating instinct. What will he call this dominating instinct, supposing he feels the need to give it a name? The answer is beyond doubt: this sovereign man calls it his *conscience*."[14] Ironically, it was this great historical drama—the advent of the responsible, conscientious, sovereign individual, an "animal soul turned against itself" so as to become worthy of "divine spectators"—that inspired Nietzsche's grandiose fantasies about the coming of an overman, a still higher and more God-like specimen of humanity who would exercise his will to power without guilt, thereby rescuing Europe from self-loathing and rendering the choice between good and evil obsolete.[15]

Alexander Bain had linked responsibility to punishment and called attention to the metonymic character of the word. Just as "crown" can stand for royalty and "miter" for episcopacy, so he believed that "response" had come to stand for something more complex: the practice of allowing accused criminals to answer the charges against them before being punished. Nietzsche, for whom responsibility was, in the first instance, at least, a cultural phenomenon rather than a philosophical concept, assigned a more creative role to pain. Etymological evidence persuaded him that punishing offenders because they could have acted differently was a late and subtle form of judgment that would have made little sense to our ancestors. Long before notions of voluntariness and just desserts appeared on the scene, punishment was an expression of unbridled rage, channeled only by a crude equivalence presumed to exist between money and pain. Nietzsche believed that in primitive times creditors unable to collect debts were compensated by giving them license to inflict bodily harm on the debtor, the degree of harm corresponding to the size of the debt. The delight of inflicting pain, he thought, "constituted the great festival pleasure" of primitive man; turned inward and directed against one's own "natural inclinations," the infliction of pain became the source of all the "good" things on which we moderns pride ourselves, including reason and responsibility. "We modern men are the heirs of the conscience-vivisection and self-torture of millennia."[16]

Nietzsche dramatized—some would say overdramatized—the historicity of responsibility, while leaving its chronology wholly indeterminate. Some stages of the (highly conjectural) developmental process he described would have had to occur in prehistoric times, others early in the Christian era, still others much more recently. The most radical of historicists, he was no historian and cared not at all about dates. Since today we still lack anything even remotely approaching a history of responsibility, no one can specify when the various elements of this form of life came into play or how fully it has been embraced by different peoples at different times and places. We have only a few scattered landmarks to help us get our bearings in time.

Max Weber, who read and respected Nietzsche, took the Protestant Reformation of the sixteenth century to be the great watershed between "traditional" and "rational" (or modern) ways of life in Europe. If Weber was right, the ascetic values that largely define responsible conduct in Western culture today were initially cultivated in monasteries and oriented to otherworldly goals, but they marched into the marketplace of everyday life and evolved in close conjunction with capitalism from the time of the Reformation forward. Any thought of a link between capitalism and rising standards of responsibility may seem paradoxical, yet Weber's point was sound: Even though market economies live by the rule of caveat emptor and deliberately shrink responsibility in some dimensions (e.g., the limited liability corporation), they also depend on a norm of promise keeping and cannot thrive without an ample supply of calculating, self-disciplined "economic men" (and women), alert to their interests and acutely attentive to the remote consequences of their conduct. It is among people of just this consequentialist cast of mind that perceptions of responsibility are most likely to flourish.[17] My assumption is not that the market elevates morality, but that the form of life fostered by the market may entail the heightened sense of agency and enlarged causal horizon without which Nietzsche's "long-willed" sovereign individual cannot function, whether for good or evil. The expansive causal imagination that enables the entrepreneur confidently to assume responsibility for constructing a profitable future is a prerequisite for ambitious projects of humanitarian reform, on the one hand, and brutal schemes of self-aggrandizement on the other.

Recent research by social historians suggests that, as a cultural and psychological phenomenon, the ethic of responsibility had not achieved dominion at all levels of European society even as late as the mid-nineteenth century. Middle-class moralists of the Victorian era no doubt indulged their own hunger for amour propre and underestimated the degree to which responsible conduct presupposes economic security, but they were probably not wrong to sense in working-class culture an attitude more fatalistic and more tolerant of irresponsibility than that of their own class. Evangelical Protestants in England certainly felt that they were fighting an uphill battle as they tried to inculcate habits of foresight, repression of impulse, and delay of gratification in working-class populations.[18] "Thinking causally" and anticipating "distant eventualities as if they belonged to the present" are not built into human nature. These traits are no less historical than the rational forms of acquisitiveness that Weber associated with the market and traced back to the worldly asceticism of the early Protestants. Such traits helped constitute the cultural phenomenon that Nietzsche thought so momentous, but the triumph of responsibility may have been more recent than either Nietzsche or Weber recognized—if, indeed, it is complete even today.

Nowhere has the developmental chronology of responsibility been more vigorously debated than in the case of ancient Greece. If there is ample room for disagreement about the timing and the uneven spread of the ethic of responsibility in modern European societies, there has until recently been nearly a consensus about its absence from the world of Homer. In a passage that rivals Nietzsche in eloquence, the Italian writer Roberto Calasso expresses a widespread view when he describes Homer's world as one in which people and events were threaded together by a logic very different from our own:

> Whenever their lives were set aflame, through desire or suffering, or even reflection, the Homeric heroes knew that a God was at work. . . . They were more cautious than anybody when it came to attributing to themselves the origins of their actions. . . . The moderns are proud above all of their responsibility, but in being so they presume to respond in a voice that they are not even sure is theirs. The Homeric heroes knew nothing of that cumbersome word *responsibility*, nor would they have believed in it if they had. For them, it was as if every crime were committed in a state of mental infirmity. But such infirmity meant that a God was present and at work. What we consider infirmity they saw as "divine infatuation" (átë). . . . Thus a people obsessed with the idea of hubris were also a people who dismissed with the utmost skepticism an agent's claim actually to *do* anything.[19]

Calasso's eloquence skates on the edge of exaggeration. Different from us though the ancients were, they did not regard one another merely as playthings of the gods or straws in the wind of fate. For the most part they saw each other as authentic actors and assigned praise and blame accordingly. True, as Calasso says, they left many an opening for divine intervention, but they were not in this respect wholly different from the Christians who came after them, who also found it difficult to reconcile human accountability with divine strength. From Pelagius in the fifth century to Arminius in the seventeenth, devout Christians quarreled about responsibility for sin and salvation in a world ruled by a God whose power was immense—so immense that in the hands of incautious commentators it could seem to crowd human responsibility out of the picture altogether, depriving humans of any rationale for doing good and threatening to make God the author even of sin. How could one credit human choices with making a difference without seeming to limit the limitless sovereignty of God? To that question the response of Aquinas was that "in all things that operate God is the cause of their operating"—yet he never meant to suggest that God's hand guided that of the assassin or the thief. The orthodox formulation, which Aquinas helped devise, was that "providence does not exclude freedom of the will," but words like these only papered over the problem that would finally break the Christian church in two.[20] When Luther and Calvin attacked "good works" and denied that the will could be free, they were recommending in regard to the paramount issue of salvation an attitude similar to that which Calasso says the Greeks displayed in all aspects of life: "skepticism about an agent's claim ever actually to *do* anything."

The difference between the Greeks and ourselves is neither the number of gods they had to accommodate nor the fact that some of their beliefs were contradictory. The past two centuries of secular social thought show that, even in the absence of any god, speculation about freedom and fate never escapes contradiction for long. Rather, the difference lies in the absence or seeming immaturity in Greek culture of concepts such as decision, will, intention, and guilt. In the passage above, Calasso echoes Nietzsche in giving the ancients credit for a certain profundity about the limits of human mastery, a profundity that is easily mistaken for superficiality. Yet even Nietzsche gave some credence to the widespread impression that, when all is said and done, there is something childlike and premoral about the ancients. In its boldest form the idea is that with a few exceptions such as Plato, Aristotle, Socrates, and some versions of the character Antigone, the Greeks were indeed children in a Piagetian tale of moral development, in which we moderns figure as the adults.[21]

This "progressivist" scenario has come under sharp attack from Bernard Williams. In *Shame and Necessity* (1993) he argues on the contrary that "many of the most basic materials of our ethical outlook are present in Homer . . . what the critics find lacking are not so much the benefits of moral maturity as the accretions of misleading philosophy." Although Homer lacked words for "intention" and "decide," the "idea is there," says Williams. Williams concedes that it makes some sense to speak of ancient

Greece as a "shame culture," but he challenges the usual distinction between shame and guilt, suggesting that internalized fear of shame functioned among the ancients in much the same way that the interior goad of guilt is said to operate in more modern psyches. At the heart of his dissatisfaction with the progressivist account are its tacitly Kantian assumptions about the nature of morality. The main thing he thinks moderns find missing in Greek thought is Kant's radical distinction between autonomy and heteronomy, which he considers religious in inspiration and largely illusory in practice. Insofar as the Greeks refused to think of morality as adherence to laws disclosed either by reason or divine illumination, Williams thinks they were not immature, but wise.[22]

Although he does not deny the existence of important differences, Williams highlights the similarity of modern and ancient thinking about human responsibility by suggesting that all judgments of responsibility consist of some combination of four elements: *cause, intention, state,* and *response:* "These are the basic elements of any conception of responsibility." Williams believes that these elements were as apparent to Homer as they are to us, and although Homer combined them in ways that are unfamiliar to us (and often unsuited to the world we now live in), we have no grounds for considering our ways superior: "There is not, and there never could be, just one appropriate way of adjusting these elements to one another."[23]

The first of the four elements, causation, is primary. "Without this," as Williams says, "there is no concept of responsibility at all." Human beings act, and their acts alter an existing state of affairs. Sometimes the alteration is intended, sometimes not. Either way, some may welcome the new state of affairs, but others may deplore it, and when it is deplored a demand may arise for some response from the originating actor. This may be a demand that the actor makes upon himself, or the demand may be made by others, or both. When the new state of affairs is welcomed, the question becomes one of praise rather than blame. In any event there will be interest in the actor's intentions, if for no other reason than to understand what has happened.[24]

These are, Williams admits, "banalities," but "universal" ones, present in any historical or cultural setting. His central point is that although any judgment of responsibility must include these four elements (giving reason some purchase on human conduct *across* boundaries of time and place), there is no one right way of relating them. There are many ways of connecting intention and state with response, many ways of deciding what qualifies as a cause. All four elements are vulnerable to various sorts of skeptical objections and each is elastic enough to shrink or expand with circumstances. Thus in matters of "strict liability," modern tort law does

13

not require the defendant to intend or really even to cause the harm in order to be held liable, but merely to be well situated to prevent it. If pragmatic policy considerations can induce us moderns to shrink two of the four building blocks of responsibility this much, we should not be surprised to find in the thinking of the ancients a similar elasticity in the service of their quite different needs and purposes.[25]

Williams's four-part scheme of analysis is illuminating, and it helps him earn one of the conclusions he aimed at, namely, that at the level of "underlying conceptions" the difference between us and the Greeks may not be as great as the progressivists suppose. But he also wanted to dispel the idea that their moral reasoning was inferior to our own and to do that he knew he needed to present a "philosophical description of an historical reality."[26] Here his success is less complete, for reasons that have to do with the diverging motives of history and philosophy. In his effort to demonstrate the conceptual continuity of responsibility across the ages, Williams empties its constituent elements of any particular content and soars to a high level of abstraction that, although appropriate to most philosophical questions, makes it exceedingly difficult to keep in focus the lived experience of actual historical actors. From this altitude there is little possibility of understanding how conceptions of responsibility change.

Consider slavery, for example. Few differences between us and the Greeks feel more profound than our repugnance for slavery and their unquestioning acceptance of it. Williams's abstract categories leave us with no adequate way of registering this profound difference. Repugnance for slavery and acceptance of slavery entail two very different assessments of responsibility for the suffering of others, but for Williams all such judgments merely rearrange the same four elements: "adjustments" vary while "underlying conceptions" remain the same. This will not do. It terminates inquiry just as things become interesting. A comparably premature termination of inquiry would occur if one were to say that, since poker and bridge are just different ways of arranging the same fifty-two card deck, the two games really come to the same thing. On the contrary: Having chosen to compare poker and bridge, one must look beyond the games' reliance on a common deck of cards and focus on the different rules by which they are played. Likewise, if one wishes to take the historicity of responsibility seriously, as Williams does, then one must recognize that nineteenth-century abolitionists and fifth-century–B.C. Greek philosophers were playing the game of responsibility very differently, and ask what could have produced such a profound change in the rules.

It is revealing that when Williams tackles the problem of change most directly, in his examination of Aristotle's decidedly premodern views on slavery, his timeless four-element conception of responsibility disappears from sight. There is no evidence that Aristotle or anyone else in the ancient world ever felt sufficiently responsible for the suffering of slaves to challenge the institution of slavery. That slaves suffered was common knowledge: To be enslaved, as Williams observes, was to the ancients "the very paradigm of bad luck" or "disaster." But the justice of slavery was seldom discussed, much less questioned, and although Aristotle distinguished himself by considering it worthy of discussion, the conclusions he reached are notoriously ambivalent and inconsistent.[27] He was content to regard some people as "natural slaves." He knew that some actual slaves did not belong in the category of "natural slave," and the enslavement of such persons was therefore in his view "against nature" and "not just." One might think that this remark goes some distance toward closing the gap between ancient and modern, but Williams is quick to admit that the appearance is deceiving. Aristotle, like his contemporaries, perceived in the master-slave relation an implacable necessity that we moderns can only strain to understand. Saying that slavery was "not just," says Williams, was not the same thing for Aristotle and his contemporaries as calling it "unjust." Having summed up the difference between Aristotle's time and ours in terms of a difference (apparent to them but not to us) between "not just" and "unjust," Williams then fails, in my view, to translate that baffling distinction into terms intelligible to a modern mind.[28]

Here is what he says: "Slavery, in most people's eyes, was not just, but necessary. Because it was necessary, it was not, as an institution, seen as unjust either: to say that it was unjust would imply that ideally, at least, it should cease to exist, and few if any, could see how that might be. If as an institution it was not seen as either just or unjust, there was not much to be said about its justice, and indeed it has often been noticed that in extant Greek literature there are very few discussions at all of the justice of slavery."[29] I have no quarrel with Williams's principal point. It is indeed self-indulgent of us to formulate the difference between the ancients and ourselves simply as a matter of their "immaturity." I also think he is onto something important when he asserts that Aristotle and his contemporaries construed slavery in such a way that its existence seemed necessary and its abolition almost literally unthinkable. But Williams's distinction between "not just" and "unjust" cannot carry the weight of his argument, and his ad hoc way of accounting for the ancients' perception of necessity is not adequate to the task he set himself.

Consider each of these two points in turn. In the passage quoted above, Williams credits the Greeks with understanding that slavery was "not just," while reserving for us moderns the view that slavery is both "not just" and also "unjust." What the ancients could have meant by distinguishing between "not just" and "unjust" is never made clear. Perhaps Williams does not think it can be.[30] At one point in the passage quoted above he identifies the modern opinion that slavery is unjust with the view that "ideally, at least, it should cease to exist." Taken by itself, this phrase would seem to imply that the crucial difference between us and Aristotle is that we possess a higher *ideal* of justice that was not available to him. The ambiguous conclusion of Williams's sentence casts doubt on this construal, however, and it is precisely the sort of interpretation he rejected in earlier pages. His stress on the universality and timelessness of the four basic elements constituting judgments of responsibility is but one example of his repeated claim that differences between us and the Greeks "*cannot* best be understood in terms of a shift in basic ethical conceptions of agency, responsibility, shame, or freedom."[31]

In subsequent pages Williams unambiguously reasserts his central claim: The crucial difference between past and present does *not* lie in the ancients' ideals or basic conceptions of justice, which were similar to ours. Instead, the difference lies in their comparative inability to imagine any course of action that would bring about the practical implementation of those ideals. Their bland acceptance of slavery is attributable, then, to what Quentin Skinner might have called "constraints upon imagination," rather than immaturity of judgment or a failure of moral insight as such. The crux of the matter for Williams is that the ancients drew differently the line that defines where the domain of necessity leaves off and human agency begins. In their eyes slavery, though not just, was irremediable. That is a matter of social psychology rather than philosophy, a matter of the limits they perceived to their own collective power of reshaping the world rather than a flawed understanding of what justice would, in principle, require.

Here nuance becomes vital and Williams should be allowed to speak for himself:

> Most people did not suppose that because slavery was necessary, it was therefore just; this, as Aristotle very clearly saw, would not be enough, and a further argument would be needed, one that he hopelessly tried to find. *The effect of the necessity was, rather, that life proceeded on the basis of slavery and left no space, effectively, for the question of its justice to be raised."*
>
> Once the question is raised, it is quite hard not to see slavery as unjust, indeed as a paradigm of injustice, in the light of considerations basically available to the Greeks themselves. . . . We, now, have no difficulty in seeing slavery as unjust: we have economic

arrangements and a conception of a society of citizens with which slavery is straightforwardly incompatible. This may stir a reflex of cultural self-congratulation, or at least satisfaction that in some dimensions there is progress. *But the main feature of the Greek attitude to slavery, I have suggested, was not a morally primitive belief in its justice, but the fact that considerations of justice and injustice were immobilised by the demands of what was seen as social and economic necessity. That phenomenon has not so much been eliminated from modern life as shifted to different places.*

We have social practices in relation to which we are in a situation much like that of the Greeks with slavery. We recognise arbitrary and brutal ways in which people are handled by society, ways which are conditioned, often, by no more than exposure to luck. We have the intellectual resources to regard the situation of these people, and the systems that allow these things, as unjust, but are uncertain whether to do so, partly because we have seen the corruption and collapse of supposedly alternative systems, partly because we have no settled opinion on the question about which Aristotle tried to contrive a settled opinion, how far the existence of a worthwhile life for some people involves the imposition of suffering on others.[32] (Emphasis added.)

In a nutshell, Williams's strategy is to insist on continuity between the Greeks and ourselves at the level of abstract ideals of what justice requires, while conceding that they differ greatly from us in perceptions of necessity and possibility. So necessary did the existence of slavery (and presumably many other features of their society) seem to the ancients, so far beyond the reach of human will did these arrangements appear to lie, that no cognitive "space" was left, effectively, for the question of justice even to be raised. Although he conspicuously avoids using the term, perhaps because of its religious connotations, what he is saying is that the ancients perceived slavery as a *necessary evil.*

This is fine as far as it goes, but it does not go far enough. To say, as Williams does, that "considerations of justice and injustice were immobilised by the demands of what was seen as social and economic necessity" is indiscriminately to lump Aristotle together with thousands of slave owners who sincerely believed, even in the midst of the American Civil War, that their entire way of life, as admirable as any other, depended on the perpetuation of slavery. Necessity is the first resort even of the lowest scoundrel. Williams needs to credit Aristotle with more than this tendentious and self-serving sort of "necessity" in order to make good on his claim that the ancients' moral judgment was not inferior to our own. If the constraints that kept Aristotle from seeing in slavery anything worse than a "necessary evil" boiled down to nothing more than this—an ideological blind spot or "immobilisation" induced by the inconvenience of doing without slave labor—then surely in this regard we moderns would be entitled to feel morally superior and the progressivist interpretation that Williams wishes to deflate would instead be vindicated.

Williams's cryptic observation that perceptions of necessary evil have not been "eliminated" in modern times, only "shifted to different places," is extremely promising, but it begs for further elaboration. He is of course right to insist that we moderns, too, have our "necessary evils." But that must not be allowed to obscure an even more important fact: The domain of necessity is perceived to be far less extensive today than it was in Aristotle's day. Its shrinkage is a dramatic difference between past and present. In that difference, I suspect, lies the grain of truth behind the persistent, but finally implausible progressivist intuition that we, the contemporaries of Adolf Hitler, Joseph Stalin, and Pol Pot, are as a group more mature moral reasoners than the author of the *Nicomachean Ethics*.

*How do "necessary evils" such as slavery come to seem remediable, thus shrinking the domain of necessity and expanding the realm within which the imperatives of responsibility can operate?* My principal complaint is that Williams fails to address this question. To answer it we need a way of thinking about responsibility that candidly acknowledges its historicity without either abandoning reason or falling back on naïve notions of moral progress. Such an approach need not run to the Nietzschean extreme of obliterating distinctions between good and evil, but neither can it embrace a linear narrative of ever closer approximations to some moral law or ideal of conduct that stands outside human history and above convention. We need to admit that moral judgment is only partly systematic (leaving room for equally competent reasoners sometimes to reach conflicting conclusions) and to recognize that, even at its most systematic, moral deliberation takes place within a given framework of assumptions, the possession of which is essentially a matter of "luck," for which individual reasoners deserve little or no personal credit. To be sure, individuals differ greatly, both in their insight into the requirements of morality and in their courage to do what is required. But even the boldest of moral innovators can do no more (it is, after all, a great deal) than revise, extend, rearrange, and apply to new situations an array of conventions that they acquire through inheritance.

No philosopher in the analytic tradition has done more than Williams to take "luck" into philosophical account, and his insistence that past and present differ less in formal prescriptions than in the perceived limits of human agency puts us on the right track.[33] In the remainder of this essay I will propose amending his formulation in two ways: by stressing (even more than he already has) the dependence of all judgments of responsibility on perceptions of causal efficacy, and by noting that causal perception, in turn, cannot help but be largely a matter of social convention, subject to all the vicissitudes of historical change. As we have seen, Williams understands full well that a perception of causal relationship between a person's act or omission and an altered state of affairs is the seed crystal without which judgments of responsibility cannot even begin to take shape. To that I would add only that causation is also the linchpin between history and morality, enabling us to understand why evils once thought to be necessary come to seem remediable as historical developments reconfigure the perceptual universe within which moral actors operate.

Consider a truism of moral philosophy, "Ought implies can." To say that "ought implies can" is, obviously, to say that we do not hold people responsible for doing what they cannot do. Less obviously, the truism also means that our sense of what people are responsible for extends no farther than our causal perception—that is, our way of sifting through the virtual infinity of consequences flowing from a person's acts and omissions, classifying only a small fraction as truly *belonging* to the actor in a morally relevant way and thus qualifying for praise or blame. At most, we hold people responsible only for evils over which we believe they have significant causal influence—ones about which they "can" do something. Even this is only an outer limit, a prerequisite that is necessary (but not sufficient) for blameworthiness, for there are many evils that people obviously *could* do something to alleviate for which we do not hold them responsible.

Convention enters crucially into what we think people "can" do, and because it does, the dependence of "ought" on "can" carries with it the further implication that convention necessarily plays a large role in moral judgment. Cause-and-effect relations pervade our thinking at every level, from high theory to the most mundane affairs of everyday life. They constitute, as a British philosopher put it, the "cement [or glue] of the universe."[34] Virtually everything we do, from checking a book out of the library to calming a frightened child, draws on our fund of knowledge about the relation of present acts to future states of the world—the relation, in other words, of cause to effect. But those relations are not given as such in raw experience; causal relationships are something we *impute* to the people, events, and things around us, and we do so in ways shaped by social convention.

To illustrate the role of convention, imagine that a great earthquake has just occurred, such as the one that struck Mexico City in 1985. In a strictly physical sense, I undoubtedly "can" stop writing this essay, board a flight to Mexico City, and help save at least one stranger's life by lifting debris and performing other emergency tasks. If I took literally the well-nigh universal rule of reciprocity, "Do unto others what you would have them do unto you," this would seem to be the only acceptable thing to do, for if I were pinned beneath a collapsed building, I would certainly want others to drop their daily routines and come to my aid. Yet I continue writing instead of going to the aid of the stranger, and no one accuses me of violating the Golden Rule. Why not? *But for* my inaction, the stranger would live. Why am I not deemed blameworthy for this death, which is undeniably among the consequences that flow from my failure to go to his aid? The answer is clear. I am not held responsible for this lamentable consequence of my inaction because, by the prevailing conventions of my time and place, this "can" is not real, not operative. Mexico City is "too far away;" going there would disrupt my life "too much."[35]

Too far and too much by what measure? Convention supplies the measure. Convention authorizes me to say I "cannot" help the stranger, at least not in this direct way, even though, in a purely physical sense, I undoubtedly possess the means of doing so. This shared, tacit under-standing that converts the "can" of physical ability into the "cannot" of acceptable moral practice, need not be arbitrary—it may be loosely related to considerations of relative cost, for example—but I am not persuaded that its rational elements could ever be strong enough to anchor it against tides of change or lift it up out of the category of convention altogether. The existence of such conventions is nothing to regret. In the absence of convention, prescriptions such as the Golden Rule would either have to be ignored altogether or taken literally, which would set standards so high that no one, no matter how scrupulous and compassionate, could live up to them. The world brims over with suffering strangers who, but for our inaction, would undeniably be better off; we cannot literally do for every suffering Other what we would have Others do for us.[36]

If ought implies can, and "can" is conventional in this sense, then it follows inexorably that our understanding of moral responsibility—of what we "ought" to do—is deeply imbedded in social practice and cannot help but be influenced, at least in broad outline, by the material circum-stances, the historical experiences, and, especially, the technological capa-bilities of the society in which we live. As our collective circumstances, experiences, and capabilities change, we should expect the conventions of moral responsibility to change as well, though not in any simple or automatic manner. The easiest way to illustrate the point is to imagine a dramatic change in what we "can" do. The invention of technology that would permit us to travel to Mexico City, or any other scene of disaster, instantaneously and at trivial expense would be very likely to alter the conventions governing moral responsibility in our society—making my failure to go to the aid of the earthquake victim morally unacceptable, at least in some quarters. Any change that stretches our causal horizons and expands the sphere within which we feel we "can" act has the potential to transform what we hitherto perceived as "necessary evils" into remediable ones. And once an evil is perceived as remediable, some people (not all, certainly) will be exposed to feelings of guilt and responsibility for suffering that previously was viewed with indifference or, at most, aroused only passive sympathy—like the sympathy the ancient Greeks felt for those who had the misfortune to be enslaved, or which the reader and I feel today for distant earthquake victims who are "too far away" to help.[37]

This is the sort of development that I believe paved the way for "modern" or "humane" or "responsible" attitudes toward slavery and many other cruel and exploitative practices. My understanding parallels Williams's at some levels while diverging at others. He is right that we moderns have nothing to teach the ancients about the requirements of justice, abstractly considered. He is also right to insist that the ancients owe us no apologies for lacking the heightened sense of agency that has prompted Europeans since the eighteenth century to perceive in slavery an evil both unjust *and* unnecessary. But these strengths of Williams's analysis need to be supplemented with a fuller acknowledgment that the element of causation, although universally present in judgments of responsibility, plays a role that is historically contingent, depending as it must on conventional understandings of what people "can" do. Of the four elements that Williams says are universal features of all judgments of responsibility, causation is the most historical; the one most likely to vary with changes in people's everyday practices, material circumstances, and technological capabilities. As causal conventions change, so must perceptions of freedom and fate, possibility and necessity. And as evils previously regarded as necessary are brought perceptually and conceptually within the reach of remedial action, people whose basic conceptions of justice may not differ from those of their ancestors may nonetheless feel obliged to act in unprecedented ways. Because the causal imagination feeds on awareness that things could be other than they are, the high rate of change and technological innovation in modern societies fosters an expansive sense of agency (and correspondingly shrunken domain of necessity) that was unthinkable in Aristotle's day.

21

This is not to give technology (even in the very capacious and wholly unmechanical sense of the word intended here) credit for being an autonomous force or unilinear process in history. Nor is it to credit technology with being a force for the moral betterment of mankind, for of course every expansion of causal horizons creates new opportunities for doing evil as well as good. It is merely to recognize that (a) people cannot feel responsible enough to do anything about ending suffering as long as they cannot imagine any practicable course of action that will reliably lead to that outcome, and (b) imagining complex, far-reaching courses of moral reform comes easiest to those who in their everyday affairs routinely witness or take part in projects that are comparably far-reaching in their effects. Whether the projects are motivated by altruism or selfish interests is not decisive; what is important is that the projects be far-reaching—not solely in a spatial sense but also in temporal scope and in the number and complexity of the qualitative transformations necessary to their accomplishment.

At the scene of a bloody accident we expect less of lay people than of physicians, who have the knowledge and skills to intervene in ways that it would be reckless for a layperson to attempt. By the same token, responsibility for all manner of institutionalized injustice weighs heaviest on people who have been acculturated to accept change as natural, to pride themselves on their demonstrated mastery of fate, and routinely to participate in or witness ambitious projects aimed at distant goals—again, "distant" not only in space or time, but also in the number and complexity of the cause-and-effect linkages necessary to their attainment. From such experience comes a person like Oscar Schindler: undistinguished in moral character, perhaps, but bold, worldly wise, and thus equipped with such wide causal horizons that he may, under the pressure of circumstance, feel responsible for the performance of humane feats of which other, more sensitive moralists would be incapable.

One reason for thinking that this feature of modern life accounts for changed attitudes toward slave suffering is the startling recency of the humanitarian phenomenon. Individual Good Samaritans go back as far as human memory. Organized efforts to rescue kinsmen or fellow-believers from slavery were common in medieval Europe. But sustained movements collectively dedicated to the relief of suffering strangers—people sharing no tie of blood, faith, or common citizenship—and aiming at the demolition of the institutional arrangements that held them down, are a phenomenon of the recent past. No slave society of which we have historical knowledge lacked voices acknowledging that slaves suffered: Aristotle knew it, Aquinas knew it, Locke knew it even as he wrote slavery into the Fundamental Constitutions of Carolina. Yet no serious opposition to the institution of slavery developed before the eighteenth century. In the entire history of responsibility, there is no fact more sobering or revealing than this. *For two millennia after Aristotle, the suffering of slaves continued to be perceived as nothing worse than a regrettable, but necessary evil.* The first people to go farther and condemn the institution outright were isolated religious zealots of the sixteenth and seventeenth centuries, all but forgotten by history and dismissed by their contemporaries as misfits. With the single exception of Jean Bodin in the sixteenth century, even Europe's most insightful moralists and philosophers did no more than acknowledge that slavery was ethically problematical—until the middle decades of the eighteenth century.[38] Then, in little more than a century, slavery was suddenly transformed from a troubling but readily defensible institution into a self-evidently intolerable relic of barbarism, noxious to decent people everywhere. On a historical scale of reckoning, this reversal of opinion occurred overnight.

Most of those who attacked slavery were fired by religious indignation, but the Christian doctrines they hurled at slave owners had for centuries been thought compatible with slave holding. We do not demean the abolitionists' labors, without which emancipation would never have been achieved, by entertaining the possibility that their crusade was made possible (not *produced,* but *made possible*) by changes in the material circumstances and technological capabilities of the society in which they lived. The historical developments that set the stage for new attitudes toward suffering and servitude lay outside the realm of "ideas," in political and especially economic changes that greatly expanded the horizon within which deliberate human action routinely took place. The upshot, I suggest, was an outward shift in the conventions governing perceptions of causation, necessity, and moral responsibility, such that what had hitherto appeared to be "necessary evils" began to seem remediable.

Before substantial numbers of people could feel outraged by the very existence of slavery and take action to uproot it, they had to be able to impute to themselves historically unprecedented powers of intervention, and they had to perceive hierarchical social arrangements and institutional structures, not as reflections of God's will or manifestations of nature's own order, but as contingent, malleable phenomena open to human influence and correction. In other words, the conventionally defined domain of necessity—that which is not construed as the consequence of any human choice, act, or omission—had to shrink. Not until slavery's evil appeared remediable would anyone, even so thoughtful a person as Aristotle, feel responsible for doing anything about it. And not until human agency seemed expansive enough to challenge even such ancient and interest-bound institutions as slavery would people feel the need for the new word "responsibility," the adoption of which was eloquent testimony to the ever wider range of consequences that by the 1780s were being traced back to human choice rather than to traditional founts of necessity such as God, Chance, Fate, Fortune, Luck, or Nature.

Here we come full circle. My speculation is that the coinage of the word "responsibility" in the late eighteenth century was one straw in the wind, registering the onset of a major upheaval in the conventions governing causal attribution in Western culture. That speculation having been ventured, it is important to notice in closing that the upheaval, if such it is, is still underway—and gaining momentum. The philosopher Hans Jonas puts his finger on its deepest sources and reminds us that its consequences are by no means entirely encouraging. Like the shell of an exploding star, responsibility swiftly expands in all directions under the continuing impulse of man's growing technological virtuosity and ever higher expectations of self-mastery and control of nature. But as it expands, obliterating perceptions of necessity wherever it reaches, the shell grows thin and brittle. A day may come when, overextended, it collapses back upon itself.

"Modern technology," warns Jonas, "informed by an ever-deeper penetration of nature and propelled by the forces of market and politics, has enhanced human power beyond anything known or even dreamed of before." "It is a power over matter, over life on earth, and over man himself; and it keeps growing at an accelerating pace. Its unfettered exercise for about two centuries now has raised the material estate of its wielders and main beneficiaries, the industrial 'West,' to heights equally unknown in the history of mankind. . . . But lately, the other side of the triumphal advance has begun to show its face, disturbing the euphoria of success with threats that are as novel as its welcomed fruits."[39]

Although expanding horizons of responsibility helped doom slavery and brought succor to untold numbers of suffering strangers who otherwise would have met with nothing better than passive sympathy, the continuation of this process is not an unmixed blessing. We have become keenly aware in recent decades that the explosion of technological innovation that propels this outward sweep of human responsibility has horrific dangers of its own, such as nuclear holocaust and ecological catastrophe. We also know that staggering ethical dilemmas lie just around the corner, as human agency penetrates still deeper into nature, unravels genetic codes, and trembles on the brink of creating life itself. In spite of all the publicity devoted to threats such as these, they are not the only ones we have to fear. The most serious may stem from the overdevelopment of the idea of responsibility itself.

Every time technical ingenuity makes new inroads against the given and the necessary, responsibility becomes more expansive, more tenuous, and more susceptible to the ancient charge of hubris. Many commentators have sensed in modern culture a growing arbitrariness, as expanding causal horizons paradoxically make us seem responsible for everything in principle and nothing in particular. As the realm of the given shrinks toward the vanishing point, evils begin to appear "necessary" only insofar as fragile conventions dignify our reluctance to disrupt our lives for the sake of rendering aid. Under these conditions, responsibility itself is transformed from a concrete relation with specific applications into a diffuse quality that floats freely through all relations, ready to be imputed manipulatively to anyone, anytime, for anything. One wonders which is worse, the paralysis that comes from acknowledging that we are, through omission, causally complicit in evils all over the world, or the cynicism that comes from knowing that only those evils that win the lottery of politics stand any chance of actually being remedied.

Other observers have noted that the ethical maxims of the past increasingly fail us because they evolved in contexts dramatically different from the one in which we now operate.[40] The goods and evils that our ancestors tried to attain or avoid were close at hand, proximate both in space and time. As Jonas says, "the effective range of action was small, the time span of foresight, goal-setting, and accountability was short, control of circumstances was limited. The long run of consequences was left to chance, fate, or providence. Ethics accordingly was of the here and now . . . the agent and the "other" of his action [shared] a common present. . . . No one was held responsible for the unintended later effects of his well-intentioned, well-considered, and well-performed act. The short arm of human power did not call for a long arm of predictive knowledge."[41]

Now, as Jonas says, "all this has decisively changed. Modern technology has introduced actions of such novel scale, objects, and consequences that the framework of former ethics can no longer contain them." We saw above that Calasso chalked it up to the wisdom and modesty of the ancient Greeks that they "dismissed with the utmost skepticism an agent's claim actually to *do* anything," but it should now be apparent that their "modesty" was inseparable from the constricted causal imagination instilled in them by a technologically limited form of life, one unequipped with the expansive sense of agency required to sustain the view that the suffering of the slave was anything worse than a necessary evil. One can only wonder what will pass for wisdom and modesty in the world of the future, in which, as Jonas says, the "lengthened reach" or "causal pregnancy" of our technological deeds will put responsibility at "the center of the ethical stage," with "no less than man's fate for its object."[42] What counts as "hubris" as we approach a condition in which necessity evaporates and all problems appear in principle to be soluble, if only enough resources are dedicated to them? The possibilities for both good and ill are incalculable—but among them is the possibility that the supposed beneficiaries of modernity's widening gyre of freedom and responsibility will rebel and do whatever it takes to reinstate the reign of necessity rather than bear the rising burden of guilt and frustration that goes with boundless causal horizons.

The question for historians (perhaps of no great moment in the larger scheme of things) is how we are to avoid letting history become Voltaire's "bag of tricks played upon the dead." Throughout the modern era conventions of responsibility have not only been in motion, they have moved at an accelerating pace, a state of affairs that make the danger of arbitrary and anachronistic judgment more acute than ever. Under conditions such as these it seems obvious that all historians, not just those specializing in the history of ideas, owe it to their audience to suspend judgment long enough to specify as clearly as they can the conventions by which their subjects lived. But achieving that goal will be hard, for it goes against the grain of the historical profession as now constituted, both intellectually and institutionally.

Conventions are not empirical entities that can be weighed or counted; they will not be found in the archives filed under "C." Controversies about them will seem frustratingly inconclusive and the profession's favorite myth—that historians' quarrels turn on hard facts rather than imponderable issues of interpretation—will become harder and harder to sustain. Ferreting out conventions will require skills of logical inference and imagination that have never figured prominently in either the recruitment or the training of historians. Taking conventions into account will complicate the stories historians tell and incur the wrath of all those— not only defenders of the status quo, but also its critics—who have a vested interest in using the past to serve present interests predictably. Skeptics who see nothing to gain from acknowledging the force of convention are numerous, both inside and outside the profession. Some of the most vociferous naysayers will be those who construe convention as an ancillary reflex of group interest. In their eyes, powerful elites, well versed in the arts of "social control" and "cultural hegemony," find it no harder to imbue subject populations with convenient conventions than to select ready-made clothing out of a mail-order catalogue.

Quentin Skinner observed over twenty years ago that "it is the limit of our imaginative grasp as well as our lack of information that makes the past a foreign country, just as it is imaginative grasp as well as control of information that makes the historian." When Skinner wrote those words he was none too sanguine that historians would come to grips with the foreignness of the past. Still greater pessimism seems warranted today, for little has changed. Just as in 1970, most historians today still believe that it is "best not to think about their subject but merely to do it, as if these were self-evidently separate activities."[43] After two decades of talk about the importance of context and the desirability of "thick description," historians have scarcely begun to scale the barriers to understanding that shifting conventions throw in their path. Nor are they likely to do so as long as they are more concerned to use the past than to understand it. To be sure, we reconstruct the past for our sake, not its own, but understanding it in its own terms is the indispensable condition of honest use.

# Democracy in the United States
## From Revolution to Civil War

## Lacy K. Ford, Jr.

From its halting beginnings in the late colonial era through its nineteenth-century denouement—the extension of voting rights to African-American males during Reconstruction—American democracy developed in response to a complex mix of ideological imperatives and practical exigencies. For most of the colonial era political privileges lay mainly in the hands of the propertied elite, both landed and commercial, who controlled the colonial legislatures and enjoyed the largest financial stake in the course of imperial relations. After 1763, however, as that propertied provincial elite felt its privileges challenged by the British government, it increasingly sought broad-based popular support for its challenge to imperial authority, which began as collective resistance and ended in successful revolution. For the most part, the Revolutionary-era gentry had no intention of siring a democratic polity, instead seeking only the broader public's deferential legitimation of their own authority.[1] But their appeals to the common folk for support released the genii of democracy into the American body politic, where it remains robust, though both abused and abusive, more than two centuries later.

The Revolutionary generation's perception of politics remained heavily influenced by the teachings of classical republicanism, which prescribed limiting full political rights to the propertied gentry. Members of the gentry possessed not only the economic wherewithal to insure their independence of judgment but also the leisure to master the art of governing. Hence colonial and early post-Revolutionary political rights, such as suffrage and office-holding, usually remained the exclusive prerogative of propertied men.[2] But here uniquely American circumstances intervened on behalf of democracy. Property requirements, which in land-scarce Britain limited the suffrage to less than one-fifth of the adult male population, proved much less restrictive when transferred without significant adjustment to land-abundant America, where as many as three-fifths of free adult males owned enough property to meet freehold suffrage requirements in most states. With a majority of free white males able to satisfy extant property requirements, the quasi-aristocratic political order that the gentry preferred contained within it an explosive popular component whose sheer energy challenged the old order and eventually replaced it with a new, more democratic one.[3]

This gradual evolution from the gentrified republicanism of the 1790s to the vigorous if immature democratic republicanism of the 1850s involved four issues central to the definition of citizenship in a republic: the right of suffrage, the apportionment of representation in legislative assemblies, the emergence of extra-constitutional partisan competition as a defining characteristic of the political culture, and the controversy over whether slavery (as it existed in the southern states) was compatible with the moral and political imperatives of republicanism as antebellum Americans understood them. Each of these questions was contested, often bitterly, at the state or national level during the first half of the nineteenth century. In these contests, the forces of democratization won at least limited and sometimes impressive victories, but on most questions conservatives mounted determined rearguard defenses that slowed or moderated the progress of democratization. These confrontations between egalitarians and conservatives served as the defining dialectic of antebellum democracy.

In the early republic, virtually every state limited the suffrage to males possessing a freehold in land or its equivalent. The freehold restriction on suffrage reflected the classical republican assumption that property provided a necessary foundation for the independence required of all citizens. Even though freehold requirements in most states were low enough that a majority of white male household heads were eligible to vote, liberalization of the suffrage emerged as a central demand of egalitarian reformers in the first decades of the nineteenth century. By 1810, the otherwise conservative states of South Carolina and Maryland eliminated freehold requirements with a minimum of controversy, but as the liberalization movement spread to other states it quickly encountered stiff opposition. When reformers in Massachusetts and New York pushed for the removal of freehold restrictions in their respective state constitutional conventions in 1820–21, they encountered entrenched and eloquent opposition.[4] Advocates of a liberalized suffrage law in Massachusetts argued that all men who paid a poll tax and performed militia duty should enjoy voting rights. Exclusion placed non-freeholders "in the situation of the slaves," and Massachusetts freemen "ought to be saved" from such "degraded feelings," Bay State reformers contended.[5] Conservative Josiah Quincy, well known for his outspoken Federalism, defended the freehold suffrage in thoroughly republican terms. Republican liberty depended on constitutional checks and balances. The freehold suffrage protected independent citizens from depredations at the hands of the dependent. The "yeomanry," Quincy insisted, would eventually value protection from hordes of manufacturing operatives who were "absolutely dependent upon their employers." If the freehold restriction was removed, Quincy continued, the day would soon come when hundreds of votes would be cast "depending on the will of one employer, one great capitalist." Quincy, however, argued in favor of a "a very low" property requirement, a sum that was "the lowest consistent with independence."[6] These arguments were echoed in New York. Reformers in the Empire State pushed for the elimination of the property requirement for voters in elections for the state senate. Egalitarian New Yorkers argued that existing voting restrictions had evolved from flawed British precedents. The prized balance of the unwritten British constitution required the protecting of the "separate interests" of that nation's three estates. But in the new American republic, reformers maintained, "there is but one estate—the people." The "virtue and morality of the people," as evidenced by paying taxes or militia service, egalitarians insisted, provided the only proper qualifications for suffrage.[7] But longtime New York equity chancellor James Kent defended the freehold requirement, claiming that the "tendency of universal suffrage is to jeopardize the rights of property." Following the argument of Quincy, Kent warned that "the crowds of dependents connected with great manufacturing and commercial establishments, and the motley and undefinable population of crowded ports" might eventually dominate the state legislature and use their voting power to plunder "men of property."[8] Martin Van Buren, the rising star of New York politics and a moderate who favored broadening the suffrage to include all taxpayers, rebutted Kent. Denying the franchise to any taxpayer, even those who did not possess a freehold, Van Buren argued, amounted to taxation without representation, the central grievance that had driven American colonists to revolution during the 1770s. Kent's argument that taxpaying non-freeholders were wisely governed by freeholders, Van Buren declared, was merely a recapitulation of the long-repudiated British idea of virtual representation.[9]

A decade after the New York and Massachusetts debates, Virginia's Constitutional Convention, whose delegates included two former presidents and one future one, as well as the sitting chief justice of the United

States Supreme Court, engaged in frank debate over liberalizing the suffrage. Virginia's existing freehold requirement disfranchised roughly half of the adult white males in the commonwealth according to some estimates.[10] In Virginia more clearly than in other states, reformers staked their case for white manhood suffrage in terms of the language of Jefferson's Declaration of Independence. Virginia egalitarians argued that militia service offered better evidence of virtue and intelligence than possession of a freehold. But Virginia conservatives countered that a freehold was the most "durable" form of property and that it linked the fate of its proprietor "by the strongest of all ties" to "the destiny of the country."[11] However, Charles Morgan, a reformer from western Virginia, made perhaps the most telling argument in favor of liberalizing the suffrage when he tied democracy for all white men to the defense of slavery. Morgan noted that South Carolina, Alabama, and other slaveholding states south of Virginia "deemed it of the utmost importance to make all free white men as free and independent as Government could make them" in order to unify their states in defense of slavery. "Is it not wise now," Morgan asked, "to call together at least every free white human being, and unite them in the same common interest and Government."[12] Whatever the relative merits of reform versus conservative arguments, most states had either abandoned property requirements or reduced them to insignificant levels by the election of the nation's first Whig president, William Henry Harrison, in 1840. Yet a few exceptions, including North Carolina, Virginia, and most notably Rhode Island retained some type of freehold requirement.[13]

In the main, however, this halting move toward liberalized suffrage included white men only. Free African-American males enjoyed the same voting opportunities as their white counterparts only in a handful of New England states (Massachusetts, New Hampshire, Vermont, and Maine). Moreover, a number of states, North and South, used their Jacksonian-era state conventions to disfranchise blacks who had previously enjoyed the suffrage. New Jersey, Pennsylvania, and Connecticut joined North Carolina and Tennessee as states that eliminated free black voting as they liberalized suffrage laws for whites.[14] In New York, the same Jeffersonian egalitarians who pushed for white manhood suffrage also sought to disfranchise blacks regardless of property, wealth, or education. Federalists, who usually received the vote of propertied blacks in New York, fought the disfranchisement effort. "Why are they [black males], who were born as free as ourselves, natives of the same country, and deriving from nature and our political institutions, the same rights and privileges which we have, now to be deprived of all those rights, and doomed to remain forever as aliens among us?" asked Federalist lawyer Peter Jay.[15] But advocates of restricting the suffrage to whites insisted that blacks were "a peculiar people, incapable . . . of exercising that privilege with any sort of discretion, prudence, or independence."[16] A compromise, engineered by Martin Van Buren, disfranchised most blacks but allowed black male freeholders who met residency requirements to vote. Thus, even in New York, expanded voting rights for whites were accompanied by tighter restrictions on black voting.[17] Race, rather than property ownership, increasingly became the principal determinant of which males could vote. By 1840, virtually the entire southern black population and over ninety percent of blacks in the North were effectively disfranchised.[18]

To egalitarian reformers, the question of legislative reapportionment rivaled democratization of the suffrage in importance. Reformers wanted to reapportion state legislatures on the basis of population rather than property. Their efforts at democratizing representation triumphed with comparative ease in newer states on or near the trans-Appalachian frontier, but in the older, seaboard states politicians from wealthy areas defended the representation of property.[19] Up and down the Atlantic coast, debate over legislative apportionment revealed the fundamental distinctions between the older conservative republicanism concerned with balanced government, checking the power of majorities, and the protection of property and a newer democratic republicanism driven by hatred of special privilege, faith in majority rule, and commitment to broad-based political participation. The egalitarians sought the full expression of popular will and saw it as the chief aim of republican government. The gentry conservatives sought to check the power of popular majorities and saw the diffusion of power as essential to the preservation of republican government.

Though details of the debate varied from state to state, the practical question centered on whether representation in the state legislatures should be based on population, property, geopolitical units, or some combination of all three. In almost every case, combination approaches prevailed. But reformers pushed for combinations weighted toward population while conservatives fought for apportionment formulas tying representation to property and political subdivisions. Most Revolution-era state constitutions simply allotted a specific number of legislative seats to specified geopolitical units and made no allowance for periodic reapportionment. Over time, these representation formulas tended to overrepresent older wealthy areas while underrepresenting newer areas with larger populations but less accumulated wealth. As reformers pushed for more equitable representation of population, conservatives emphasized the importance of property to the American definition of independence.[20]

After considerable public debate lasting more than a decade, South Carolina, despite the power of its wealthy Lowcountry elite, found a ready compromise on the representation issue as early as 1808. In that year, the legislature ratified a constitutional amendment apportioning representation in the South Carolina House of Representatives according to a formula giving equal weight to white population and taxes paid while giving each of the state's political subdivisions one state senator. This compromise increased the power of the white majority in the Upcountry in the state's House of Representatives but left the state senate firmly under the control of the Lowcountry. This carefully crafted compromise created a balance of power between the Palmetto State's two major subregions, giving each informal veto power in the legislature.[21] Such political balance between subregions emerged in other states, but usually the shaping of such accommodations proved decidedly more acrimonious than it did in South Carolina.

In the Massachusetts Convention of 1820–21, Jeffersonians moved to change the basis for apportioning the state senate from taxes paid to population. "Our government is one of the people, not a government of property," Massachusetts reformers declared. Moreover, as reformer Levi Lincoln asserted, "It is only necessary that all who are taxed should be represented, and not that they should be represented in proportion to their tax."[22] The proposed shift to a popular basis for the state senate called forth emphatic opposition from the convention's most learned conservatives. Making his first speech to the convention, former President John Adams contended that the "great object" of republican government was "to render property secure." Republics survived, Adams claimed, only as long as "the balance between property and numbers" was maintained.[23] Conservative Joseph Story argued that government "stands on a combination of interest and circumstances" and that the protection of property against the "inroads of poverty and vice" remained of the utmost importance.[24] Daniel Webster, known in 1820 as a brilliant Boston attorney, insisted that American republicanism drew its strength from property, which secured the independence and virtue of the people. Thus it was "entirely just that property should have its due weight and consideration in political arrangements."[25] Despite initial support for the popular basis, the conservative arguments eventually prevailed and the Massachusetts convention adopted taxes paid as the basis for apportioning the state senate, balancing the town population basis used in apportioning the Massachusetts House.

Nowhere in antebellum America did the battle over legislative apportionment rage more fiercely than at the Virginia Constitutional Convention of 1829–30. Reformers, mostly from the Valley and trans-Allegheny regions in the western portion of the state where there were few slaves, argued in favor of the white basis for representation, while slave-holding Tidewater conservatives, who enjoyed disproportionate power in the existing legislature, vehemently defended the principle that property deserved representation. Shenandoah Valley reformer John R. Cocke advanced the white basis proposal by appealing explicitly to Virginia's Revolutionary and Jeffersonian heritage, which he claimed "laid deep the foundation of our Republic on the sovereignty of the people and the equal-ity of men."[26] But conservative Abel P. Upshur, later secretary of state under President John Tyler, countered with a penetrating critique of popular majorities that anticipated the future work of South Carolina's John C. Calhoun. Upshur contended that there were two kinds of majorities, a "majority in interest, as well as a majority in number." The power of elect-ed majorities over minorities presented fatal dangers to republicanism. The logical check on numerical majorities, Upshur continued, was the repre-sentation of property in political assemblies. "Persons and property," Upshur insisted, "comprised the constitutional elements of society," and legislative apportionment should effectively balance their sometimes con-flicting interests.[27] Outspoken egalitarian Philip Doddridge, a Congressman from western Virginia, replied to Upshur, arguing that conservatives denied to the white majority the same rights they claimed for the minority. The conservative argument reduced to its naked form, Doddridge claimed, con-sisted of nothing more than the principle that "the owner of slave proper-ty must possess all the power of Government" in order "to secure that prop-erty from the rapacity of an overgrown majority of white men." Such a principle, Doddridge concluded, "makes me a slave."[28]

Eccentric conservative John Randolph of Roanoke, in his last public address, ridiculed advocates of the white basis as foolish subjects of "King Numbers," in whose realm "a negro boy with a knife and a tally-stick is a Statesman."[29] Cooler heads, led by Chief Justice John Marshall, supported a compromise plan basing representation on the so-called Federal ratio (all whites and three-fifths of all slaves) and urged both sides to "meet on mid-dle ground."[30] Eventually, after tense negotiations marked by frayed tempers on all sides, the Virginia Convention reluctantly approved a compromise plan that arbitrarily allocated roughly equal representation to the four major geographic regions of the state, the Tidewater, the Piedmont, the Valley, and the trans-Allegheny. This plan strengthened the Piedmont and Valley at the expense of the Tidewater, which still enjoyed disproportionate legislative influence despite a small white population, and increased the representation of the predominately white counties west of the Blue Ridge but left that area with less representation than they would have enjoyed under the white basis. Thus the western delegates voted overwhelmingly against the compromise, but it carried the convention anyway with the strong support of former President James Madison, arguably the republic's foremost constitutional theorist.[31]

The compromise on apportionment in Virginia produced a slightly more democratic legislature than the existing basis, but it was, on balance, a defeat for reformers. Seldom had egalitarian champions of the white basis accepted such an unsatisfactory compromise. Five years later, the North Carolina Constitutional Convention found a compromise on the representation question that apportioned the state senate on the basis of taxes paid and the lower house on the basis of the federal ratio. In 1837, Maryland's legislature, after tempestuous debate, amended its constitution to apportion the state's lower house by the federal ratio and give each county equal representation in the state senate. Again, seaboard states had adopted modestly more democratic formulas for allocating representation but stopped well short of the white basis scheme favored by radical egalitarians. By contrast, in Tennessee and Alabama the white basis prevailed in the lower houses.[32]

On the whole, democratic reformers of the Jacksonian era secured greater representation for population, but in many eases, especially in the original thirteen states and others created before 1800, they had to accept compromise representation formulas that took property (whether as taxes paid or slaves) and political subdivisions into account. These reforms left state legislatures of the Jacksonian era decidedly more democratic than those of the 1790s, but balanced the legislative power of numbers with the representation of wealth and geopolitical units (such as counties, parishes, and even towns). These mixed bases of representation reflected the republican emphasis on balanced government and the continuing suspicion of unrestrained democracy among men of substantial property.

In other ways, however, the constitutional reforms of the 1820s and 1830s ushered in powerful democratic forces that proved more difficult to restrain than either white manhood suffrage or representation based on white population. The democratization of local government, giving voters the right to elect sheriffs, justices of the peace, and other county officers, and popular election of judges invigorated popular government in most states during this era, but the reforms that truly succeeded in politicizing the masses were state constitutional amendments calling for the popular election of presidential electors and governors. By 1832, every state except South Carolina had adopted popular statewide elections as their method of choosing presidential electors, and by 1844, every state except Virginia and South Carolina had given the election of the governor to the people rather than the legislature. Together with the liberalization of the suffrage, these reforms mobilized American voters and nurtured the formation of political parties as vehicles for advancing candidates in national, state, and local races. The process of party formation during the Jacksonian era, the rise of the so-called Second American Party System, may have had its substantive roots in the policies of Andrew Jackson's administration and the concerted opposition to them, but the massive popular mobilization that characterized the rise of parties during the 1830s owed much to an expanded electorate and popular voting for governors and presidential electors. This "altered environment of politics," combined with improved transportation and communication, helped make political parties viable. Partisan competition spurred voter turnout. In 1824, when Andrew Jackson made his first bid for the presidency in the era of one-party Republican domination, only about one-fourth of all eligible voters cast ballots, but by 1840, in perhaps the first clear partisan contest between Democrats and Whigs, roughly 80 percent of all those eligible voted. Similar dramatic increases in turnout occurred in state gubernatorial elections, and even in South Carolina, which remained outside the vortex of party competition, the critical elections of the nullification era generated voter turnouts in excess of 80 percent.[33]

The intense competitiveness of the Second American Party system transformed the nation's political culture. The influence of local notables gave way to party organization. Calculated reticence on the part of aspirants for office yielded to vigorous canvassing. And early republican aversion to political parties gradually evolved into an open embrace of party competition as an instrument of popular choice and democracy. With party competition came all the machinery of party organization, including a partisan press, the party caucus in legislatures, and party conventions to nominate slates of party candidates. Moreover, as Richard McCormick pointed out, the Jacksonian party system was extremely competitive in almost every state.[34] The closeness of contests reenforced voter enthusiasm. The dynamic of party choice mobilized the electorate and energized American democracy even as it narrowed the range of electoral options.

Fundamental ideological differences also sustained party competition during the Jacksonian era. The Democrats, initially defined by Jackson's hostility to the national bank, opposition to federally financed internal improvements, and advocacy of cheap public land, wanted to use the power of the government negatively to defend the independent producer from dangerous concentrations of power, such as corporations and other aristocracies of wealth. The Whig party, united originally by opposition to Jackson, wanted to use the power of government positively to encourage entrepreneurship and education. Committed to the idea of moral and material improvement, the Whigs, despite significant state-to-state variations, established themselves as the party of a national bank, internal improvements, protective tariffs, public schools, hospitals, and insane asylums. Whigs wanted to enhance liberty as well as maintain it and saw democracy as a process rather than an end. By contrast, Democrats focused on protecting independent citizens from Whiggish good intentions, either by opposing Whig proposals outright or insisting that they were the responsibility of individual states rather than the federal government. Democrats saw liberty as an existing condition that need vigilant protection and saw democracy as the majority's instrument for defending its liberty. Ideologically charged campaigns, coupled with full party mobilization, produced the fierce partisan combat of the 1840s.[35]

Yet for all its partisan bitterness, the Second American Party System focused political disagreement on economic rather than sectional issues, and, as a result, kept growing tensions over slavery effectively bottled up until the outbreak of the Mexican War. During the 1846 Congressional debate over war appropriations, however, the question of whether or not slavery would be allowed to expand into western territories, including any territory acquired from Mexico as a result of the war, quickly exploded to the surface. The ensuing debate over slavery divided both national parties internally and shifted political debate away from economic issues and toward sectional ones. Slavery had long presented thorny problems for American democracy. Few northerners supported slavery outright but many acquiesced in its existence as the price of Union. In the upper South, many defended slavery only as a necessary evil, but usually these defenders emphasized the necessary and slighted the evil. In the lower South, slaveholders increasingly defended slavery as a positive good, an institution that formed the firmest foundation for white democracy while defining the region's dependent black working class out of the body politic.

When the issue shifted from the outright abolition of slavery to a prohibition against expansion into new territory, however, a popular majority in the North gradually coalesced behind the so-called "free soil" movement. After 1854, when the Whig party disintegrated due to sectional differences over the right of slaveholders to take their slaves into the territories, the second party system collapsed, and a new party, based entirely in the North, emerged to challenge the Democrats. Calling itself the party of "free soil, free labor, and free men," the newly formed Republican party celebrated the free labor society of the North for its apparent willingness to reward hard work with upward social mobility.[36] As former Illinois Whig and future Republican president Abraham Lincoln explained in 1859, the North recognized "no permanent class of hired laborers. . . . The hired laborer of yesterday, labors on his account today, and will hire others to labor for him tomorrow."[37] The free-labor party also developed a coherent critique of the South as a backward, unrepublican society where an aristocratic Slave Power rather than an independent citizenry ruled. Southerners, increasingly found concentrated in the antiantislavery Democratic party or touting the formation of a new proslavery sectional party, responded by characterizing the North as a corrupt industrial society where greedy capitalists and speculators ruled masses of dependent laborers (wage slaves). Rooted in conflicting views of slavery, competing sectional ideologies emerged. The North and the South each judged itself the true champion of democracy and the other as a retrograde aristocracy that threatened republican liberty.[38] This volatile ideological atmosphere soon exploded in civil war.

Yet well before sectional conflict erupted into civil war, the northern antislavery movement had generated another challenge to the traditional tenets of American democracy. After the religious resurgence known as the Second Great Awakening occurred during the first decades of the nineteenth century, middle-class northern women, through churches and voluntary associations, took an increasingly active role in social reform movements. Their activities on behalf of Sunday schools, temperance, and eventually abolition helped spread bourgeois morality throughout the region, but the censorious tinge to this middle-class ideology also generated a backlash from immigrant and other working-class communities. Even the abolitionists were badly divided among themselves over precisely what role women should play. Drawing on their ambivalent experience within the abolition movement, where they found their help wanted but their role circumscribed, a radical minority of women reformers recognized the need to push for a larger public role for women in American society, for the application of egalitarian ideology to the issue of gender, for what soon became known as women's rights.[39] None of the rights demanded by radical women generated more controversy than their demand for the right to vote. At the 1848 Seneca Falls Convention for women's rights, Elizabeth Cady Stanton proposed that women "secure to themselves the sacred right to the elective franchise."[40] But other women at the convention thought the idea too radical, and Stanton's motion passed by a very narrow margin. Soon thereafter, however, women reformers united behind the idea that "the one cardinal demand" of their movement was "for the right of suffrage."[41]

Outside the women's movement, however, most Americans viewed the call for women's suffrage as radical indeed. In the North, many states revised property laws that discriminated against women during the 1850s, but refused to grant voting rights. In the South, virtually all whites equated women's rights with abolition and considered women's suffrage an entering wedge for African-American suffrage. In a scathing conservative critique of nineteenth-century feminism, South Carolinian Louisa McCord, an accomplished intellectual, denounced women's suffrage as "entirely a Yankee notion" and ridiculed its advocates as "petticoated despisers of their sex" who entered the public arena "cheek by jowl with the abolitionists." McCord defended a defiantly conservative view of women as "neither man's equal nor inferior only his different." A woman, McCord insisted, could find "at her own fire-side . . . duties enough, cares enough, troubles enough, thought enough, wisdom enough, to fit a martyr for the stake, a philosopher for life, or a saint for heaven." In seeking the vote, McCord believed, women demeaned rather than elevated themselves. Yet the crux of the problem for McCord was not so much the battle of the sexes as the struggle for white supremacy. The causes of women's rights and abolition were so interlocked in her mind that her most vivid images denigrating suffragettes involved women "scuffling with Cuffee for a vote" and "elbowing Sambo for the stump."[42] Northern opponents of women's suffrage may or may not have shared Louisa McCord's caustic racism, but they almost all agreed that voting women represented a mortal threat to patriarchal authority in antebellum America.

But the American people would have to resolve the fate of the republic before they could ponder a full-fledged challenge to its long-standing patriarchal politics. The cotton states of the Deep South seceded from the Union in the four months following the election of a free-labor Republican president, Abraham Lincoln, who had carried every northern state but garnered an insignificant vote in the slaveholding states. Hardly an abolitionist, Lincoln nevertheless criticized slavery as a "monstrous injustice" and pledged during the 1860 campaign to prevent the expansion of slavery into any area where it did not already exist.[43] White southerners generally belittled the distinction between outright abolitionists and "free-soil" Republicans and believed the latter's determination to exclude slaveholders from the western territories implicitly reduced all white southerners to the status of second-class citizenship. Rather than face such degradation, a majority supported secession, which some southerners justified as a constitutional right and others acknowledged as tantamount to revolution. But despite their fundamental disagreements over slavery and its expansion, and without minimizing the significant moral outrage against slavery that existed among northerners, both the North and South believed that they were fighting for the cause of white man's democracy. The genius of the free-labor ideology lay in its ability to combine moral opposition to slavery with the economic self-interest of ordinary white northerners by pledging to keep the territories free of slave competition. The majority of white northerners firmly opposed the expansion of slavery, but they were also wary of abolition. On both fronts, they sought to maximize economic opportunity for white northerners by keeping blacks, whether slave or free, out of the West and North. White southerners saw slavery as a guarantee of white democracy since it served as an institutional foundation for white supremacy and an economic hindrance to the emergence of a dependent, free working class in the region. Slavery for blacks insured independence for whites. A threat to one by definition constituted a threat to the other.[44]

Even as military conflict began, Lincoln doubted that blacks were capable of exercising the full rights of citizens. But the momentum of the war and its terrible human cost drove Lincoln and other northerners to reconsider old prejudices, and by late 1862 the president was ready to do what he had said in 1860 he would not do—emancipate slaves in areas where slavery had long existed. But even after he issued the Emancipation Proclamation freeing all slaves behind Confederate lines, Lincoln approached the idea of black suffrage cautiously. In his highly publicized prewar debates with Stephen Douglas in 1858, Lincoln averred that he had never favored "making voters or jurors of negroes" and insisted he opposed "bringing about in any way the social and political equality of the white and black races. "[45]

By 1864, Lincoln's position had evolved, but only slightly. Lincoln privately asked the "first free-state governor" of Louisiana if the state's constitutional convention might give the suffrage to "some of the colored people." The president recommended "the very intelligent" and "those who have fought gallantly in our ranks."[46] Indeed, courageous service by African Americans (including former slaves) in the Union army merged with the partisan Republican need to build a viable base in the postwar South to convince radical Republicans to insist on black voting rights as a precondition for the readmission of the defeated southern states to the Union. The Fourteenth Amendment to the United States Constitution, ratified in 1868, left the question of whether to enfranchise blacks entirely up to the states, but gave Congress the right to reduce the representation of states that denied the suffrage on racial grounds. This amendment went further toward black suffrage than Lincoln had gone publicly before his death but stopped short of an outright ban on racial discrimination in voting rights because moderate Republicans feared that pushing black suffrage would lead to political losses in the numerous northern states which still limited suffrage to whites.[47]

By 1869, however, the value of the black vote in the southern states convinced northern Republicans, who also expected to win the lion's share of a significant black vote in the northern and border states if racial restrictions on voting became unconstitutional, to seek a national ban on racial discrimination at the ballot box. Congress passed the Fifteenth Amendment, which prohibited denying the franchise to anyone on the basis of race, color, or previous condition of servitude on February 26, 1869, and by early 1870 enough states had ratified the amendment to make it the law of the land. This amendment, which made black male suffrage a national right, carried nineteenth-century American democracy to its most inclusive moment. But the amendment had its conservative as well as its egalitarian thrust, because it was as remarkable for what it did not say as for what it did. It did not even hint at granting women's suffrage despite ongoing pressure from feminists, leaving that question to the states until the twentieth century. And by focusing on race alone, it did not prohibit voting qualifications based on property, taxes, education, or literacy.[48] In the years after Reconstruction, white southerners, with northern acquiescence, used all of these means as well as violence and intimidation to effectively disfranchise blacks despite the Fourteenth and Fifteenth Amendments.[49] The full expansion of democracy across the boundaries of race and gender did not come until the twentieth century, when the women's suffrage amendment of 1920 and the Voting Rights Act of 1965 would finally bring full political rights to all adult Americans.

# The Enlightenment and Evangelical Intellectual Life in the Nineteenth Century

## Mark A. Noll

During the nineteenth century, all English-speaking regions of North America, as well as many regions of the European Continent, witnessed a great expansion of evangelical Protestantism. Beginning with an upsurge of Pietism in German-speaking areas of Europe and broadening out rapidly through revivals in Britain and North America—most notably the Methodist movement in Britain and the Great Awakening in the colonies—evangelicalism rapidly became the dominant form of Protestant Christianity in these areas.[1] Defining evangelicalism precisely is notoriously difficult, because the movement was always guided much more by the innovations of leaders and the shape of personal expedience than by traditional ecclesiastical organizations, creeds, or even consistent political affiliations. While fluidity always characterized the movement, evangelicals were still marked by several common characteristics. The British historian David Bebbington has defined these as conversionism (an emphasis on the "new birth" as a life-changing religious experience), biblicism (a reliance on the Bible as ultimate religious authority), activism (a concern for sharing the Christian faith), and crucicentrism (a focus on Christ's redeeming work on the cross).[2]

In the United States, evangelical Protestantism came to exert considerable cultural influence, especially through revival and the voluntary agency. Evangelicalism in one variety or the other was the religion to which many nineteenth-century presidents deferred; it was the religion that created American public education and dominated it into the twentieth century;[3] it was the religion that, until much later in the twentieth century than once was thought, established the ethos for American higher education;[4] it was the religion that, of all American faiths, enjoyed closest connections with mainstream publishing; and it was the religion that foreign visitors like Lord Bryce and Andre Siegfried, along with articulate immigrants like Philip Schaff, always singled out as a, if not the, driving force of American culture.[5]

Since evangelicals differed substantially by race, region, era, class, denomination, and gender, a full history of nineteenth-century evangelical thought would have to reflect a wide range of influences, relationships, and responses to events, including, at a minimum, the effects of democratization, conservative confessionalism, the division over slavery, the Civil War, nationalism, antagonism against Roman Catholics, and habits of voluntary organization.[6] At the same time, however, on the level of formal ideas, nineteenth-century evangelical thought was surprisingly uniform. That uniformity was created by the enduring influence of intellectual assumptions, thought processes, and methodological commitments rooted in the American Enlightenment. While the story could be told in other ways, a focus on the Enlightenment provides an unusually comprehensive account of nineteenth-century evangelical intellectual life. In particular, this focus enables us to see how evangelicalism, a religion of marginal influence during the American Revolution, emerged as the nation's dominant faith by the early decades of the nineteenth century; how evangelicals put to use the forms of the Enlightenment to express their faith; and, finally, how intellectual crises in the period from the Civil War to World War I, especially the epistemologically charged issues of evolution and biblical criticism, were addressed along lines dictated by the earlier commitment to the Enlightenment.

## The Enlightenment to the Rescue of Protestantism, 1776–1860

The key matter of definition is to remember that the American history of the Enlightenment was not the same as the European.[7] For this purpose, Henry May's *The Enlightenment in America* is critical, especially its argument that eighteenth-century Americans perceived several Enlightenments, rather than just one.[8] Americans in general held in high regard, but from afar, what May calls the *moderate* Enlightenment exemplified by Isaac Newton and John Locke. By contrast, evangelicals in America came to repudiate two other forms of European Enlightenment, *skeptical* as defined by Voltaire and David Hume, and *revolutionary* as in the work of Rousseau, William Godwin, and (after 1780) Tom Paine. A fourth variety of Enlightenment, however, received a very different reception in Protestant America. This *didactic*

Enlightenment, which has recently been the subject of fresh scholarly attention, was largely a product of Scotland.[9] There, three generations of philosophers and moralists—among whom Francis Hutcheson, Thomas Reid, Adam Smith, and Dugald Stewart were the leaders—struggled to restore intellectual confidence and social cohesion to the Enlightenment ideal. They achieved these goals by showing that all humans possessed naturally a common set of capacities—both epistemological and ethical—by which they could grasp the basic realities of nature and morality. Moreover, these human capacities could be studied as scientifically as Newton studied the physical world. Such rigorous study, especially of consciousness, would yield laws for human behavior and ethics every bit as scientific as Newton's conclusions about nature. In the United States this form of Enlightenment came to dominate intellectual life for more than the first half century of its existence.

The influence of this didactic Enlightenment stretched broadly in the population at large, from Jefferson and Madison in the White House to the first professional scientists in the United States as well as to the literary pioneers of the new nation.[10] But the most articulate spokesmen for the common-sense principles of the American Enlightenment were Protestant educators and ministers. These principles provided the basis for collegiate instruction at Unitarian Harvard, Baptist Brown, Congregationalist Yale, Presbyterian Princeton, and the rest of the nation's rapidly growing network of colleges, still at this stage almost exclusively the preserve of the churches. They defined mental habits for evangelicals North and South, for dignified urban ministers and enterprising preachers on the frontier, for sober doctrinal conservatives and populist democratic polemicists.[11]

A wealth of outstanding writing has recently illuminated the way in which evangelicals made the Enlightenment their own. But still there is something of a mystery about it. This was a Protestant tradition descended from the Reformation and recently renewed by the New Light revivalism of John Wesley, George Whitefield, and Jonathan Edwards, with Reformation and revival both stressing human disability as much as human capability, noetic deficiency as much as epistemic capacity, historical realism as much as social optimism. Yet it came to express itself without reserve in the language of the Enlightenment.

At the middle of the eighteenth century America's most important evangelical thinker set himself resolutely against what James Ward Smith once called the "deeper spirit" of the Enlightenment.[12] Jonathan Edwards's books on free will and original sin and especially his *The Nature of True Virtue* called into question the natural moral capacities that were so important in the ethics of the Enlightenment and especially of Scottish moral philosophy.

Edwards also repudiated the metaphysical dualism that Newton took for granted, that stood at the heart of Locke's epistemology, and that grounded the thinking of the Scots. In opposition to the philosophy of common sense, Edwards held that the physics of Newton required an idealistic metaphysics everywhere dependent on God, and he believed that true virtue arose not from a natural moral sense but from the supernatural grace of God.

In addition, Edwards and other evangelicals in the mid-eighteenth century defended the Reformation conception of human nature that repudiated the high view of natural moral capacities underlying the ethics of the Scottish philosophy.[13] In particular, their view of ethics was conversionist; it divided sharply the whole of humanity between the redeemed, in whom God had implanted a "new sense of the heart" to know and love the ultimately virtuous, and the rest of humankind, which had to be content with self-centered or self-serving imitations of true virtue. This Augustinian picture of human nature was much more than the intellectual plaything of pedants, for it had provided the theology for the colonial Great Awakening of the 1740s, which some historians now regard as the single most influential event in pre-Revolutionary America.[14]

Finally, it is also pertinent to note that in Scotland the philosophy of Common Sense was linked to a Moderate Party in the Kirk that self-styled "evangelicals" resisted and even ridiculed. Moderate thought, one of the evangelicals spoofed, "has been . . . well licked into form and method by the late immortal Mr. Hutcheson."[15] The author of that sally was John Witherspoon, who migrated to America in 1768 to become president of Princeton. One might be forgiven for thinking that Witherspoon's rapid rise in the esteem of his fellow Americans would have inhibited the spread here of the Scottish Enlightenment that was so organically linked to his moderate opponents in Scotland. (The reality was just the opposite.)

A problem, therefore, exists in explaining why American evangelicals came so rapidly and so thoroughly to embrace the Enlightenment in its Scottish form.[16] The Reformation in which American Protestantism was rooted, the Puritan tradition that provided Americans their most articulate theological heritage, the Great Awakening through the writings of its leading exponents, and the newer influence of immigrant Scots who had opposed the Moderate Party all make it harder rather than easier to see why American evangelicals by 1800 would everywhere champion the naturalism, the optimism, and the scientific rationality that, albeit "pressed . . . into the service of traditional values,"[17] nonetheless still characterized their Enlightenment.

The answer to this puzzle is that the Scottish Enlightenment offered evangelicals and other Americans exactly what they needed to master the tumults of the Revolutionary era. In the midst of what Nathan Hatch has called "a cultural ferment over the meaning of freedom," the intuitive, sensationalist ethics provided by the Scots offered an intellectually respectable way to establish public virtue in a society that was busily repudiating the props upon which virtue had traditionally rested—tradition itself, divine revelation, history, social hierarchy, an inherited government, and the authority of religious denominations.[18] As Norman Fiering has put it, the "moral philosophy" of the eighteenth-century Scottish Enlightenment "was uniquely suited to the needs of an era still strongly committed to traditional religious values and yet searching for alternative modes of justification for those values."[19] For evangelicals who wanted to preserve traditional forms of Christianity without having to appeal to traditional religious authorities, the common-sense reasoning of the Scottish Enlightenment was the answer.

Two great political tasks confronted the Revolutionary generation, and a third equally great difficulty faced the Protestants who joined the patriot cause. The first was to justify the break with Great Britain. The second was to establish principles of social order for a new nation that was repudiating autocratic government, hierarchical political assumptions, and automatic deference to tradition. The third task, for Protestant leaders, was to preserve the hereditary position of Christianity in a culture that denied absolute sovereignty to any authority and that was turning against the structures of traditional religion (like the political episcopate or the establishment of Congregational churches in New England) as actively as it was turning against other inherited authorities.

For each of these tasks the reasoning of the Scottish Enlightenment proved irresistibly appealing. The general influence of the Revolution on American thought was such that the form of reasoning by which patriots justified their rebellion against the crown instinctively became also the form of reasoning by which political and religious leaders sought a stable social order for the new nation and by which evangelical spokesmen defended the place of traditional faith in a traditionless society.

The particularly Enlightenment character of this reasoning was its trust in objectivity, its devotion to a principle of privileged scientific inquiry. Protestant commitment to this form of the Enlightenment was thoroughgoing because it seemed to work so well—it could justify the rebellion, it did establish social order in a Constitution infused with the principles of moral philosophy, and it did make way for nearly a century's triumphant vindication of traditional Protestantism. Evangelical commitment to this form of the Enlightenment became deeply engrained, not only because it was so successful, but also because it was so intuitive, so instinctual, so much a part of second nature. For much of the history of the United States, evangelicals denied that they had a philosophy. They were merely pursuing common sense.[20]

The utility of this kind of Enlightenment reasoning was apparent. It was, most obviously, a mainstay of political argument. What weight could the traditional authority of the King in Parliament carry against the "self-evident truths," the "unalienable rights," or "the laws of nature" proclaimed by the Declaration of Independence? What need was there for a careful rebuttal of authorities, or even a careful perusal of Scripture, to justify rebellion, if it was transparent to the moral sense that such a rebellion was necessary?[21]

For evangelicals, Enlightenment patterns of thought had even more uses than they did for the statesmen who were employing common-sense arguments to establish a new government. Guardians of American public virtue could now rely on the "moral sense" to restate traditional morality in a scientific form without having recourse to the traditional props for ethics, including even the special revelation of the Bible. Witherspoon, who as professor of moral philosophy at Princeton turned to the work of his former bête noir Francis Hutcheson for the content of his lectures, claimed that when we study our own minds, we end up with the proper principles for a just and stable society. He hoped that "a time may come when men, treating moral philosophy as Newton and his successors have done natural [philosophy], may arrive at greater precision" on ethical matters.[22]

Witherspoon's successor as president of Princeton, Samuel Stanhope Smith, was the most capable early systematizer of the American Enlightenment. In a work from 1787 defending the unity of humanity Smith left no doubts about his faith in the power of the new moral philosophy to move from an examination of one's own heart to universally valid principles of social order, a power that would be destroyed if humanity did not constitute a unified species:

> The science of morals would be absurd; the law of nature and nations would be annihilated; no general principles of human conduct, of religion, or of policy could be framed; for, human nature . . . could not be comprehended in any system. The rules which would result from the study of our own nature, would not apply to the natives of other countries who would be of different species. . . . Such principles tend to confound all science, as well as piety; and leave us in the world uncertain whom to trust, or what opinions to frame of others. The doctrine of one race, removes this uncertainty, renders human nature susceptible of system, illustrates the powers of physical causes, and opens a rich and extensive field for moral science.[23]

The paths marked out by Witherspoon and Stanhope Smith were followed by most of the country's major educators in the years before the Civil War.[24] Exceptionally able books by Wilson Smith, Daniel Walker Howe, and D. H. Meyer have shown how deeply engrained this trust in Enlightenment procedure became.[25] Explicit in the lectures and textbooks of the nation's Protestant leaders was the Enlightenment belief that Americans could find within themselves resources, compatible with Christianity, to bring social order out of the rootlessness and confusion of the new nation.

## The Enlightenment and the Shape of Evangelical Thought

The extent of evangelical incorporation of the Enlightenment, however, went much further than merely its utility for the moral direction of society. In fact, when we observe how deeply this kind of Enlightenment entered into the fabric of evangelical thought, we begin to see why the tie between evangelicalism and the Enlightenment was so enduring. At the levels of high culture that tie shaped apologetics and theology. For all major evangelical groups it influenced expectations concerning revival. And among both common people and the elite it provided the framework for appropriating Scripture.

For evangelical leaders, principles of the didactic Enlightenment arrived just in time. A modern, respectable defense of the faith seemed absolutely essential for the survival of Protestantism in Revolutionary America. The American Revolution differed from the later Revolution in France in part because of the ability of American evangelicals to align faith in reason with faith in God. The intellectual goal of evangelicals in the struggle against the irreligion and disorder of the Revolutionary period was, In Witherspoon's words, "to meet [infidels] upon their own ground,—and to show them from reason itself, the fallacy of their principles."[26] In the 1790s and for several decades thereafter evangelicals relied heavily on the imported apologetics of William Paley to secure their case.[27]

Later, as they began to develop their own defenses for Christianity, evangelicals drew ever more directly on the methods of the didactic Enlightenment. Examples of apologetics grounded on scientific rationality abounded in the early national period. It was a part of Timothy Dwight's armament that proved immediately useful when he became president of Yale in 1795 and confronted undergraduate doubts about the veracity of the Bible.[28] Widespread as the recourse to scientific demonstration was among the Congregationalists, it was the Presbyterians who excelled at what T. D. Bozeman has called a "Baconian" approach to the faith.[29] In divinity, rigorous empiricism became the standard for justifying belief in God, revelation, and the Trinity. In the moral sciences, it marked out the royal road to ethical certainty. It also provided a key for using physical science itself as a demonstration of religious truths.[30] In every case the appeal was, as Stanhope Smith put it, "to the evidence of facts, and to conclusions resulting from these facts which . . . every genuine disciple of nature will acknowledge to be legitimately drawn from her own fountain."[31] Among both Congregationalists and Presbyterians, the most theologically articulate evangelicals in the early republic, this approach guided responses to Paine's *Age of Reason* in the 1790s, and to other infidels thereafter.[32] This kind of "supernatural rationalism" was also useful for counteracting the impious use of science by making possible the harmonization of first the Bible and astronomy, and then Scripture and geology.[33]

Closely related to the evangelical reliance upon scientific reason was dependence upon intuitive common sense, for common sense was everywhere considered the basis for reliable knowledge. Nothing worked better at squelching the deism that Tom Paine promoted, said the lay activist Elias Boudinot, than simply "the rules of common sense."[34] Timothy Dwight praised common sense as "the most valuable faculty . . . of man" and regularly used it both to begin and sustain arguments.[35] The same faith in intuition served the New Haven Theology as it counterattacked the Unitarians and modified Edwards's theory of the will. To accomplish the latter, Nathaniel William Taylor urged, "Let a man look into his own breast, and he cannot but perceive . . . *inward freedom*—for if freedom be not in the mind it is nowhere. And liberty in the mind implies self-determination."[36]

So basic did this reasoning become that even self-consciously orthodox Evangelicals had no qualms about resting the entire edifice of the faith on the principles of the Scottish Enlightenment. Archibald Alexander, longtime professor at the confessional Presbyterian seminary in Princeton, year by year told the first-year students: "To prove that our faculties are not so constituted as to misguide us, some have had recourse to the *goodness* and *truth of God* our creator, but this argument is unnecessary. We are as certain of these intuitive truths as we can be. . . . Besides, we must be sure that we exist, and that the world exists, before we can be certain that there is a God, for it is from these *data* that we prove his existence."[37]

The range and development of antebellum theology more generally is too complicated to sum up briefly. But even an abbreviated account of the New England tradition of trinitarian Congregationalism, which Bruce Kuklick calls "the most sustained intellectual tradition the United States has produced," may suggest the alterations that occurred when, even among those most solicitous of preserving historic faith, evangelicals became partners in the American Enlightenment.[38]

Jonathan Edwards's immediate heirs, Joseph Bellamy and Samuel Hopkins, dearly tried their best to preserve the master's teaching in the age of Enlightenment that was dawning about them. Yet the need they felt to defer to the impersonal, lawlike character of the universe (as in Bellamy's governmental theory of the atonement) or to stake everything on an empirical approach to the moral world (as in Hopkins's belief that God willed sin as an advantage to the universe) marked the path of the future.[39] Their turning had nothing in it of a disavowal; it was rather a gradual substitution of an Enlightenment mentality of celestial accounts for Edwards's preoccupation with the prerogatives of deity. In the next generation, Timothy Dwight and Jonathan Edwards, Jr., came more explicitly to trust in natural intuition, the unacknowledged source from which Bellamy's and Hopkins's sense of universal fitness had also emerged. Although Dwight was the most effective experimental Calvinist in the early United States, he yet relied directly on "common sense" to shape his beliefs about what was possible in the moral world, and on "natural ability" to begin a course of action.[40] In the mature thought of N. W. Taylor, Dwight's successor, orthodoxy no longer stood on its own, but was dependent upon "reason . . . our only guide in religion, in examining the evidences of revelation, in ascertaining its import, in believing its doctrines, and in obeying its precepts."[41]

In the next generation, the last of the great defenders of the New England theological tradition, Edwards Amasa Park, spelled out exactly how that theology had developed. The context for his account was a long argument with Charles Hodge of Princeton who accused the New England Congregationalists of giving away essential doctrines of traditional Calvinism. Park acknowledged that later New Englanders had adjusted Jonathan Edwards's convictions concerning free will, the imputation of Adam's guilt, and the nature of human sinfulness, but he felt they had good reason for doing so. After Edwards's day, "a philosophical theory, on the freedom and worth of the human soul" had made a welcome contribution to New England theology. The New England "scheme" was still rooted in Edwards, but its expression also benefited, as Park put it, from "the philosophy of Reid, Oswald, Campbell, Beattie, Stewart . . . *the philosophy of common sense.*" These Scottish philosophers had been able "to develop 'the fundamental laws of human belief.'" Their contribution "has aided our writers in shaping their faith according to those ethical axioms, which so many fathers in the church have undervalued." The result was that "the metaphysics of New England Theology . . . is the metaphysics of common sense." As a follower of this theology, Park could also take pride in the fact that "the New England system is not only scriptural, but is scriptural *science.*"[42] The end result of the sort of changes described by Park has been well summarized by Bruce Kuklick: "Disinterested benevolence showed the movement of Congregationalists away from a mysterious divine cosmos to a human-centered one, just as the theology itself relied less on mystery and more on what appeared reasonable for divines to believe. Hopkins's ethics responded to the same forces as Paley's utilitarianism. In the nineteenth century Congregational theology continued to grow humanistic."[43]

Other evangelical traditions in America developed differently, but in almost all of the major systems of the era—Princeton Presbyterianism, the Oberlin perfectionism of Asa Mahan and Charles Finney, and the frontier Restorationism of Alexander Campbell and Barton Stone—similar evidence was present, though often in contrasting ways, to show the shaping significance of the didactic Enlightenment on theology.[44]

Revivalism, perhaps the least likely feature of antebellum Protestantism to reflect the influence of the Enlightenment, nonetheless took on a new shape because of that influence. The push even in the realms of the Spirit, was to rationality and scientific predictability.[45] Charles G. Finney, the greatest evangelist of the antebellum period and one of the most influential Americans of his generation, did not speak for all. But the elements of Enlightenment thinking in his revivalism suggest how pervasive its principles had become. His *Lectures on Revivals of Religion* (1835) summarized a new approach to evangelism. Since God had established reliable laws in the natural world, we know that he has also done so in the spiritual world. To activate the proper causes for revivals was to produce the proper effect: "The connection between the right use of means for a revival and a revival is as philosophically [i.e., scientifically] sure as between the right use of means to raise grain and a crop of wheat. I believe, in fact, it is more certain, and there are fewer instances of failure."[46] Because the world spiritual was analogous to the world natural, observable cause and effect must work in religion as well as in physics.

Nowhere did the marriage between Protestantism and the Enlightenment produce a more lively offspring than in the American appropriation of the Bible. Traditional interpretations of Scripture may have come under attack in the new United States and traditions of biblical exposition or elitist assumptions about how much study was necessary before someone could publicly preach the Bible were gleefully disregarded, but there was no retreat from the Scripture itself. For reasons that have yet to be probed satisfactorily, the "Bible alone" (in both senses of the term) survived the assault on tradition that characterized the era. What Nathan Hatch has written about populist religion in the early republic was true as well for almost all evangelicals: "In a culture that mounted a frontal assault upon tradition, medi-

51

ating elites, and institutions, the Bible very easily became . . . 'a book dropped from the skies for all sorts of men to use in their own way.'"[47]

Virtually every aspect of the profound evangelical attachment to the Bible was shaped by the Enlightenment. Convincing theological arguments, like Andover's Moses Stuart's 1833 rebuttal of the notion of innate inheritable depravity, could rest on the fact that the erroneous view was "plainly at variance with the explicit declarations of the Scriptures . . . and with the first dictates of our unbiased feelings and our reason."[48] The orthodox Congregationalist, Leonard Woods, Jr., wrote in 1822 that the best method of Bible study was "that which is pursued in the science of physics," regulated "by the maxims of Bacon and Newton." Newtonian method, Woods said, "is as applicable in theology as in physics, although in theology we have an extra-aid, the revelation of the Bible. But in each science reasoning is the same—we inquire for facts and from them arrive at general truths."[49] Southern Presbyterian Robert Breckinridge wrote in 1847 that theology derived from the Bible could be a science expressed as "uncontrovertibly as I would write geometry."[50] The best-known statement of Enlightenment biblicism appeared after the Civil War in Charles Hodge's *Systematic Theology:* "The Bible is to the theologian what nature is to the man of science. It is his store-house of facts; and his method of ascertaining what the Bible teaches, is the same as that which the natural philosopher adopts to ascertain what nature teaches. . . . The duty of the Christian theologian is to ascertain, collect, and combine all the facts which God has revealed concerning himself and our relation to him. These facts are all in the Bible."[51]

Such attitudes were by no means limited to the established denominations with reputations to protect. A recent study of Alexander Campbell and the Restorationist movement, which led to the founding of the Disciples of Christ, the Churches of Christ, and the Christian Churches, argues convincingly that "the Campbell movement was as dear an expression of the spirit of common sense rationalism as one could hope to find in American religion in the early nineteenth century."[52] Nowhere does that rationalism appear more evidently than in Restorationist use of Scripture. At (Francis) Bacon College, which Disciples founded in 1836, students were instructed in how to study the Bible by the example of Campbell: "I have endeavored to read the Scriptures as though no one had read them before me." Other Restorationist leaders, like Tolbert Fanning, expressed the boundless methodological confidence of the age when he asserted that "the Scriptures fairly translated need no explanation." Another Restorationist, James S. Lamar, published in 1859 his *Organon of Scripture: Or the Inductive Method of Biblical Interpretation* in which the impress of the Enlightenment was unmistakable: "the Scriptures admit of being studied and expounded upon the principles of the inductive method; and . . . when thus interpreted they speak to us in a voice as certain and unmistakable as the language of nature heard in the experiments and observations of science."[53]

One final feature of early natural affinities came powerfully into play as American evangelicals embraced the didactic Enlightenment. In ways that have been probed extensively by a wealth of historical works, the process that witnessed Protestant alignment with the Enlightenment witnessed also Protestant alignment with the United States.[54] The contrast with Revolutionary France could not have been greater. In France, liberty, the people, the Enlightenment, and the new sense of French national destiny stood over against the church. In the United States, evangelicalism identified itself with the people, the Enlightenment, democracy, republicanism, economic liberalism, and the sense of American manifest destiny.[55] This identification had profound intellectual effects. Evangelical identity in America could no more be separated from its commitment to Enlightenment rationalism than from its belief in the divine character of the country and in God's ordination of democratic liberalism. All of the elements that went into the making of an American evangelical Enlightenment were melted together indistinguishably in the crucible from which also emerged the American nation.

## The Enlightenment and the Division of Protestant Thought, 1865–1914

If the antebellum bond between the Enlightenment and evangelicalism was as secure as I have suggested, the intellectual situation in 1920 looks like a puzzle. By that time a very different kind of science had replaced the earlier doxological Baconianism, and the academy had grown inhospitable to the earlier cultural alliance between science and Protestantism. In this situation there was an unprecedented intellectual division among evangelicals caused in large part by contrasting opinions on the merits of the new science. Through a complicated set of maneuvers in which the role of the churches is only beginning to be studied, the academy was encouraging new forms of science at the same time that it was replacing the traditional religious framework for a more secular one.[56] Nothing less than an intellectual revolution was underway. Nonetheless, despite very significant changes, the earlier habits of Enlightenment thought continued to shape the intellectual life of evangelicalism, even as evangelicalism itself broke apart into liberal and fundamentalist parties.

Several possible reasons may be given for the rapid shift in American intellectual life after the Civil War, including new scholars, new influences from Europe, new configurations in the American economy, and new social expectations for mass culture.[57] Whatever the exact role of Protestants in bringing about the altered state of affairs, it is abundantly clear that a new intellectual world had dawned. Views of science were changing from static and mechanistic to developmental and organic, attitudes toward academic work from teleological and doxological to progressive and functional, perspectives on religion from particularistic and theistic to universalistic and agnostic.

Painful decisions faced the heirs of those who before midcentury had operated from a base of Christian faith and scientific rationality in restful harmony. A threefold division of nineteenth-century evangelicalism came about in response to the new challenge. First, the more liberal evangelicals moved with the times, conceded the hegemony of the new science, and sought to preserve in a new form the old harmonies of the American Protestant Enlightenment.[58] For them irrelevancy threatened as their theology was superseded by the university's new intellectual conventions.

By contrast, populist evangelicals, the later fundamentalists, made a more complicated response.[59] They moved both with and against the times—with, by adopting the new applied technologies of mass media and public marketing,[60] against, by resisting the evolution of the old science into the new. They too attempted to preserve the American Protestant Enlightenment, but with its old content as well as its old form. For them loomed Kulturkampf or at least the frustrations of those who defend a paradigm after the authorities on normal science had decreed it was lapsed.

By far the majority of evangelical Protestants vacillated in the middle, nostalgic for the old intellectual harmonies, unsettled by the tendency of the new science to dismiss traditional Christian convictions, but unwilling to decide decisively for either the old paradigm with its tethered science and commandeering faith or the new with its liberated science and second-class faith.[61]

Because of the general intellectual situation and the nature of evangelical responses to that situation, the Protestant-Enlightenment synthesis, though battered, did survive. The new American university posed major problems of fact to evangelicals, but did not call forth reconsiderations of method. This set of circumstances—new problems within the context of old opinions about how to solve problems—is best illustrated by evangelical responses to Darwin and to biblical criticism.

The historic commitment by American evangelicals to the harmony of science and theology had everything to do with responses to Darwin's *Origin*.[62] Until the American scientific community itself embraced a version of organic evolution, Protestant leaders of widely varying theological persuasions (including advanced thinkers like Horace Bushnell, moderates like Phillips Brooks, and conservatives like Charles Hodge) could unite in rejecting Darwin's transmutation hypothesis as simply bad science. The few individuals like Harvard's Asa Gray, who felt he could reconcile Darwinism with a reasonably evangelical theology, were in a distinct minority during the 1860s.

When, however, American scientists accepted the broad outlines of organic evolution in the 1870s, the situation changed dramatically. Now evangelicals had to decide whether to follow their practice of more than a century—by adjusting Christian doctrines to evolution as they had earlier done in response to proposals about the age of the earth and the nebular hypothesis—or to draw the line against this new challenge.[63] Three positions developed in the last quarter of the century. Conservative naysayers rejected evolution out of hand, primarily for religious reasons—because it did not square with their understanding of the Bible. But that understanding of the Bible was also influenced by earlier commitments to Baconian science and eighteenth-century formulations of the Argument from Design.

Those who found it possible to align evolution with their Protestant faith divided into two additional groups. Theologically conservative evolutionists, of whom Oberlin's George Frederick Wright and Princeton's B. B. Warfield were the preeminent examples, thought it was possible to affirm evolution without making substantial changes in historic Christian doctrines.

By far the majority who embraced evolution, however, did so as part of a major adjustment in theology. The reinterpretation that evolutionary ideas advanced drew also on the higher criticism of the Bible, a new trust in religious consciousness, and a growing confidence in the progressive advancement of the human race. Following these trends, which amounted to an adjustment in the content of the Enlightenment, Protestant evolutionists came to defend an immanent conception of God, to redefine the Bible as an expression of evolving religious consciousness, and to recast Christian notions of redemption in terms borrowed from organic evolution.

It is precisely the historic evangelical-Enlightenment synthesis that makes sense of these responses. The debate over evolution in the last third of the nineteenth century was fateful because of the importance science had assumed for evangelicals in a post-Revolutionary, democratic culture. The ability to demonstrate scientifically the existence of God and the truths of the Bible was far more important for American evangelicals than for their counterparts in Europe, where traditional authorities continued to support, in varying degrees, traditional Christianity. Hence, conservative British and European Protestants never divided over evolution in the same way that

Americans did.[64] In these terms, the intellectual debate over evolution was also a debate over the role of Protestantism in a culture that had foresworn tradition. The failure of either proponents or opponents to question historic Protestant commitments to that bond between Enlightenment rationalism and Christianity also testified, however, to the continuing power of Enlightenment ideals among American evangelicals.

Much the same conclusions may be reached for Protestant divisions over the higher criticism of Scripture. The consensus that had once prevailed among Protestants on the nature of the Bible began to change during the last third of the nineteenth century.[65] Conclusions from both "textual criticism" (comparative study of the manuscript evidence for the original words of the New and Old Testaments) and "higher criticism" (the application of modern philosophical notions to the Bible) were calling settled opinions into question. The appearance of new views on the American scene corresponded with a surge of professionalization in the country's universities. In the 1870s and 1880s, graduate study on the European model began to be offered at older universities like Harvard and newer ones like Johns Hopkins. At such centers objectivist science was exalted as the royal road to truth, and the new professional academics reacted scornfully to what were perceived as parochial, uninformed, and outmoded scholarship. All fields, including the study of the Bible, were to be unfettered for free inquiry. In keeping with newer intellectual fashions, this scholarship relied heavily upon evolutionary notions. It was commonly assumed that histories, stories, and writings all evolved over time, as did religious consciousness itself. The new intellectual climate was also skeptical about the miraculous and reflected the view that the religious experience of Jews and Christians was not essentially different from other peoples in the ancient world.

For our purposes the salient feature of Protestant responses to the new views of the Bible was their uniformly scientific character. The inaugural public discussion of the new views occurred between Presbyterian conservatives and moderates from 1881 to 1883 in the pages of the *Presbyterian Review*. Both sides, as would almost all who followed in their train, tried as if by instinct to secure for themselves the high ground of scientific credibility. The moderates, led by Charles A. Briggs, were committed to "the principles of Scientific Induction." Since Old Testament studies had "been greatly enlarged by the advances in linguistic and historical science which marks our century," it was only proper to take this new evidence into account. To these Presbyterian intellectuals the situation, as Briggs saw it, was clear: "The great majority of professional Biblical scholars in the various Universities and Theological Halls of the world, embracing those of the greatest learning, industry, and piety, demand a revision of traditional theories of the Bible on account of a large induction of new facts from the Bible and history."[66]

The conservatives were just as determined to enlist science on their side. As A. A. Hodge and Benjamin B. Warfield put it at the start of the exchange: "[We] are sincerely convinced of the perfect soundness of the great Catholic doctrine of Biblical Inspiration . . . and hence that all [the Scriptures'] elements and all their affirmations are absolutely errorless, and binding the faith and obedience of men. Nevertheless we admit that the question between ourselves and the advocates of [modern criticism], is one of fact, to be decided only by an exhaustive and impartial examination of all the sources of evidence, i.e., the claims and the phenomena of the Scriptures themselves."

Their colleague, William Henry Green, chose not to examine W. Robertson Smith's "presumptions" that led him to adopt critical views of the Old Testament, but rather chose the way of induction: "We shall concern ourselves simply with duly certified facts." And Willis J. Beecher contended that the "mere hypotheses" of the new views proved nothing. 'Without some element of positive evidence, a hypothesis or a hundred hypotheses fail of themselves. . . . Any author is uncritical if he indulges in assertions which are based on mere hypotheses."[67] In this debate, both sides recognized the role of presuppositions—they were what kept the other side from seeing the truth.

Once the terms of the debate were set in this scientific form, there was little deviation. On the right, the populist scholars continued without hesitation to apply standards of the early American Enlightenment to the Bible. R. A. Torrey's *What the Bible Teaches* provided in 1898, for example, a book whose method was "rigidly inductive," where "the methods of modern science are applied to Bible study—thorough analysis followed by careful synthesis." The result was "a careful, unbiased, systematic, thorough-going, *inductive* study and statement of Bible truth."[68] Academic conservatives followed the same path. Robert Dick Wilson of Princeton Seminary, for instance, published in 1926 a work titled *A Scientific Investigation of the Old Testament* in which he chose not to use prophecy or miracles to support his traditional conclusions about the Hebrew Scriptures. Rather, he would use "the evidential method . . . the Laws of Evidence as applied to documents admitted in our courts of law . . . the evidence of manuscripts and versions and of the Egyptian, Babylonian, and other documents outside the Bible" to demonstrate the truth of traditional opinions.[69]

For their part, moderate and liberal evangelicals who defended the new views were no less committed to the authority of detached scientific effort, although, of course, science in the new mode instead of the old. Shirley Jackson Case at the University of Chicago justified renovation of older views on Scripture, because of the demands of science. Secular and religious historians alike employed a "method of procedure which is strictly inductive; all [their] conclusions are to be derived from concrete and empirically verifiable data." A true scholar sticks to "experimentally ascertainable facts," shuns "metaphysical speculation and worships at the shrine of empiricism." The best way of proceeding is "under the conviction—that religion can be best understood by giving first attention, not to its theoretical aspects, but to its actual historical research manifestations, and when speculative interpretations and historical research meet on common grounds he will insist that all hypotheses be judged at the bar of his science."[70] Liberal scholarship on the Bible still stood upon the older privileges of scientific inquiry.

A special irony attended the sway of the Enlightenment among at least some of those who promoted new views of the Bible. In the early years of critical scholarship Shirley Jackson Case and Shailer Mathews, both of the University of Chicago, were especially important influences. But although they promoted new views, they did so with traditional attitudes toward method. What William J. Hynes has called an "anti-metaphysical and anti-philosophical bias" characterized their work. Influenced first by Albrecht Ritschl and later by the scientific ideal of the "socio-historical" method, both scholars, again in Hynes's words, seemed to "prefer that philosophical questions be bracketed with respect to Christianity and theological methods."[71] Case and Mathews made no secret of their desire to replace fundamentalist views of the Bible with scientific, enlightened views. But the irony of their situation is that their aversion to philosophical self-consciousness followed exactly the path of nineteenth-century traditionalists who were also proud of having no preconceptions and simply letting the facts speak for themselves. At Chicago, the content of biblical interpretation shifted dramatically from previous patterns, but the power of Enlightenment assumptions about method remained pretty much the same.

In the end, therefore, questions about Darwinism and biblical criticism divided evangelicals. But they remained struggles over facts (and also over control of schools and denominations) that did not disturb hereditary Protestant confidence in Enlightenment rationality. Because it was an age of unquestioned hegemony for science—an age that fully embodied the optimism, this-worldliness, and scientific confidence of the early evangelical Enlightenment—and because evangelicals for a century had known no other world, it was second nature to address new problems with the old certainties of the first American Enlightenment. Moderates maintained the form of the old system; conservatives, both form and content. In the early American Enlightenment, evangelicals had been able to unite a commitment to authority from the people with a commitment to authority from science. In response to shifting intellectual conditions after the Civil War, fundamentalists tried to retain the old populist science, liberal evangelicals opted instead for an elite new science over against the old populism, but both, with the multitudes in between, did not challenge the older conceptions of self-justifying authority or the dictates of common sense.

Nineteenth-century evangelicalism was both broader and narrower than American evangelicalism has become at the end of the twentieth century. It was broader because it took in almost the entire Protestant spectrum. It was narrower because its intellectual base was tightly bound to the intellectual conventions of the didactic Enlightenment. What now seems like an anomaly—the harmony of Enlightenment science and evangelical faith—was then the commonplace that defined an era.

# Ideas behind
# the Women's Movement
## Beginning with Wollstonecraft

## Ruth Nadelhaft

In the mid-twentieth century, the United States women's movement developed new power and urgency, growing out of the successes of the civil rights movement, the antiwar movement focused on the United States' involvement in Southeast Asia, and a spreading disenchantment among predominantly white and middle-class women described by Betty Friedan in her book *The Feminine Mystique* as "the problem that has no name."[1] Although the thrust of this essay will be directed towards the identification and analysis of the nineteenth- and twentieth-century ideas informing the women's movement, I am convinced that we must begin with Mary Wollstonecraft's *A Vindication of the Rights of Woman,* published in England in 1792, reprinted in the United States in the 1790s.[2] This intense, hurried, and often repetitive text contains many of the under-pinnings, both theoretical and personal, upon which nineteenth- and twentieth-century activists and theorists based their commitment to the women's movement. Indeed, Wollstonecraft's book illustrates not only the intellectual categories and approaches that had much to do with the formation of later ideas and platforms. The book (and its uneasy place in Wollstonecraft's experience) serves still to illustrate the difficulties as well as the satisfactions in examining the place of women and the costs of social and political analysis and change.

Perhaps the most salient idea informing the women's movement and the development of feminist thought is the understanding that gender, as differentiated from sex, is a social and cultural construction. The meaning of gender, for many thinkers and activists in the women's movement, gives it centrality; for, if gender is indeed largely a construction of social and cultural experience, the nature of that social and cultural world has everything to do with the formation of girls, women, and society itself. Wollstonecraft did not distinguish, as our contemporaries do, between sex and gender. But she did clearly distinguish between those behaviors and characteristics that she viewed as "innate" and those she understood to result from the social, intellectual, religious, and personal influences to which women were subjected and to which—most importantly—they contributed as mothers of the next generation.

Wollstonecraft wrote from the perspective of an Enlightenment liberal, a believer in the improvement, if not the perfectibility, of human beings and thus of human society. She wrote from both a political and a moral perspective, taking for granted the conjunction between individual and society; she looked for improvement both within the human heart and through the agency of political and social change. It might be an oversimplification to describe Wollstonecraft as the source of what came to be known as Liberal feminism, but she must certainly be understood as the significant voice in the development of ideas underlying feminist thought of the nineteenth and twentieth centuries.

Wollstonecraft dedicated her *Vindication* to Talleyrand because, as she notes, she thought that he would understand her. That understanding would rest not on Talleyrand's commitment to the rights of women but on his sense of the necessary connection between moral education and national character. Wollstonecraft looked to the education and moral development of women both as rights and as responsibilities. Identifying women with humanity, attesting to the capacity of humans to choose the right and grow towards rationality, Wollstonecraft constructed several frameworks upon which later feminist thought, and generations of the women's movement, were to rely.

Wollstonecraft, early in her book, considers the fundamental question of innate differences between the sexes. She takes a firm position in favor of women's essential similarity to men as human souls; she contends, as later women's rights advocates were to contend, that nurture accounts for the observable differences in women's tastes and behavior. Here she argues consciously against Jean-Jacques Rousseau who wished men to benefit from women's softness, guilefulness, and outward obedience; for Wollstonecraft, women's deference towards men whose tempers and tastes were depraved constituted a form of slavery. Slavishness, she recognized, depraved both master and slave. Education she wrote, "is such

61

an exercise of the understanding as is best calculated to strengthen the body and form the heart. Or, in other words, to enable the individual to attain such habits of virtue as will render it independent."[3]

Wollstonecraft prized the notion of "independence," recognizing both from her personal experience and from the general conditions of her time the perils of dependence for women. Her desire to see women educated both practically and intellectually represents another of the fundamental tenets of the later women's movement. Wollstonecraft's concern was rooted in her politics as much as in her philosophical background. The European Enlightenment shaped Wollstonecraft's assumptions about human nature and the human capacity to learn and grow. The political theory of Locke, Godwin, and Paine looked to the sanctity of the enlightened citizen whose capacity to reason would contribute to the appropriate division of responsibility within the family and towards the responsible behavior of the state.

For Wollstonecraft, women's roles as wives, mothers, and teachers were paramount. So significant was the calling of mother and educator for Wollstonecraft that women must be properly educated in order to carry out the sacred responsibilities associated with child rearing. Critical issues about the nature of motherhood continue to engage the thought of feminists and women's rights activists to this day: In Wollstonecraft's identification of patriotism with the role of the mother in the home, she anticipates much recent discussion about the personal as political. She anticipates, as well, the thinking of such contemporary philosophers as Dorothy Dinnerstein and Sara Ruddick who argue that domestic arrangements shape the capacity of children to become agents for peaceful change.[4]

A fundamental issue for feminists was and continues to be the nature of women's sexuality and its proper place in both the public and the private sphere. Here Wollstonecraft anticipates some of the issues and judgments that perplex and divide the women's movement throughout its later history. Wollstonecraft taxes women with their sexuality and their romanticism. In women's narcissism and preoccupation with sexual attractiveness and the trappings of appearance, Wollstonecraft sees their undoing. Relations with men, to Wollstonecraft, if not based upon the firm ground of friendship and intellectual exchange, must result in exploitation and—most dangerous—dependency.

The women's movement that followed the time of Wollstonecraft has struggled to arrive at an understanding of women's sexuality and women's notions of personal appeal. For Wollstonecraft, middle-class women contributed to their own intellectual and moral inferiority by misdirecting their energies towards adornment and frivolity. Herself caught up in the heady and disastrous consequences of a passionate liaison, Wollstonecraft was precise and incisive in pointing out the risks and follies of relationships based upon sexual and romantic attraction.

Western culture has long differentiated between the angelic and the natural conditions of womanhood. Through Wollstonecraft, as through many other women writers and thinkers, women committed to the women's movement struggled, and struggle still, to describe and to respect the complex condition of women's sexuality. (In our own time, thinkers such as Sarah Blaffer Hrdy, in her book *The Woman That Never Evolved*, locate sexual behavior in thoughtful observation of primate relations.)[5] Many, like Wollstonecraft, strove to redirect the emotional and physical intensity towards motherhood and the domestic sphere. In the nineteenth century, the notion of separate spheres engaged many thoughtful members of the women's movement. Sarah Moore Grimké, in 1838, might have been continuing the thought of Wollstonecraft when she wrote about women that "the passion for dress, which so generally characterizes them, is one cause why there is so little of that solid achievement and weight of character which might be acquired under almost any circumstances, if the mind were not occupied by the love of admiration and the desire to gratify personal vanity."[6] In the middle of the nineteenth century, correspondence between Elizabeth Cady Stanton and her cousin, Gerrit Smith, testifies to the continuing association between the notion of "personal vanity" and the awareness of women's dependence upon—or oppression by—men. Smith writes to his cousin, "voluntarily wearing, in common with their sex, a dress which imprisons and cripples them, they nevertheless, follow up this absurdity with the greater one of coveting and demanding a social position no less full of admitted rights, and a relation to the other sex no less full of independence, than such position and relation would naturally and necessarily have been, had they scorned a dress which leaves them less than half their personal power of self-subsistence and uselessness. I admit that the mass of women are not chargeable with this latter absurdity of cherishing aspirations and urging claims so wholly and so glaringly at war with this voluntary imprisonment and this self-degradation. They are content in their helplessness and poverty and destitution of rights."[7]

Here Wollstonecraft's insight takes on new urgency, and its latent suggestion of blaming the victim—holding women responsible for the fashions and social constrictions that imprison them—flowers into the accusation of intellectual inconsistency and overwhelming vanity. Wollstonecraft's sense that the material conditions of women's lives, epitomized by their dress, their educational deprivation, and their habits, must be consciously addressed has developed into a misplaced fury directed against women's fashionableness: "Were women to throw off the dress, which, in the eye of chivalry and gallantry, is so well adapted to womanly gracefulness and womanly helplessness, and to put on a dress that would leave her free to work her own way through the world, I see not but that chivalry and gallantry would nearly or quite die out."[8] Women, it appears, by their acquiescence to the codes of fashion, have become responsible for their own oppression. Smith recognizes the deep similarity between the oppressiveness of Western dress and the "cramped foot" of the Chinese woman. But he focuses his outrage on the Western trappings that, he believes, testify to deliberate and mistaken choice by women who daily relinquish any notions of equality and power.

In her response, Elizabeth Cady Stanton articulates a strong nineteenth-century liberal feminism. To begin, she reminds her cousin that women have a perspective on such matters that derives from their experience of being women; she anticipates here later theory that focuses directly upon the notion of gender as perhaps the salient force affecting the formation of personality. Stanton reminds her cousin that equality under the law, regarding the right to hold property, the right to vote, the right to speak in public, represents the cure for inequality. Fashion, she asserts, "may be doffed or donned at the will of the individual; but institutions, supported by laws, can be overturned but by revolution." And, she points out, slaves dress with the utmost freedom and simplicity—in their slavery. This focus on adornment and dress, in other words, serves as camouflage for a lack of true chivalry that would see beyond the appearance of youth and attractiveness to the human soul.[9]

Wollstonecraft thus laid the groundwork for continued discussion of the issue of dress, personal adornment, and inequality. For Wollstonecraft, slavery or despotism corrupts humanity; like the nineteenth-century American abolitionists who attempted to link the pursuit of voting rights for women to the pursuit of human rights for slaves, Wollstonecraft understood the connection between the oppression of women and a caste system.

In the nineteenth century, American women working for the abolition of slavery also worked consciously for the emancipation of women. As Wollstonecraft understood the master-slave relationship to be at work in the marriage of dependency, activists such as Lucretia Mott pointed to the network of social complicity that accounted for the continuing existence of black slavery in America.[10] What Wollstonecraft describes as the indolence of gentlewomen comes from their having become "softened rather than refined by civilization.[11] Such women, like those Lucretia Mott sought to change, perpetuated the ills of the world by restricting their own minds and capabilities, devoting themselves to trivia rather than taking an active role in the moral and intellectual development of themselves and their children.[12]

These early and challenging accounts of the connection between domestic life and the health of the body politic provide some of the underpinning for the significant assertion in the twentieth-century women's movement that the personal is the political. This idea, along with the understanding that gender is socially and culturally constructed, provides one of the vital supports of the women's movement. On one level, this link between the domestic and the public worlds elevates and dignifies an element of women's traditional experience, giving to it a significance perhaps not otherwise apparent to those whose experience it has been. At the same time, the explicit connection between the private and the public worlds conforms to Wollstonecraft's claim that it is on the domestic hearth that notions of the public good, "patriotism," are engendered. A recent feminist analysis of curriculum development, Madeline R. Grumet' s *Bitter Milk*, suggests that parenting and teaching are essentially about "reproducing ourselves," not simply as families but as "the reproduction of culture, the linking of generations, . . . extending the traditions and conventions with which it was parented. But by situating reproduction in culture we need not collapse it into the habits, aversions, and appetites that testify to the persuasions of ideology. For reproducing ourselves also brings a critical dimension to biological and ideological reproduction by suggesting the reflexive capacity of parents to reconceive our own childhoods and education as well as our own situations as adults and choose another way for ourselves expressed in the nurture of our progeny."[13] Though Grumet's work does not refer to Wollstonecraft, her thinking derives from the approach Wollstonecraft argued at the end of the eighteenth century: In the reproduction and education of children lie the grounds for revolution.

Much of the energy of the nineteenth- and twentieth-century women's movements has focused upon the meaning and responsibility of motherhood. As Susan Gorsky points out in her study of women and literature in the nineteenth century, *Femininity to Feminism,* the nineteenth-century "idea that women reigned in the home is part truth, part myth, part lie; but the literature of the day implies that it is all truth."[14] Recent theorists and activists in the women's movement, working from the realization that the images of motherhood have taken possession of the cultural mainstream, have focused especially upon the pressures towards reproduction that, coupled with advances in the world of reproductive biology, have resulted in such expensive and exhausting processes as in vitro fertilization, embryo transplants, and surrogate motherhood. Feminists struggle to distinguish genuine empowerment from cultural conditioning as they consider again the options and demands of new forms of reproduction. Gena Corea, in her 1985 book *The Mother Machine,* asserted firmly that "reproductive technology is a product of the male reality. The values expressed in the technology—objectification, domination—are typical of the male culture." She acknowledges the presence of women in the world of reproductive technology, as nurses, doctors, technicians, and "entrepreneurs," but she is firm in her conviction that the industry is male in its ethos and its practice.[15]

*Choice* for women, whether in regard to reproduction or to the construction of social reality, is one of the key issues in twentieth-century feminist thought. Gena Corea's argument exemplifies the complexity of the issues that now confront women. While Wollstonecraft could represent early feminism in a unified line of argument, subsequent feminists, whose base of knowledge has expanded far beyond that available to Wollstonecraft, may not so easily settle on a consistent position in regard to reproductive choice. "With regard to the formation of the foetus in the womb, we are very ignorant," says Wollstonecraft.[16] Increased knowledge has led to more complex arguments and thus to divisions and dissent within the women's movement itself.

In turn, division within the women's movement of the nineteenth and twentieth centuries has resulted in a necessary rethinking about feminism itself; theorists and activists now understand that there must be as many varieties of feminist thought (and the women's movement) as there are many varieties of feminists. Wollstonecraft, who could focus her thought and her rhetoric on the emerging middle class in England, could simply exclude working-class and upper-class women from her consideration. As nineteenth-century feminists discovered, the identity of interests once assumed among women fractured with the twin movements towards emancipation of African Americans and voting rights for white women. In our own time, attitudes towards such fundamental concepts as reproductive choice must take into account the differing needs and campaigns of women from a variety of classes and ethnic backgrounds. "Gender, race and class" has become a unified concept that underlies the feminism of our time, demanding that serious feminist analysis recognize the inherent limitations and contradictions that these categories may unveil in glib and quick generalities.

Within reproductive technology itself, tests that reveal the sex of the fetus have presented new issues to the women's movement. Tests that allow women to learn whether the fetus they carry suffers potentially disabling defects also allow women to learn the sex of the fetus. This technology, in patriarchal culture, may well result (and does result, in India, for example), in the termination of many pregnancies that would otherwise result in the birth of healthy female infants. Feminists and other activists within the contemporary women's movement must thus mediate between the determination to make available to women the tools for self-determination and choice, and their recognition of the presence of patriarchy in both the development and the use of the tools of reproductive technology.

Members of the women's movement have hailed the development of theory focused on women's domain, women's ways of knowing, as it were. The women's movement has hoped that such theory would provide for men and women alike the alternative systems of thought with which to encounter the new complexities posed by advances in science, and women's changing roles in the workplace and in the family. The development of theory such as Carol Gilligan's revision of Lawrence Kulberg's hierarchy of moral values, articulated most fully in her book *In a Different Voice*, once again posits for women a kind of experience and a set of values that are *rational* rather than *individual*.[17] Morality for women thus seems to depend on modes of feeling and evaluating that have their origin in the domain of caring and compassion. Gilligan's work has been enormously influential but has also been sharply criticized precisely because it does not take race and class into consideration and seems to present women's moral development as a consistent response to an alternate theory of male development. In her book *Maternal Thinking: Towards a Politics of Peace*, Sara Ruddick grapples with such overly deterministic characterization of the moral perspective of women. This project necessarily means that Ruddick must disentangle ideas about motherhood from the psychoanalytic interpretations that originated with Freud but found their full expression because of the earlier assumptions that supported the ideas of Mary Wollstonecraft. For Ruddick, "Psychoanalytic theories regale us with the passions of family life told from a child's point of view." (Many contemporary feminist critics of psychoanalysis protest, of course, the refusal of Freud to hear the story of the female child when the story condemns patriarchy.) Ruddick understands the "romanticizing" of psychoanalytic theory to lie in its acceptance of the child's vision of the mother's power, a vision that must fail to comprehend the constraints upon the mother that come from her subjection to patriarchal power. "Fortunately," Ruddick writes, "in the feminist tradition numerous writers neither fear nor romanticize mothers and their work. These feminist writers distinguish the experience of mothering from the oppressive, confining, isolating institutions of motherhood that spoil that experience for many women." She quotes Mary Helen Washington, just one African-American feminist writer among many, who urge daughters to see their mothers not as icons or as projections but as "separate, individuated beings(s) whose daughters cannot even begin to imagine the mysteries of" their lives.[18]

It is one of the major tasks of the contemporary women's movement to disentangle the thought and behavior of feminism from the context of patriarchal culture in which individual and collective women think. It may be that this enterprise constitutes one of the most important ideas underlying the developing women's movement of the late twentieth century. Recognizing (and valuing) the particular characteristics of social and political contexts, many feminist theorists nevertheless search for some consistent thought patterns that can explain women to one another and distinguish their common experience. Many contemporary feminists turn to the use of language itself, constructed and employed in the service of patriarchy, to provide a new level of understanding as we attempt to carry the women's movement forward.

Although Mary Wollstonecraft wrote what we would now call social and political theory, her grounding was in criticism and in literature; her highest aspiration was to write fiction, and she left behind, unfinished, a novel that was intended to anatomize and to reconstruct and reinvent motherhood and the development of a woman named Mary, caught in the unjust imprisonment of a mental institution.

It is in the analysis of language itself that the contemporary women's movement connects with and departs from the life and work of Mary Wollstonecraft. For feminist theorists who consider the analysis of language and literature fundamental to our new understanding of the cultural and political world in which women come to be women, analysis of the construction of language is the analysis of politics. In her unfinished and perplexing novel, *Mary*, Wollstonecraft thought that it was through the construction of narrative that she could refashion social reality.[19] Most recently, some feminist theorists have shown that the use of language in effect *is* the narrative.

Susan Bordo, in her 1993 study *Unbearable Weight: Feminism, Western Culture, and the Body*, confronts the long-standing "mythologies" about women's bodies that have served throughout Western history to construct "a *practical* metaphysics that has been deployed and socially embodied in medicine, law, literary and artistic representations, the psychological construction of self, interpersonal relationships, popular culture, and advertisements—a metaphysics of the institutions and practices that sustain it."[20] Early in her text, Bordo acknowledges Wollstonecraft's insight into the primacy of the female body as the source and the objectification of the condition of women.

At the heart of Bordo's analysis lies her investigation into the idea of personhood, subjective identity. Simone DeBeauvoir's identification of the notion of women as "other," an observation invaluable to the development of the twentieth-century women's movement and to feminist thought, provides the point of departure for Bordo's chapter "Reproductive Rights and the Politics of Subjectivity." Here Bordo begins with the question, Are mothers persons? Considering key legal decisions, and most particularly the language in which, by which, they are constructed, Bordo suggests that the political answer to that question has been, No.

A sharp focus on language contributes to a sense of continuing urgency for the late-twentieth-century women's movement. Given the demographic shifts in the work force, the integration of women into industries, professions, and political organizations from which they had been conspicuously absent in earlier times, it has been possible for observers to suggest that a continuing preoccupation with the condition of women constituted an unwillingness to concede progress or to acknowledge the accomplishment of a veritable revolution. If language itself testifies to the preservation of the *idea* of women that is lodged in much earlier and less favorable understanding of women's reality, then the analysis of language becomes that much more pressing for contemporary feminists.

In the domain of "reproductive control," language has formed the issues in ways that remain to confront us at this moment in the late twentieth century, suggesting that the women's movement still has much to reckon with within itself, in its concern with diversity as described by the investigation of "gender, race and class," and as issues of ageism raised by important members of the women's movement themselves. But outside of the women's movement, issues remain that must be understood before they can be addressed by those who continue to work for women's rights and responsibilities.

Bordo focuses on the legal notion of bodily integrity that informs legal history in the United States. However, the strong, straightforward, and single-minded articulation of the right to bodily integrity, "'the right to one's person may be said to be a right of complete immunity: to be let alone,'" as expressed by a justice of the Supreme Court more than a hundred years ago, applies almost entirely to the notion of the male body.[21] Bodily integrity has been held sacrosanct in cases involving male subjects who have been protected from procedures understood by the courts to be invasive, to breach the security, in other words, of the envelope of skin within which the *person* resides.

The doctrine of informed consent, now observed virtually universally in hospital procedures, assumes this notion of bodily integrity, one Bordo considers extremely subjective. Requiring "a suspected drug dealer . . . to regurgitate two capsules he had swallowed" was described by an outraged justice in language deliberately evocative of both Medieval torture devices and the Holocaust. This doctrine, however, which is generally understood to be at the heart of both our contemporary medical and judicial systems, fails to appear in the language used to describe and to justify the very different treatment of women in regard to their reproductive lives. Here, as Bordo points out, the junction of gender, race, and class provides undeclared sanction for invasive procedures ranging from the preservation of comatose women so that they might be delivered of viable fetuses to the forced carrying out of Caesarean sections on women whose religious faith forbids such surgical intervention. Information from a 1987 issue of the *New England Journal of Medicine* illustrates this conjunction of gender, race, and class as the explanation for court-ordered obstetrical interventions in 86 percent of the cases in which they were sought: "Eighty-one percent of the women involved were black, Asian, or Hispanic."[22]

The language employed by court orders, justices, and the legal system in general focuses on "convenience" and "desires" when the issues involve women resisting, or attempting to resist, various forms of surgical interventions; such language differs to a remarkable degree from the language of torture, invasion, and intrusion ordinarily associated with violation of bodily integrity in cases involving men.

Increasingly, feminist theorists must concern themselves with images in language and in visual iconography that construct identity for women in ways that make true subjectivity difficult to attain. Wollstonecraft's insight into the ways in which socialization and education construct female identity extends deeply into the current thinking of the women's movement. Increasingly, scholars must use the resources of art history, anthropology, and communication theory to investigate and understand the ways in which gender is constructed, defended, and defined, often at the expense of the individual woman. Perhaps the most recent "idea" of the women's movement is the notion that any study of women must be cross-disciplinary, must indeed become a new kind of discipline that goes by the name of women's studies.

Certainly it is clear that the contemporary women's movement is much more complex than the conception of women's vindication advanced by Mary Wollstonecraft two centuries ago. At the same time, it is evident that her analysis and her identification of the issues of women's subordination were both accurate for her time and essential to the development of the ideas of the women's movement in the nineteenth and twentieth centuries. Wollstonecraft's concerns with the integration of private and public education, with the redefinition of maternal power and authority, and with the necessity of an altered relationship between men and women continue to be vital to the women's movement. In our time, the strands of the women's movement have necessarily become more separate and more tangled. Investigation of women's communication strategies leads both to a better understanding of difference and to the articulation of strategies for bridging such differences. Gender identity as a social and cultural construction has been differentiated from sexual identity in ways that take Woll-stonecraft's analysis far beyond her formulation. But the strands of continuity persist, offering both hope and disappointment: in that continuity and connection we may find the sources of many of our current and recurrent problems as well as the construction of the arguments that will help us to understand them and perhaps to bring about change.

One of the continuing challenges to the women's movement has been simply to continue as a visible movement. Our ability to trace some of the key ideas of the movement testifies both to its endurance and to its intellectual integrity.

# Ideas of the American Labor Movement, 1880–1950

## Gary Gerstle

For many years, scholars of the American labor movement were preoccupied with an ideology—socialism—that seemed curiously absent from the ranks of American workers. At a time when socialism and later communism were winning the hearts of the European masses, American workers seemed indifferent or antagonistic to it. To the extent to which they participated in the labor movement, they did so in organizations, such as the American Federation of Labor (AFL), that were avowedly antisocialist. The explanations of this exceptionalism varied, with Werner Sombart stressing the affluence of American workers, Louis Hartz emphasizing the absence of a feudal inheritance, and Marc Karson underscoring the conservative influence of Catholicism on a predominately Catholic working class.[1] But no one seemed to doubt socialism's marginality to American labor and American politics. A close corollary of this view was that class did not have the same salience here as it did in Europe.

In such exceptional circumstances, these same observers agreed, there arose a distinctively American brand of trade unionism. Variously labeled "bread and butter," "pure and simple," and "job-conscious" unionism, this American phenomenon, associated with the American Federation of Labor and its iron-willed, ex-Marxist leader, Samuel Gompers, was invariably described as hostile not only to socialism but to ideas and intellectuals of all persuasions. This labor movement was depicted—and often depicted itself—as hard-nosed rather than idealistic, practical rather than visionary, oriented toward the interests of ordinary workers rather than to those of dreamy radicals. Its goal was to get

American workers what they most wanted and what the American cultural and political environment most encouraged its people to seek: "More!" in Gompers's famous declaration.[2] Some observers praised this development as a wise adaptation to the circumstances of American life and wished the AFL and Gompers well; others deplored it as an abdication of labor's mission to transform social and political life. But virtually all conceded that "bread and butter unionism" was indeed the defining characteristic of American labor.

## The Challenge of Republicanism

This view came under attack in the 1970s and 1980s, largely by practitioners of the "new labor history," by social historians, and by historians of socialism. These scholars, at first, did not so much challenge the earlier portrait of the AFL as question the centrality of the AFL to the history of American labor. Turning their backs on Gompers, they began recovering the history of other groups of workers and labor organizations that earlier scholars had either ignored or dismissed as insignificant. Melvyn Dubofsky's meticulous history of the Industrial Workers of the World revealed the importance of syndicalism between 1900 and 1920. Nick Salvatore's gripping biography of Eugene Debs, in which he was able to show Debs's rootedness in American political and religious traditions, persuaded historians to accord more significance to American socialism than they once had. Herbert Gutman's stunning studies of long-forgotten Gilded Age labor struggles made that era seem far more turbulent, class conscious, and radical than previous accounts had suggested. Alan Dawley's and Sean Wilentz's studies of workingmen brought a similar perspective to the antebellum era. Leon Fink rehabilitated the Knights of Labor, a late-nineteenth-century labor organization that earlier scholars had written off as thoroughly impractical, unworkable, and thus inconsequential. In Fink's telling, the Knights were effective organizers, politically shrewd, and radical in their resistance to capitalist development and wage-dependency. In the 1880s, in Fink's judgment, the Knights "built the largest and most representative labor body until its time" and "probably the single largest unionizing movement in the Western world in the 1880s."[3] And until the 1890s, it was far more successful than Gompers's fledgling AFL.

David Montgomery carried this revisionist perspective into the history of the AFL itself. In his magisterial *The Fall of the House of Labor*, Montgomery convincingly demonstrated that the AFL was a house with many mansions. Bread and butter unionists, many concentrated in the building trades, controlled some of the more imposing mansions, to be sure. But the AFL was full of socialists who comprised as much as a third of its membership. And, at certain points, the socialists challenged Gompers's control, actually ousting him from leadership in 1893 and almost securing in that year adoption of a plank calling for the nationalization of American industry; in 1921, they challenged once again, and almost succeeded.[4]

Twenty-five years of research by the new labor historians produced a historical stage crowded with labor organizations of varied compositions and ambitions. These organizations brought many ideas to the American labor movement: several kinds of socialism and syndicalism, some built on a desire for what Montgomery had labeled "workers' control."[5] Equally important were the efforts by native-born and foreign-born workers alike to transform religious and ethnocultural traditions into tools of working-class protest. Herbert Gutman stressed the importance of the "Christian spirit" in enabling workers to counterpose values of justice, dignity, and compassion to the exploitative and demeaning character of capitalist development. Immigrant Catholics brought notions of moral economy, a just wage, and fair price to bear on the market forces that bore down hard upon them. Immigrants of all sorts transformed Old World traditions of resistance into tools of anticapitalist protest.[6]

In these studies, one idea seemed more important than the rest: republicanism. Taking their cue from colonial scholars such as J. G. A. Pocock, Bernard Bailyn, and Gordon Wood, labor historians began to argue that republicanism was the true legacy of the American Revolution.[7] In the republican vision, the nation would be comprised of independent citizens united by their commitment toward preserving liberty for all. Unlike liberalism, which defined liberty in terms of the right of each individual to pursue his private interest, republicanism emphasized the importance of a rich, vital public realm in which citizens would exercise their democratic rights, cultivate habits of cooperation and virtue, and enrich each other's experience of liberty. In order for this republican realm to flourish, citizens had to be intellectually and economically independent. Hence, republicanism's most ardent supporters, such as Thomas Jefferson, argued that a proprietary democracy, a political society comprised of farmers, artisans, and other producers who controlled their own labor and property, stood the best chance of sustaining the republican dream. Jefferson and others became increasingly vocal critics of capitalism, a system they viewed as stripping farmers and artisans of their economic independence and reducing them to the servile status of wage laborers. Capitalism concentrated power in the hands of a few and mired the masses in relations of economic dependency; in such circumstances, democracy could not survive. Power would drive out virtue and corrupt liberty, and the republic would fall. It was this belief that explains the presence of this remarkable statement in the preamble to the Knights of Labor constitution: "We declare an inevitable and irresistible conflict between the wage-system of labor and the republican system of government."[8]

The new labor historians found the republican critique of capitalism everywhere in the nineteenth century: in the workingmen's movements of the antebellum years, in the labor and populist agitation of the 1880s and 1890s, and even in the American Federation of Labor and the Socialist Party of the early twentieth century. American workers, far from being preoccupied with material gain, seem to have been inspired by a glorious idea: that those who labored were to control their economic destiny, and through such control preserve the American republic, the world's most remarkable experiment in popular liberty.[9]

The architects of this view, such as Wilentz, hoped to show that republicanism constituted a mature class consciousness, and thus that class conflict was as fully developed and fully articulated here as it was in any of the industrializing nations of western Europe. But this effort cannot be regarded as more than partially successful. Republicanism never was the coherent class-conscious ideology that some claimed it to have been. The labor republicanism of the nineteenth century was, in fact, a complex and shifting amalgam of ideologies. In addition to a healthy portion of classical republicanism, its ingredients included a good measure of natural rights liberalism and, as Leon Fink has shrewdly pointed out, a strong lacing of Anglo-American fraternalism. For this reason, it was compatible with a variety of social visions, some markedly less class-conscious than others. Labor republicanism could and did sustain collective visions of escape from wage labor, visions in which workers were imagined to be pooling their resources to free themselves from their employers and establish cooperatively owned and operated industries. But labor republicanism supported with equal vigor individualist formulas for escape. Countless nineteenth- and twentieth-century Americans have expressed their distaste for wage labor and their yearning for independence not through trade unionism but through independent proprietorship. They became farmers, small businessmen and manufacturers, shopkeepers, bar-owners, professionals—occupations in which they could be their own bosses, in charge of their own labor. They swelled the ranks of small businessmen (and of the Republican Party) as much as they did the ranks of class-conscious workers. The ease with which "class-conscious" labor leaders such as Terence Powderly, John Lewis, and others moved from militant labor organization to independent proprietorship and back again reveals particularly well how the republican thirst for economic independence could lead the same individuals in profoundly different directions.[10]

This same obsession with independence also justified a range of conservative, even reactionary, positions vis-à-vis blacks, women, immigrants, and the unskilled. A detestation of dependence accompanied the high regard for independence. Such disgust could and did prompt some labor republicans to launch movements to raise the dependent classes to a proud and independent status. A good deal of the energy flowing into the suffrage movement, the Knights of Labor, and Populism can be understood in these terms.[11] But what if dependence was thought to be rooted in biological weakness rather than in exploitative social relations? What if women were deemed unsuited by "nature" for republican citizenship or if African Americans, Slavs, the Chinese, or some other group was thought to be constitutionally incapable of achieving independence? Republican-ism offered those who thought in these racialist terms a rationale for depriving the "dependent" classes of their civil rights and excluding them from citizenship ranks. The very strength of republicanism helps to explain how this "land of liberty" could "thrive" while keeping large portions of its population in various kinds of servitude. Its discursive power makes sense as well of the hysterical fear of dependence—far more extreme than in Europe—that seems to fasten itself periodically on the nation's political imagination.[12]

## The Question of Socialism Reconsidered

By arguing that republicanism was as class-conscious an ideology as socialism, Wilentz and others intended to render the whole question of socialism in America obsolete. For, if American workers already had republicanism, they evidently did not need socialism. But if republicanism, in fact, was a poorer vehicle for class consciousness and one that broke down with distressing frequency—and Wilentz's own work on New York City artisans offers one of the most detailed records of this breakdown—then the question of socialism in America necessarily resurfaces, especially in regard to the years from 1890 to 1920, when rapid industrialization unleashed the nation's biggest crisis since the Civil War. The huge size of corporations and their extraordinary political power seemed to make a mockery of American republican institutions. The "labor question" bore down upon the country's politics with increasing urgency, especially as labor and capital engaged in a series of battles—the 1877 railroad strikes, the 1886 Haymarket bombing, the 1892 Homestead ironworkers and Coeur d'Alene miners strikes, the 1893 Pullman strike, and the 1913 Ludlow Massacre of 1913—that were among the most violent in the industrializing world.[13] Once the Knights of Labor, the Populists, and other popular movements that had based their protest on a republican critique had failed, increasing numbers of workers, farmers, and middle-class critics began gravitating to socialism.

Socialism, in the early years of the twentieth century, came in several forms: the democratic socialism of Eugene Debs; the revolutionary syndicalism of William Haywood, Elizabeth Gurley Flynn, and Carlo Tresca; the agrarian socialism of Oscar Ameringer and Julius Wayland; and the technocratic socialism of Richard Ely, Edward Bellamy, Walter Lippmann, and Florence Kelley. Socialists were well represented in labor unions, including several of the AFL's largest (the United Mine Workers and the United Association of Machinists, for example). By 1912, Debs had made the Socialist Party of America a serious contender in American politics. Not only did Debs receive 6 percent of the national presidential vote that year; his agitation about the excessive concentration of power in the hands of monopolists profoundly influenced Theodore Roosevelt and Woodrow Wilson, both of whom made the fate of the "Trusts" the most important issue of political debate. Recent works by Alan Dawley and Tom Knock argue persuasively that a powerful left-liberal alliance took shape in the years from 1912 to America's entry into war, compelling Wilson to push through Congress a series of domestic reforms that gave individual wage earners protection against market forces and corporate power. If socialism was not as strong in America as it was in Europe, it was nevertheless gaining in power and pushing American politics in a "European" direction.[14]

Still, important differences between Europe and America remained. American socialism seemed far more dependent, than did its European counterparts, on an older language of republicanism. In fact, one can argue that insofar as socialists, and later communists, made headway in the United States, they did so by couching their politics in the language of the American republic. This was Salvatore's most startling revelation about Debs. Soon after Debs was released from a Chicago jail in 1895—an incarceration that had completed his transformation from craft unionist to socialist—he began an address to an assembled throng of 100,000 with these words: "Manifestly the spirit of '76 still survives. The fires of liberty and noble aspirations are not yet extinguished. . . . The vindication and glorification of American principles of government, as proclaimed to the world in the Declaration of Independence is the high purpose of this convocation."[15] This kind of language remained a constant throughout the next twenty years when Debs built the American socialist movement into something of political consequence. And, subsequently, in the Communist Party's brief moment of significance in the 1930s and early 1940s, the distinctive language of American politics was equally in evidence, nowhere more so than in Earl Browder's incantation, "Communism is Twentieth-Century Americanism."[16]

This tendency to couch ideas in the language of Americanism was equally manifest among liberal reformers and labor leaders who were inclined toward socialism. Sometimes individuals such as John Dewey, Florence Kelley, Jane Addams, Sidney Hillman, and Frederick Howe called themselves socialists, but more often they did not. In Europe, they undoubtedly would have joined socialist or labor parties. In America, though they flirted with socialism and sometimes belonged to the Socialist Party, they generally preferred to keep the socialist label at some distance from their politics. They remained Democrats and Republicans or members of a third party that avoided the word "socialism" in its title, usually by putting the more ambiguous moniker, "progressive," in its place. They sought to describe their political agenda in terms that communicated the substance but not the rhetoric of socialism.[17] This was true of the labor movement, too. By 1921, the self-styled "progressive" bloc within the AFL, which seemed poised to oust Gompers from the federation's leadership, had endorsed a "`sweeping program' of `government ownership and democratic control' of American industry." Among their aims were the nationalization of railroads and coal mines, national health insurance, the establishment of a labor party, and ironclad government guarantees for the rights of workers to organize and bargain collectively with their employers. But they preferred not to call this socialist agenda by its real name.[18]

The phrase most commonly substituted for socialism—other than progressivism—was industrial democracy. It seemed to be spoken everywhere in the 1910s, by a wide variety of speakers with diverse political agendas. For shop-floor radicals, it provided a justification for their radical ambitions to wrest control of their workplaces from their foremen and employers—the first step, they imagined, toward working-class revolution. For more moderate trade unionists and middle-class reformers, it symbolized an alternative to revolution, a sharing of power between workers and employers that would introduce at least some measure of democracy into punishing and autocratic mass production regimes. It inspired all sorts of visions—collective bargaining, work councils, employee representation plans, stock distributions, profit-sharing, corporate parliaments—of how industry might be reconstructed in ways that increased the workers' sense of involvement, improved efficiency, and enlarged employer profits. Even socialists found the phrase irresistible. In 1919, the Intercollegiate Socialist Society changed its name to the League for Industrial Democracy, and, by the mid-1920s, Norman Thomas, Debs's successor as Socialist Party leader, found it a useful term for describing the thorough transformation of society that he hoped his Socialist Party would one day accomplish.[19]

What made the phrase so attractive was the opportunity it gave its advocates to link their controversial struggles to the revered American revolution. In a favorite formulation, radicals and reformers alike argued that the achievements of 1776, most notably the establishment of political democracy, were in danger of being subverted by industrial autocracy. Only the extension of democracy to industry could preserve the American experiment in freedom. "Political Democracy is an illusion," declared Frank Walsh, a left Progressive and chairman of the National War Labor Board, in 1918, "unless builded upon and guaranteed by a free and virile Industrial Democracy." In 1926, W. Jett Lauck, an economist and long-time advisor to John L. Lewis, president of the United Mine Workers, kept Walsh's idea alive with a book-length treatise on the inseparability of political and industrial democracy. And sure enough, when American trade unionism revived in the 1930s, Lewis, Lauck, and others hailed it as a "great movement for industrial democracy."[20]

The very prominence of the phrase industrial democracy, I am arguing, reveals a discomfort with the language of socialism. Even in the tumultuous period from 1890 to 1920, when American politics most resembled European politics, class conflict, it seems, could not be easily expressed through socialist language. This is not the same observation made by the early students of American labor such as Sombart. By and large they did not treat language as a medium independent of class relations. To their way of thinking, a working-class interest in socialism reflected the existence of class conflict; conversely, the lack of interest revealed the absence of class conflict. A situation such as existed in the United States—the presence of class conflict but an aversion to socialism—was a phenomenon that, intellectually, they were not prepared to recognize.

## The Language of American Nationalism

Why, given the presence of class conflict, was socialist language suspect? The answer lies, I believe, in the very strength and character of the American language of nationalism. America was an invented nation. It lacked an ancient attachment to the land; it lacked, too, a homogeneous population with a common history, religion, or ethnicity. Its identity depended, therefore, on the story of its invention (the revolution of 1776), and the justification of that invention in terms of a universal creed of equal rights, liberty, and democracy that would benefit all humankind. This story of the Revolution had to be constantly retold and the creed reiterated so that all Americans—especially the 35 million who came from abroad in the years from 1820 to 1920—would come to know them well. A willingness to measure progress by reference to the Founding Fathers and their ideals became a precondition for entering American politics, and political discussions often took the form of whether the ideals were being honored or breached. Upholding "republican" or "American" principles, then, entailed more than allegiance to discrete political ideas. It marked a willingness to involve oneself in the American nation. Constituent parts of the language of nationalism, these principles—liberty, equality, democracy—were the very sinews of nationhood. To abandon the principles was, thus, not simply to reject an ideology but to sever oneself from the nation. This peculiarly American predicament helps to explain why someone such as Debs always insisted that his socialism was to be understood as a continuation of the principles of 1776.

The situation in the industrializing nations of western Europe was markedly different. A French socialist, for example, might find republicanism useful to his critique of capitalism but it was not vital to his sense of being French. Some Frenchmen revered the Revolution of 1789, others reviled it; but fidelity to its principles did not become a test of "Frenchness." An opponent of the Revolution did not risk the charge of being "un-French," any more than did a supporter of the French Socialist or Communist Party. The notion that a Frenchman could injure his nation through the espousal of "un-French" doctrines was a strange idea. Freed of the obligation to provide the nation with its cohesion, ideology in France enjoyed a kind of autonomy that in America it never had.

The language of American nationalism was a remarkably flexible instrument, able to serve as a vehicle for a wide range of ideologies and political programs. Had it not been so flexible, it would not have survived the major changes in economics, politics, and demography that transpired in the two hundred years following the American revolution. But this language was not infinitely elastic. Two beliefs proved particularly difficult to reconfigure: a suspicion of government power and proprietary notions of independence.

The American revolutionaries viewed unchecked government power—it appeared to them in the form of George III—as the greatest threat to personal liberty, and they were determined to establish a republic immune to such tyranny. This hostility to state power was a crucial part of the story they told about themselves and, over time, it acquired the status of a founding myth. This myth proved to be a huge obstacle to the progress of socialism, an ideology built on a belief that only a strong, centralized state could vanquish private economic power (the most dire threat to personal liberty, in socialist eyes). Even the greatest moments of state-building in America—the Progressive era, the New Deal and World War II, the 1960s—were hampered by a continuing resistance to a strong state. Ambitious policies were often scaled back in Congress, or made dependent on private cooperation, or eviscerated through inadequate funding. This resistance was more than ideological; it took structural form in America's decentralized governing system, a system meant, from its eighteenth-century inception, to fragment state power (both within the federal government and between the federal government and the states) and to allow a proper scope for private liberty. This ideological and structural resistance to centralized state power made socialism a particularly hard sell.[21]

It was also difficult to overcome proprietary, some would say bourgeois, notions of independence. The original Jeffersonian vision of republicanism—the one revered by subsequent generations of labor and farmer militants—had been one grounded in notions of proprietary democracy. The archetypal citizen was the man who owned his land, tools, or shop. When the slaves claimed their freedom in the 1860s they thought not about establishing cooperative farms but about each getting his own "forty acres and a mule." This proprietary vision, too, was sustained by a material reality. A large yeoman farm sector persisted well into the twentieth century, as did a vibrant small business sector comprised of retailers, small manufacturers, and service providers. Thus, those who strove to redefine independence in collective terms, as arising from the common action of individuals seeking the establishment of communal institutions of freedom, had to struggle against the proprietary individualism rooted deep in American nationalism and sustained by particular patterns of American economic development.[22]

Other than the Civil War, the early-twentieth-century's industrialization crisis was the one moment when the power of this language of American nationalism might have been broken. The collapse of the Knights and of the Populists placed notions of proprietary democracy under unprecedented pressure. The immensity of corporate power made the notion that government posed the gravest threat to personal liberty look rather preposterous. The presence of so many immigrants infused American politics with a critical mass of freshly imported ideas for reorganizing society. But the hold of American nationalism, or "Americanism," a word that was uttered with increasing frequency, was not broken. With slogans such as "New Nationalism" and "New Freedom," influential reformers managed to adapt the language of American nationalism to a new age. The stronger the European ideological presence became, the more reformers intensified their Americanization campaigns. The uncharacteristically centralized state institutions established under Wilson during the First World War did violate the injunction against concentrated state power, but they were all torn down within months after the war had ended. Only an American military defeat in the First World War and accompanying economic devastation—the circumstances that produced revolutions in Russia and Germany and brought labor to power in Great Britain—would have shattered the mold. But the United States emerged the big winner in 1918, its capitalism vibrant, its nationalism proud, its antistatism intact, its socialists defeated, censored, scattered. This was the world in which American labor would have to live.[23]

## Industrial Democracy, Social Democracy, and the CIO

In the 1920s, 1930s, and 1940s, trade unionists offered two very different visions of labor's place in American society. One was a backward-looking proprietary vision that found its natural home in the post-1920 American Federation of Labor. This vision saw American workers as collections of craft workers who possessed highly developed skills and often owned their own tools and whose labor market power gave them a sense of personal independence. In the minds of those who subscribed to this vision, work, autonomy, and independence were bundled tightly together; nineteenth-century notions of republicanism still resonated. They were suspicious of a strong state, too, not so much because of foundational myths but because their real experience with government power had taught them that the state could not be relied upon to enhance their liberty. They were, in sum, a defensive group, conscious that they were a remnant of an earlier age and that most American workers labored in circumstances dramatically different from their own. Their defensiveness showed in their reluctance to bring the unskilled into the ranks, in their xenophobic fear of immigrant workers, especially those from southern and eastern Europe, and in their deep-seated racism towards African-American workers. They expended more energy on shoring up their collapsing world than on building a new and inclusive trade union movement.

The other vision was progressive and social democratic. It first emerged as the "new unionism" within AFL unions in the 1910s, and remained a fitful part of that federation until the early 1930s, when its leaders established an independent institutional base, the Committee (later Congress) of Industrial Organizations. The architects of this vision regarded the presence of powerful corporations and their armies of semiskilled and unskilled wage laborers as accomplished facts. It was these workers that they sought to organize. While conceding that factory workers could not enjoy the kind of workplace independence or control that nineteenth-century craftsmen had achieved, progressive unionists insisted that the wage-earning masses would benefit from the introduction of "industrial democracy" to the workplace. Industrial democracy, in their rendering, embodied an ambition to extend the rule of law and the consent of the governed to the workplace. Workers would be represented by a union that would bargain with employers not just on wages and benefits but on job descriptions, work rules, piece rates, hiring and firing, and perhaps even the marketing of corporate products and the investment of corporate profits. The resulting trade agreement (later called the collective bargaining agreement) would function as a constitution, stipulating the rights of both employers and workers and establishing mechanisms for resolving disputes through law and negotiation rather than by force and fiat. William Leiserson, an influential economist and labor relations expert, was so impressed with some early experiments in this "industrial jurisprudence" that he deemed them worthy of comparison to England's parliamentary system.[24]

Unions, in this vision, would not only represent worker interests, but would actively train them in their rights and responsibilities. Thus, unions were expected to restrain shop-floor militants who displayed little regard for the time-tested techniques of parliamentary democracy (elections, petitions, negotiations) and to undertake the vital task of Americanizing the masses of ignorant immigrants who were thought to be woefully unfamiliar with constitutional forms of government. When Sidney Hillman, the leader of the Amalgamated Clothing Workers (ACW) and later a key architect of the CIO, first observed the success of the ACW's Americanization programs in 1914, he could barely contain his delight: "To see these people, only a few years ago from lands where factories were unknown, meeting to discuss problems of the rights and wrongs of shop discipline, of changing prices, of the rightfulness of discharge is a thing to fill one with the hope for the future of democracy."[25]

At times, this view of industrial relations seemed not too dissimilar from what far-seeing corporate leaders envisioned. Frightened by the labor disturbances of World War I, these industrialists recognized the need to give workers more of a stake in their enterprises. They were not motivated simply—or even primarily—by a desire to spread democracy or justice. First, and foremost, they were interested in procuring industrial peace and raising corporate profits. They had become convinced that those workers who had a stake in their firm, who believed that they had some say in the conditions of their own labor, would work harder, more efficiently, and thus increase corporate productivity.[26]

Gary Gerstle

In practice, however, the trade union proponents of industrial democracy clashed with corporate managers over what kind of constitutional order factories should have and over how rights and responsibilities were to be distributed between managers and workers. The pioneering systems set up in the garment industry succeeded in large part because clothing manufacturers viewed unions as a crucial source of stability in an industry racked by uncontrollable competition. A national union, they hoped, would bring a uniformity to wage and piece rates, benefits, and work rules that thousands of garment manufacturers had been unable to achieve on their own. Employers were willing to tolerate the loss of unilateral managerial control that union power entailed as long as labor-management cooperation boosted, rather than hurt, revenues and profits.[27]

But the major sectors of American industry were not like the garment industry. Auto, steel, and rubber manufactures, to take three examples, were characterized by oligopolistic control rather than competition. The dominant firms in each industry believed that they could achieve corporate stability on their own, without the aid of unions; and their sheer industrial might made them contemptuous of the thought of conceding any power to shop-floor militants. The Great Depression gravely injured the confidence, resources, and power of these firms, of course, and trade unionists were quick to take advantage of their weakness. Labor-management relations became increasingly contentious and threatening to corporate control. The federal government hoped to direct this labor turbulence into more orderly and constitutional channels by passing the National Labor Relations Act (NLRA) in 1935, legislation that established clear and enforceable procedures for workers to choose unions as their bargaining agents and for unions and employers to negotiate a mutually agreed-upon contract. But the NLRA left several crucial issues frustratingly vague. For example, the precise nature of employee or employer rights was nowhere specified, nor did the NLRA establish a mechanism that would allow management and labor to adjudicate contract disputes. Thus, in the five years following the NLRA's passage, a variety of workplace regimes developed, their character usually reflecting the strength or weakness of particular unions. Where industrial unions were strong, workers were able to translate NLRA law into elaborate systems for the democratization of industrial authority. In Rhode Island by 1941, for example, well-organized textile unionists had democratized virtually every element of shop-floor life. The hiring, firing and transfer of workers, the distribution of available work and the determination of work loads, the introduction of new technology and alterations in piece rates: all these tasks, once the sole province of employers, were now to be jointly undertaken by management and labor. But where unions were weak, little constitutionalism developed, and employers remained lords of the shop floor.[28]

The imperatives of war mobilization made this uneven pattern of development intolerable. In 1941, the Roosevelt administration established the War Labor Board (WLB) to standardize rules of labor-management relations throughout American manufacturing. The WLB reinforced workers' basic collective bargaining rights—to join a union, to bargain collectively with employers over wages, hours, and benefits—and thus abetted the spread of unionism to ever wider circles of American industry. By the war's end, fifteen million workers, representing a full 35 percent of the nation's nonagricultural work force, enjoyed union representation, and the access to decent wages, job security, and benefits such as vacations and health insurance that union membership provided. But the WLB simultaneously carved out a sphere of what it called "managerial prerogatives"—aspects of corporate production, distribution, and investment in which all power would continue to reside with the employers. Workers could no longer hope that their consent would be needed in matters of technological change, the character and amount of investment, the prices that corporations would charge for their goods. General Motors workers under the leadership of United Auto Workers (UAW) president Walter Reuther staged a bold strike in 1946 to undo what the WLB had wrought. Specifically, they insisted that GM commit itself both to an 18-percent wage increase for its workers and to holding the price of its automobiles to their existing levels. GM was willing to grant the wage increase but not union meddling in the pricing of its products—a practice that it considered the prerogative of the corporation alone. Rather than capitulate, GM weathered a 113-day strike in the midst of a new model season, outlasting the workers who finally agreed to return to work under conditions set by GM. The UAW had received no support from the government, which considered product pricing outside the scope of collective bargaining. This strike thus made clear that the precedents established during war would continue during the peace. The result, at GM and elsewhere, was a truncated kind of constitutionalism that fell far short of the aspirations of the early visionaries of industrial democracy.[29]

The progressive unionism put forward by Sidney Hillman and others in the 1920s and 1930s had another component, however: a grand plan for reorganizing the American economy around the principles of high wages and high consumption. These progressive trade unionists wanted each American worker to be paid wages high enough to escape poverty, to achieve security for himself and his family, and to participate in the satisfactions of an ever expanding and alluring consumer marketplace. They argued that these goals, if achieved, would not only benefit workers but the whole of the American economy. High wages would spur consumer expenditures, invigorate markets, stimulate production, and thus increase corporate revenues and profits. As the depression worsened and corporate profits shrank, these progressives made their case with ever more fervor. They argued that the American economy was suffering from a case of chronic underconsumption, by which they meant that consumers did not possess the resources necessary to purchase enough of what American industry could produce. The surest road to recovery was, simply, to increase consumer purchasing power.

Seen in these terms alone, this economic recovery plan posed little threat to the nation's existing corporate structure. But once the progressive trade unionists began discussing how consumer purchasing power was to be increased, their challenge to a capitalist economy came into focus. Not only would extensive unionization be required to wrest wage increases from unwilling employers, a development that demanded government endorsement and protection of labor organizations, but the government would have to embark on a plan to redistribute wealth from the richest Americans to the poorest, in order to insure that a higher proportion of the nation's income would flow into consumption channels. Progressive taxation, social welfare spending, and public works investments, in the eyes of Hillman and his associates, were all techniques that would accomplish this downward redistribution and thus augment the working class's purchasing power. The deployment of these techniques, of course, could only be done by a strong national government with broad powers to control fiscal policy and to regulate capitalist financial and labor markets. The federal government would have to be enlarged, its economic powers enhanced, its role in economic planning legitimated. Ultimately, progressive unionists hoped to establish a tripartite corporatist system of industrial governance in which the leaders of American labor would meet with those of American industry and government and jointly plan the future of the American economy. In Europe this system came to be known as social democracy. American unionists, still worried about too close an association with the socialist label, substituted their favorite and hopelessly overworked phrase, "industrial democracy."[30]

This version of industrial democracy required unionists to reformulate two key aspects of the country's nationalist language. First, they had to justify a strong state as quintessentially American, as fulfilling the original aims of the Founding Fathers. This they did by using the argument that Lewis and others had set forth in the 1910s and 1920s, that political democracy would fail unless accompanied by the democratization of industry. Industrial democracy, they insisted, embodied the spirit of liberty unleashed in 1776. The labor leaders were given a boost by Roosevelt's and the Democratic Party's parallel efforts to claim that their innovative social policies and commitment to a large state constituted "a true Americanism," one that the Minute Men of Lexington and Concord would have recognized as necessary to the completion of the struggle that they had begun.[31] Second, the progressive unionists had to argue that the satisfactions of American workers would no longer come through work itself but through the earnings that work made possible. Progressive unionists were genuinely excited about the possibilities opened by a consumer society. They believed that the psychological rewards of leisure could compensate for the inadequate rewards of work, especially for the armies of mass production workers whose jobs held few intrinsic attractions. They thus began to detach themselves from the old republican belief that individuals derived their sense of self and citizenship from the nature and quality of their labor. In its place they asked Americans to commit themselves to an "American Standard of Living," by which they meant an income that would enable each American worker to participate fully in the alluring American marketplace. This reorientation was a dangerous one for an American labor movement to undertake, not just because it violated older and still cherished republican principles but also because it risked making the very idea of a *labor* movement obsolete. For once labor came to be seen in instrumental terms, as simply a means to affluence, security, and leisure rather than as integral to an ontological quest for honor, pride, and satisfaction, then it might lose its special claim on America's moral and democratic imagination.

But these were long-term and rather abstract considerations that, in the context of the Great Depression, seemed beside the point. The immediate concern was developing a political strategy that would enable the labor movement to gain state power and implement its vision. That strategy took shape as an alliance with Franklin Roosevelt, once Roosevelt in 1935, in response to labor's growing militancy, welcomed labor into his Democratic Party coalition and turned his New Deal in a decidedly pro-labor and "underconsumptionist" direction. He lent his support to the NLRA, a massive public works program, a national social welfare program (Social Security), and sharply graduated tax on the wealthy. In return, labor unions worked all-out for his reelection in 1936 and helped him achieve a smashing victory. In 1936 and 1937, labor's friends flooded into the administration and established control over such key federal agencies as the National Labor Relations Board, the Interior Department, the Works Progress Administration, the National Resources Planning Board, the Rural Electrification Agency, and the Federal Reserve. The CIO's ranks swelled under the friendly gaze of this incipient welfare state, and social democracy no longer appeared so far-fetched a dream.[32]

But in 1937, this state-labor alliance lost its momentum. The Supreme Court's continuing resistance to New Deal policies prompted Roosevelt to embark on his ill-advised and politically damaging court-packing scheme. Labor's spreading militancy—apparent both in a wave of sit-down strikes and the CIO's 1937 decision to carry its fight to the South (still the nation's most antiunion region)—further invigorated conservative opposition. When the sharp recession of 1937 dashed hopes for economic recovery yet again, many Americans had had enough of New Deal experimentation and sent a large contingent of conservative, antilabor representatives to Congress. New Deal reform was thus stalemated: Existing social programs were stripped of funds, new ones failed to move out of Congressional committees, the "underconsumptionists" lost their influence over fiscal policy, and labor's most ardent supporters lost their control of the National Labor Relations Board. The march toward a corporatist state was halted and then reversed. Hopes revived during World War II, when war exigencies seemed to demand the kind of democratic national planning that progressive unionists had been advocating since the mid-1930s. Indeed, the War Production Board and related state institutions seemed to embody the kind of tripartite corporatist arrangements that CIO leaders desired. In fact, however, labor was very much a junior partner in these government arrangements, unable to challenge the superior power of capital, a superiority that the Roosevelt administration had pledged to protect.[33]

Labor vigorously challenged capitalism's restored power once the war ended. The year 1946 saw the greatest strike wave in American history. At the same time, labor embarked on Operation Dixie, its second major effort in a decade to organize southern workers and to develop electoral strength in a region that wielded enormous legislative power. But its efforts failed. An American capitalism rejuvenated by the war was in no mood to share its corporate power. The outbreak of the Cold War and the accompanying ideological hysteria made it easy for labor's opponents to stigmatize any labor militancy as "communist" and thus "un-American." The Taft-Hartley Law of 1947 curtailed labor's rights to organize and stripped any union led by a communist of its government-guaranteed rights. Nine CIO unions, representing 900,000 CIO members, were led by communists, and, in 1949, the CIO expelled them from its federation. The CIO would not easily recover from this amputation. The AFL, meanwhile, had been rejuvenated by the favorable labor laws that the CIO movement had achieved, and it was further strengthened by its devout opposition to communism, to state planning, and other CIO "sins." It held the upper hand in merger negotiations with the hobbled CIO, which is why an AFL rather than a CIO man became head of the merged labor federation in 1955.[34]

Certain features of the CIO endured. Mass production industries were organized on an enduring basis for the first time in America history. The CIO had lifted a whole section of working-class America out of poverty, and integrated them, economically and culturally, into the nation. The CIO had helped to legitimate the idea of a welfare state. But the CIO's more ambitious schemes had been defeated. National democratic planning, the constitutionalization of shop-floor life, a strong social welfare state that would provide income security, pensions, and health care to all Americans, not just those who were unionized: each of these ambitions was scuttled. The CIO had succeeded in moderating but not in overcoming an entrenched American suspicion of a strong state; it had muted but not eliminated American hostility to collective institutions of freedom. The Cold War became the occasion for corporate America to unleash a vigorous ideological attack on even the modest advances that the CIO had achieved. American labor's perch, even in the years of its greatest security, was precarious. The CIO's ideas had been bold, its strategy of presenting them as an updated Americanism shrewd, but its success had still been limited.[35]

It is tempting to suggest that the CIO would have fared better had it not temporized. But little evidence suggests that labor organizations that resisted the pull of a nationalist language and refused to dilute their radical purity enjoyed better success. The world into which the CIO was born, the language of American nationalism it inherited, were not of its own making. That language could be spoken in different ways, its words could be used to construct rival "Americanisms"; but its influence could not be escaped, and its hostility to socialism never entirely overcome.

# From Child Labor to Child Work
## Changing Cultural Conceptions of
## Children's Economic Roles, 1870s–1930s

### Viviana A. Zelizer

The 1900 U.S. Census reported that one child out of every six between the ages of ten and fifteen was gainfully employed. It was an undercount: the total figure of 1,750,178 excluded many child laborers under ten as well as the children "helping out" their parents in sweatshops and on farms, before or after school hours. Ten years later, the official estimate of working children reached 1,990,225. But by 1930, the economic participation of children had dwindled dramatically. Census figures registered 667,118 laborers under fifteen years of age. The decline was particularly marked among younger children. Between 1900 and 1930, the number of children ten to thirteen years old in nonagricultural occupations alone decreased more than six fold, from 186,358 to under 30,000.[1]

The exclusion of children from the marketplace involved a difficult and prolonged battle lasting almost half a century from the 1870s to the 1930s. It was partly an economic confrontation and partly a legal dispute, but it was also a profound "moral revolution."[2] Two groups with sharply conflicting views of childhood struggled to impose their definition of children's proper place. For child labor reformers children's early labor was a violation of children's sentimental value. As one official of the National Child Labor Committee explained in 1914, a laboring child "is simply a producer, worth so much in dollars and cents, with no standard of value as a human being. . . . How do you calculate your standard of a child's value? . . . as something precious beyond all money standard."[3] On the other hand, opponents of child labor reform were just as vehement in

90

their support of the productive child, "I say it is a tragic thing to contemplate if the Federal Government closes the doors of the factories and you send that little child back, empty-handed; that brave little boy that was looking forward to get money for his mother for something to eat."[4]

This paper is about the profound cultural transformation in the economic and sentimental value of children—fourteen years of age or younger—in the early twentieth century; more specifically, the emergence of the economically "worthless" but emotionally "priceless" child. While in the nineteenth century, the market value of children was culturally acceptable, the new normative ideal of the child as an exclusively emotional asset precluded instrumental considerations. In an increasingly commercialized world, children were reserved a separate noncommercial place, *extra commercium*. The economic and sentimental values of children were thereby declared to be radically incompatible. Only mercenary or insensitive parents violated the boundary by accepting the wages or labor contributions of a useful child. Properly loved children, regardless of social class, belonged in a domesticated nonproductive world of lessons, games, and token money.

It was not a simple process. At every step, working-class and middle-class advocates of a useful childhood battled the social construction of the economically useless child. This paper will examine two aspects of the public reassessment of children's economic participation at the turn of the century: first, the controversy over the legitimacy of early labor, and second, the differentiation between child work and child labor.

## The Useful Child: From Family Asset to Social Problem

In recent studies, economists and historians have documented the vital significance of child labor for working-class families in the late nineteenth century. Using extensive national data from the 1880s and 1890s, Michael Haines concludes that child labor "appears to have been the main source of additional support for the late nineteenth-century urban family under economic stress."[5] Unlike the mid-twentieth century when married women entered the labor force, in the late nineteenth century a child, not a wife, was likely to become the family's secondary wage earner. To use children as active participants in the household economy of the working class was not only economically indispensable but also a legitimate social practice.

Child labor was not a nineteenth-century invention. American children had always worked. In his classic study of family life in Plymouth Colony, John Demos suggests that by the time children turned six or eight, they were expected to assume the role of "little adults," engaged in useful tasks in their own homes, or apprenticed elsewhere.[6] By the mid-nineteenth century, however, the construction of the economically worthless child was completed among the urban middle class. Concern shifted to education as the determinant of future marketplace worth. Yet the economic value of the working-class child increased, rather than decreased in the nineteenth century. Rapid industrialization multiplied job opportunities for children, and according to the 1870 census, about one out of every eight children was employed.

By 1900 middle-class reformers began indicting children's economic cooperation as unjustified parental exploitation: child labor emerged for the first time as a major social problem in the United States. There had been some concern before, but the occasional attempts to regulate the work of children had been largely ineffective and unable to galvanize public opinion. Existing state laws were so lax and vague as to be unenforceable. In fact, they were not even intended to put children out of work. Instead, early child labor legislation was primarily concerned with assuring a minimum of education for working children.

Child labor only gradually achieved national visibility. In 1870, for the first time, the U.S. Census provided a separate count of adult and child workers. Bureaus of labor statistics were organized in ten states between 1869 and 1883, producing and distributing data on child workers. Child labor rapidly established itself as a priority item in the political agenda of Progressive social reformers. Organizational growth was impressive. The first Child Labor Committee was formed in 1901; by 1910 there were twenty-five state and local committees in existence. A National Child Labor Committee was established in 1904. These groups sponsored and indefatigably publicized exposés of child labor conditions.

Why did twentieth-century child labor lose its nineteenth-century good reputation? What explains the sudden vehemence and urgency to remove all children from the labor market? Most historical interpretations focus on the effect of structural, economic, and technological change on child labor trends between the 1870s and the 1930s. The success of industrial capitalism is assigned primary responsibility for putting children out of work and into schools to satisfy the growing demand for a skilled, educated labor force. Rising real incomes, on the other hand, explain the reduced need for children's wages. As the standard of living steadily improved between the late nineteenth century and the 1920s, child labor declined simply because families could afford to keep their children in school. Stricter and better-enforced compulsory education laws further accelerated the unemployment of children.[7]

In his analysis of changes in the youth labor market, Paul Osterman contends that children were "pushed out of industry" not only by the declining demand for unskilled labor but also by a simultaneous increase in its supply. The tide of immigrants at the turn of the century began to compete with child laborers.[8] Joan Huber similarly points to a conflict of interest between age groups created by the new economic system. In an agrarian economy, as in the early stages of industrialization, the labor of "little work people," was a welcome alternative that freed men for agriculture. But by the turn of the century, a cheap labor supply threatened to depress adult wages.[9] Demand for child laborers was further undermined by new technology. For example, in late-nineteenth-century department stores, such as Macy's and Marshall Field's, one-third of the labor force was composed of cash girls or cash boys, young children busily involved in transporting money and goods between sales clerks, the wrapping desk, and the cashier. By 1905, the newly invented pneumatic tube and the adoption of cash registers had usurped most children's jobs.[10]

The issue of child labor, however, cannot be reduced to neat economic equations. If the inevitable outcome of a reduced demand plus the increased supply of unskilled labor was the unemployment of children, why then was their exclusion from the market such a complex and controversial process?

## The Child Labor Controversy

The history of American child labor legislation is a chronicle of obstacles and defeats. At every step of a battle that lasted some fifty years, the sustained efforts of child labor reformers were blocked by an equally determined, vocal, and highly effective opposition. Until 1938, every major attempt to pass national regulation of child labor was defeated. Although the battle did involve organizations such as the National Association of Manufacturers and the American Farm Bureau Federation whose members were reluctant to forgo the profitable labor of their many child employees, it also included a wide range of other participants: from clergymen, educators, and journalists to prominent citizen organizations and even the parents of child laborers. The child labor dispute, therefore, cannot be dismissed simply as a struggle between greedy employers determined to increase profits and humane reformers committed to stop the exploitation of children. At issue was a profound cultural uncertainty and dissent over the proper economic roles for young children.

Opponents of child labor legislation defended the pragmatic and moral legitimacy of a useful child. As a controversial article in the *Saturday Evening Post* asserted, "The work of the world has to be done; and these children have their share. . . . Why should we . . . place the emphasis on . . . prohi-

93

bitions? . . . We don t want to rear up a generation of nonworkers, what we want is workers and more workers."[11] From this perspective, regulatory legislation introduced an unwelcome and dangerous "work prohibition." The consequences would be dire: "If a child is not trained to useful work before the age of 18, we shall have a nation of paupers and thieves." Child labor, insisted its supporters, was safer than "child-idleness."[12]

For working-class families, the usefulness of their children was supported by need and custom. When parents were questioned as to why their children left school early to get to work, it was often "perplexing" for the mother to assign a reason for such an "absolutely natural proceeding—'he's of an age to work, why shouldn't he?'" As one mother who employed her young children in homework told an investigator, "Everybody does it. Other people's children help—why not ours?"[13] Government reports occasionally provide glimpses of the legitimacy of child labor: a mother boasting that her baby—a boy of seven—could "make more money than any of them picking shrimp," or an older sister apologizing for her seven-year-old brother who was unable to work in a shrimp cannery "because he couldn't reach the car to shuck."[14] Work was a socializer: it kept children busy and out of mischief. As the father of two children who worked at home wiring rosary beads explained, "keep a kid at home, save shoe leather, make better manners."[15]

Reformers sympathized with the financial hardships of the working class, yet they rarely understood and seldom condoned working-class economic strategies. Instead, parents were depicted as suspect collaborators in the exploitation of their own children. A child's contribution to the family economy was interpreted as the mercenary exploitation of parents "who coin shameful dollars from . . . their own flesh and blood."[16] Advocates of child labor legislation were determined to regulate not only factory hours, but family feeling. They introduced a new cultural equation: if children were useful and produced money, they were not being properly loved. When family relations are materialistic, warned a National Child Labor Committee leaflet, "it is rare to find a family governed by affection."[17] By excluding children from the "cash nexus," reformers promised to restore proper parental love. "It is the new view of the child," wrote Edward T. Devine, editor of *Charities and the Commons*, a leading reform magazine, "that the child is worthy of the parent's sacrifice."[18]

Thus, the conflict over child labor involved a profound cultural dispute over the proper economic and sentimental value of children. While opponents of child labor legislation hailed the usefulness of children, advocates of child labor legislation campaigned for their uselessness.

## From Child Labor to Child Work

The battle line between proponents and opponents of legislation, however, was confounded by imprecise and ambivalent cultural definitions of child labor. As one observer noted, "Ask a dozen persons 'what is child labor?' and you will get a dozen answers."[19] Opponents of legislation insisted on children's right to work, yet discriminated against certain forms of employment. Reformers' passionate advocacy of the useless child was similarly qualified. Accused of giving work a "black eye," they defensively retorted that the anti–child labor movement was also pro-work. Raymond Fuller, director of research at the National Child Labor Committee and one of the most vocal spokesmen for child labor reform, explained that "nothing could be farther from the truth than the . . . widespread notion that child labor reform is predicated on the assumption that children should have no work."[20]

Yet where could the useless, unemployed child find useful outlets? The solution was to devise formal criteria that would differentiate between legitimate and illegitimate economic roles for children. Child labor reform would not simply be an absolutist anti–child labor campaign, but instead a pro–"good" child work movement.

It was a difficult task. As one perplexed contemporary observer noted, "To work or not to work—that is the question. But nobody agrees upon the answer. . . . Who among the controversialists is wrong? And just what is work anyway? When and where does it step across the dead line and become exploitation?"[21] At what age, for instance, was the line crossed? By nineteenth-century standards, the employment of a nine- or ten-year-old had been legitimate and for the most part legal. In fact, age was not considered a terribly important criterion of legitimacy until after the 1860s. Before then, only four states limited the age of employed children. Critics objected against a legal requirement to keep children useless until twelve and protested even more forcefully against an age limit of fourteen.

If it was difficult to establish a proper age boundary, it became even more complex to differentiate between types of jobs. Industrial child labor was the most obvious category of illegitimate employment. Farm labor on the other hand, was almost blindly and romantically categorized as "good" work. Even though by 1900 sixty percent of all gainfully employed children (ten to fifteen years old) were agricultural workers, their labor was not defined as a social problem.

Between the extremes of industrial child labor and farm work, there were a variety of other occupations for children of a much more uncertain status and with different claims to legitimacy. Working as a Senate page, for instance, was a prestigious occupation for children. Working as a cash-girl or cash-boy in a department store also promised an attractive and legitimate entry into business life. Street work and particularly newsboys presented child welfare workers with a unique dilemma. As Raymond Fuller explained in his book *Child Labor and the Constitution*, "Many of us . . . are rather strongly prejudiced in favor of it, finding ourselves obliged to overcome serious difficulties in order to recognize it as child labor."[22] Legislatures similarly hesitated to challenge the legitimacy of street work. While other occupations gradually established fourteen as a minimum age limit, children in street work could legally start work at ten or twelve, and many started as young as six or seven. Why, wondered an observer, did people condemn child labor in the factories, yet "tolerate and even approve of it in the street?"[23] Why did factory work transform a child into a slave, yet street work somehow qualified him as a respectable "little merchant"?

Child labor in the home raised even more complex and confusing definitional problems. It also involved a different population; while selling newspapers or bootblacking was a boy's job, home occupations were largely, although not exclusively, a female's domain. Unlike a factory, or a street, or a store, the home was sanctioned by reformers as a proper workplace. Officially, domestic activities were not even considered "real" work. Instruction to census enumerators specified that "children who work for their parents at home merely on general household work, on chores . . . should be reported as having no occupation."[24]

But what about industrial homework? It was factory work done at home mostly by mothers with their young children. By the late nineteenth century, it had become one of the most prevalent forms of child labor. Yet many employers claimed that since "the little helpers work alongside of mother," they were not really employed.[25] Parents themselves praised an occupation that kept their children busy and safely off the streets. The industrialized home forced reformers to reassess the meaning of domestic child labor. What distinguished tenement homework from legitimate housework? As an article significantly titled "Ideal Child Labor in the Home" suggested, "The home will understand the educational necessity of work . . . and will allow each child . . . to contribute to the welfare of his family as a group and provide for his best development through the performance of a desirable amount of daily constructive work."[26] The solution was not to remove all child work from the home, but only to exclude illegitimate housework. Once again, the boundaries of legitimacy shifted and reformers differentiated more closely between types of "housework".

Child actors triggered one of the most highly publicized and controversial definitional battles in the child labor controversy. In a bizarre turnabout, some of the most prominent child labor reformers were suddenly the leading advocates of child labor on the stage. The "public craze" over child stars began in the late nineteenth century, after the smashing success of Elsie Leslie and Tommy Russell in "Editha's Burglar" and "Little Lord Fauntleroy."[27] Consequently, annoyance with child labor laws regulating stage work for children intensified. By 1910, theater managers and their many illustrious sympathizers mounted a national and highly organized campaign to exempt acting from child labor legislation. The national and state child labor committees in turn rallied their supporters to counter what they considered to be an unacceptable and dangerous challenge to child labor legislation.

For its opponents, a child actor was no different from any other child worker. Indeed, in a landmark decision, the Supreme Court of Massachusetts held in 1910 that acting was work. Theater advocates were accused of repeating the same arguments used by other employers of children. Supporters of stage work, on the other hand, refused to categorize the child actor as a child worker. Francis Wilson, a leading actor of the period, insisted that "by some mistake of wording, the factory laws . . . have been made to include the stage-child. To place this royally paid child of the stage, with his few moments of mental effort, on the same level with the under-paid overburdened child of the factory is flagrantly unjust."[28]

The conflict over child acting could be characterized as another economic struggle: a conflict of interest between theater managers eager to increase box-office returns and reformers determined to prevent child labor. Yet the evidence shows that allegiances did not follow these predictable patterns; interest in child welfare did not necessarily mean opposition to child labor on the stage. The persecution of child actors by some as well as their absolution by others reflected, more than any other facet of child labor, the changing interaction between the economic and sentimental value of children in twentieth-century America.

Children on the stage created a curious paradox: they were child laborers paid to represent a new, sentimentalized view of children. They worked to portray the useless child. The Little Lord Fauntleroys captivated by creating "emotional havoc" in theater audiences that were largely composed of women. In a widely distributed booklet published in 1911, theater enthusiasts raved about the "child-value" of a play: "the emanation of the spirit of childhood; an emanation that only a little child can convincingly give forth."[29] In this celebration of the sentimental value of children, the work role of child actors was ironically camouflaged by their fictional roles. They succeeded as popular symbols of the new sentimentalized child.

This very sentimentalization of childhood on stage that seduced theater advocates infuriated its opponents. Child labor committee members spent so much time and energy on what was numerically an insignificant sideline of the child labor problem, precisely because acting transformed childishness itself into a commercial asset. While in other forms of labor, children's tasks received monetary value, in acting the "appeal of childhood is the commodity actually offered for sale to a sentimental and unthinking public."[30] If acting was defined as "good work" by those who saw the young actor or actress as a symbol of the new "sacred," nonworking child, it was condemned as illegitimate labor by others who defined it as a profanation of children's new sentimental appeal.

## House Chores and Allowances: The Economic World of the Useless Child

By 1930, most children under fourteen were out of the labor market and into schools. Yet, significantly, federal regulation of child labor contained some exceptions. The most important statute in the field of child labor, the Fair Labor Standards Act of 1938, allowed children under fourteen to work in newspaper distribution and in motion pictures and the theater. Except for manufacturing and mining, children also remained legally entitled to work for their parents. Agricultural labor, which still employed the largest number of children was only semi-regulated as children were permitted to work outside of school hours.

To be sure, the cultural and legal immunity of certain occupations was partly dictated by market considerations: in particular, the powerful farming, newspaper, and entertainment industries. They were also based on a radically revised concept of child work. As twentieth-century American children became defined by their sentimental, noneconomic value, child work could no longer remain "real" work; it was justifiable only as a form of education or a sort of game. The useful labor of the nineteenth-century useful child was replaced by educational work for the useless child. Labor on the home farm, for instance, was condoned "for the unselfishness and the sense of family solidarity it develops."[31] Newspaper work was a legitimate "character-building" occupation. Acting, claimed its advocates, was not work at all but a liberal education and above all, a joyful child's game.

As child work shifted from instrumental to instructional, special consideration was given to domestic chores. So, when an article appearing in *Home Progress* advised parents, "Let your children work," it referred to "some little household task," not too difficult of course, "for their tender bodies."[32] House chores were not intended to be "real" work but lessons in helpfulness, order, and unselfishness. Above all, warned *Parents' Magazine*,

98

one should "never give . . . children cause to suspect us of making use of them to save ourselves work."[33] While child labor had been exclusively a working class issue, the rules and problems of child work cut across classes, equally applicable to all unemployed children. *The Journal of Home Economics* noted the extent to which parents of former child laborers were "entirely unprepared to cope with the situation, having little means of home employment for their children."[34]

As children's involvement with work changed, so did their relationship to money. The wages of a working child had been considered legitimate family property. Yet children often regained a small portion of their wages in the form of a spending allowance. If a working child earned money through labor, what was to be the source of income once children stopped working? As the American economy turned out thousands of new consumer items, many of them directed at a juvenile audience, children's money became increasingly problematic. Working-class parents not only were relinquishing the income of their children, but also assumed significant new expenses of clothing and school supplies. Concerned with children's "fever for spending," surveys investigated the "financiering of the child who is not a regular wage-earner." Articles began appearing with titles like "The Child's Idea of Money," "The Child and Money," or "How Children Spend Their Money."[35]

To be sure, middle- and upper-class children were already veteran paupers. As the *Outlook* remarked in 1903, "Servants, bootblacks, and the poorest class are rich in comparison with many young people who are dependent for their pennies." Children, observed the article, "are often at their wits' ends to know how to get a dollar together."[36] When children from affluent families were asked how they obtained spending money, most responded: "It's given me" but not without first having to tease and cajole their parents or else beg "sympathetic relatives or friends, expecting a donation."[37]

The proposed solution to the economic insolvency of young children was an allowance to be provided by parents on a regular weekly basis. This new form of allowance, however, differed in significant ways from the traditional allowance. The spending money of a working child had been in effect a portion of his or her earned wages, while the allowance for the unemployed consumer child was largely an unearned "free" gift of money. This modernized version of the allowance was a middle-class invention, yet it was advocated by child care experts and others as a solution for all children, regardless of class.

But how could poor parents afford this additional gift of money? Although the evidence is limited, it suggests that the allowance became an expectation and sometimes a reality even among working-class families. As children lost their economic value, the nineteenth-century economic contract between parents and children had to be revised. Thus, parents were not only expected to forgo their children's wages but they were expected to subsidize children's expanding spending habits.

It was difficult, however, to develop proper guidelines for the allowance money of a nonworking child. If wages were contingent on work, what did an allowance depend on? Could money be divorced from labor, and should it? From the start, the allowance was justified as educational money. By 1930, for instance, *Parents' Magazine* expressed quite explicitly the noneconomic functions of children's money: "A sense of values is what we wish to develop in our children by the use of money. The way any one spends his income indicates what he considers valuable."[38]

Converting money into an educational and moral instrument, however, was not easily accomplished. In order to preserve the traditional association of money with labor, the allowance was sometimes justified as an earned wage. *Harper's Bazaar*, for instance, recommended that children be trained "in the way in which money should come to any one—as the reward of labor." It suggested paying children "by the day or week for keeping their rooms or bureau drawers in order, for being punctual at their meals, for having clean hands . . . or for performing small duties about the house."[39]

The preferred solution was to firmly establish the allowance as "free" educational money just as domestic chores were expected to remain "free" unpaid instructional child work. By the 1930s the differentiation of allowance from wages was unequivocally endorsed. While recognizing that "it is not easy for either parent or child to draw a clear, logical line between allowance and earnings," the *Journal of Home Economics* concluded that a child's allowance "is of the nature of a right rather than a wage. He has earned the privilege of recognized membership in the family and of this status an allowance is a symbol."[40]

Thus, between the 1870s and 1930s, as children became defined as exclusively sentimental assets, their economic world was transformed. Working-class children joined their middle-class counterparts in a new nonproductive world of childhood, a world in which the sanctity and emotional value of a child made child labor taboo. To make profit out of children, declared Felix Adler in 1905, was to "touch profanely a sacred thing."[41] Excluded from productive roles, children's position in the household economy shifted from contributor to consumer. Child labor was replaced by child work and child wages with a weekly allowance. A child's new job and income were validated more by moral and educational than economic criteria.

To be sure, child labor did not magically and totally vanish. In the 1920s and 1930s, some children under fourteen still worked in rural areas and in street trades. Moreover, the Great Depression temporarily restored the need for a useful child even in some middle-class households. But the overall trend was unmistakable. In the first three decades of the twentieth century, the economically useful child became numerically and culturally an exception. Although during this period the most dramatic changes took place among the working class, the sentimentalization of child life intensified even among the already "useless" middle-class children.

# The Rights of the Elderly as a Social Movement in the United States
## The Story till 1980

### Eleanor Bruchey

Historians are fairly well in agreement that some time in the latter part of the nineteenth century the elderly in the United States suffered an increasing decline in status. By contrast, in the eighteenth century there had been a reverence for age. In an agrarian economy where land was inherited, the elderly commanded wealth and respect by their land holdings. Land enabled the elderly to exert substantial control over younger generations. In the nineteenth century, with the gradual reshaping of the economy and society by means of increased industrialization and urbanization, old age declined in status as it lost its landed power base.[1]

In an industrial society the elderly tended to be viewed as superannuated. There was generally no fund of experience or wisdom that could be respected and passed down to younger working men. Indeed, just the opposite was the case. Age was not an advantage in factory work. It was harder for older workers to keep pace with new and faster technologies. Ageism developed, fortified by medical views current in the late nineteenth century. Furthermore, at the turn of the century the values of efficiency and progress were stressed, arguing for the retirement of older workers. This view was adamantly expressed by Dr. William Osler, the world famous physician, on his own retirement from Johns Hopkins Medical School.[2] With retirement urged so emphatically for the elderly, their financial plight began to come more into focus. Very few workers could expect a retirement pension by the turn of the century. Fortunately, few actually faced mandatory retirement.[3]

Despite the apparent smoothness of these sweeping generalizations, historians themselves are not at all in agreement about the role of ideas in the analytical framework sketched above. They debate whether the prejudicial ideas emerging in the late nineteenth century were primarily responsible for the loss of status of the elderly. Some insist that the ageism which was so apparent was really due to the fundamental changes in the economy and society and the rise in the number of elderly in the population. Most, however, have turned away from previously popular structural explanation to focus on cultural values as an explanation for the decline in status of the elderly.[4]

Throughout the eighteenth and nineteenth centuries the family had traditionally cared for its older members. However, those without living relatives close enough geographically to provide care ultimately ended up in an almshouse run by the town or the county. This became the predominant pattern in the nineteenth century. However, beginning in the 1880s, the senile elderly were increasingly placed in state mental hospitals. Mental hospitals thus became in part old age homes for those aged who lacked alternatives. At the turn of the century many states passed legislation mandating state financial responsibility for all mentally ill persons. This relieved almshouses of the expense of caring for many senile elderly who could simply be reclassified as mentally ill. Thus the idea developed that the elderly should be cared for by the state rather than the family or the local community.[5]

The earliest major social movement in support of the rights of the elderly arose in connection with the Civil War federal pension. Veterans' organizations formed an effective lobby to pressure Congress for expansions and improvements in the pension. These organizations tapped into broad public sympathy for Civil War veterans disabled in the war and for widows and orphans of soldiers who had died for the cause. Here was a precursor of the idea of the right to a federal pension that was supported by a specific interest group and backed by broad social support.[6]

Aside from veterans, however, there was scant interest in a government pension for the general population. The prevailing view was that the individual should provide for his old age by saving. The family would care for a needy aged person and the final safety net would be the local government almshouses or the state's mental institutions for emergencies.[7] The 1912 platform of the Progressive Party called for a nationwide pension for the elderly and every year thereafter a bill was introduced in Congress but little interest was sparked. Furthermore, public opinion had soured because of the mismanagement of the Civil War pension system. A few efforts to provide a state pension for the disabled, which included the aged, were modestly successful at the state level but were administered begrudgingly as poor relief.[8]

In the 1920s and 1930s however, a more forceful movement for old age pensions developed. The aim was to replace relief by the local government with cash benefits paid by the state and national government so that the elderly could care for themselves.[9] A number of groups succeeded in arousing support for the idea of a right to a pension. The Fraternal Order of Eagles pushed actively for old age pensions in a well-publicized campaign. Although initially conceived as a means of increasing its own flagging membership, it was very successful not only in drumming up support for its own organization but also in its lobbying efforts in state legislatures. Eagles clubs joined with labor unions, and this increased the spread of popular support. Eventually by 1929 the AFL joined in support of state pensions. Organized labor reversed its initial insistence on union pensions when it faced increasing numbers of older workers and realized the severity of the financial strain pensions placed on their organizations. They therefore came over to the idea of old age pensions funded by a state tax.[10]

Three more groups emerged by the 1920s advocating old age pensions administered by the state. They were primarily groups of experts. The National Social Welfare Assembly included many social workers such as Jane Addams who supported the idea of old-age and mothers' pensions funded by state treasuries. This was known as the "relief and charity" approach to the problem of old age dependence. The American Association for Old Age Security (AAOAS), founded in 1927 by Abraham Epstein, was a major group pressing for old age pensions as a matter of right. Epstein maintained that they should be funded by contributions from workers, employers, and the government. Thus the benefits he envisioned were distinct from charity. Similar views had been worked out earlier by Isaac Rubinow with concepts borrowed from European systems of social insurance. One of the goals was to redistribute the national income. The third group was the American Association for Labor Legislation (AALL) which had been founded in the early 1900s by Professor John R. Commons of the University of Wisconsin. His protégé John Andrews led the organization. Their approach envisaged old age pensions funded by employers who were required to create reserve funds.

Due to the efforts of these various groups, twenty-five states passed some sort of pension law and by 1932 about 100,000 people received state old age pensions. However, it was a fragile victory since many of the laws were very weak. Often means tests or long residency or advanced age requirements limited coverage. In addition, when the depression of the 1930s worsened, the states became very hard pressed to continue, let alone expand, such insurance.[11]

Some important interests, however, had opposed the idea of state pensions from the outset because of the higher taxes that would be required. By the 1920s a number of large corporations in such industries as railroads, oil, banking, insurance, and public utilities had instituted private pension plans. Beyond these industries, however, few business firms offered a pension. Even those that did mounted precarious plans at best, many of them collapsing in times of economic downturn. As the depression deepened, however, some business leaders became convinced of the need for a national pension plan in the face of inadequate business and union programs and the overwhelming burdens put on the state legislatures.[12]

Both expert pressure groups, the AAOAS and the AALL, shifted their efforts to the national level when it became clear that the states were extremely hard pressed financially. In 1932 and 1933, Abraham Epstein's proposal that the federal government subsidize by one-third the state old age pensions was introduced into Congress. Both efforts failed. The AALL approach was introduced into Congress in 1933 but it likewise failed. With that, both groups changed to more indirect tactics. They tried to influence the Committee on Economic Security, the federal administrative agency that the Roosevelt administration had created at cabinet level. The Social Security Administration Act that ultimately was enacted was the creation of the Committee on Economic Security.[13] The committee designed the Social Security system partly to free jobs in the depression for younger workers by providing a retirement system along the lines of the civil service retirement system of the 1910s and the railroad retirement system of the 1930s.[14] The Social Security Act did not represent the views of either the AAOSA or the AALL. At the signing ceremony in August 1935 only a representative of the Fraternal Order of the Eagles was invited to be present.

Both the AAOSA and the AALL failed to expand the pension movement to appeal to a broader public. This failure was due in part to the sharp infighting within the pension movement as early as the 1920s, most notably among Epstein, the Eagles, and Andrews. In part it may also have been due to the limited symbolism in their rhetoric, which repeatedly stressed the negatives of the almshouses rather than the broader economic and societal significance of old age pensions for the population at large. Furthermore, surprisingly, they did not even attempt to drum up mass support of the elderly themselves.

By contrast, the Townsend movement enjoyed broad popular support from much of the general public as well as from large numbers of the elderly. Founded in 1934 in California by a retired doctor, Francis E. Townsend, it came on the scene too late to substantially influence the Social Security Act. Its central proposal was to provide a $200 a month pension to anyone more than 60 years old who would retire from work. It was to be funded by a federal tax on business transactions. It was not only a pension plan but also a cure for the depression by giving the elderly buying power. The movement tapped directly into the frustration of the elderly themselves. Hundreds of thousands became dues-paying members.

The pension groups aroused some popular awareness but none were directly responsible for the Social Security Act. Many of Abraham Epstein's ideas in particular became part of the final system, especially after the 1939 amendment, but he was not allowed to participate in the Committee on Economic Security, probably because some of his ideas were considered too controversial. The term "Social Security" was his, and he changed the name of his organization to the American Association for Social Security. Another of his contributions to the final act was the approach that old age pensions should be regarded as a right of the elderly and not dependent on a means test. The pension program should be based on contributory insurance. Thus the role of ideas as reflected in the disjunctive groups pushing for old age pensions seems to have been helpful but essentially subordinate in effecting the enactment of the Social Security Act.

After the passage of the Social Security Act the various pressure groups suffered a decline and several years later ceased their activities. The death of their leaders seriously undercut these organizations and hastened their demise. But all of the problems of the elderly had by no means been solved, and by the 1950s groups of concerned experts inside and outside of the federal government pressed ahead with research, new publications, conferences and congressional committee hearings. In addition, there was a little stirring of awareness of common problems among the elderly themselves, especially among those who began to go to senior centers. These centers were encouraged by both governmental and private welfare agencies. Although the centers were not active politically, they laid a foundation for the exchange of information about rights and common problems. Lastly, a number of large industrial labor unions joined in promoting an increased awareness of and concern for the problems of the elderly by establishing organizations of retired workers.[15]

During this relatively dormant period, it was not just the concern for physical needs such as income and affordable health care that stirred the elderly. More fundamental was the concern for ideas of dignity and self-respect. Many elderly felt tossed aside as worthless by a society that valued the individual according to his or her job: "What our retired olders yearn for more than anything else is involvement. They are crushed with the feeling of no longer being wanted, useful or important to others. They have been stripped of their value."[16] "We are not discards!" shouted an elderly man at a 1959 hearing of Senator Patrick McNamara's subcommittee on problems of the aged and aging.[17]

In the 1960s the elderly became activated politically, particularly on the issue of health care. "Senior Citizens for Kennedy," a three-month effort in the 1960 campaign of Kennedy and Johnson had a surprisingly effective impact. Some of the Democratic party leaders recognized a changing mood toward social change among the elderly. Motivated by concern to enact Medicare, a network of volunteer groups of the elderly spread over forty states to help elect Kennedy in the last months of his campaign. Their efforts brought about a new appreciation in both political parties of the elderly as an effective, outspoken group. The Democratic party especially woke up to a realization that the elderly were potentially a basis of support. Previously, the party had tended to write off the elderly vote as solidly in the Republican camp.

Frustration on the part of the elderly was increasing due to the confluence of a number of factors. One long-term factor continued to be the increased mobility of families and hence the isolation of the elderly. Inflation was another important problem for the elderly. Unfortunately, most older Americans had to rely on their Social Security benefits because of the inadequacy of private pension plans and personal savings. Inflation then cut down the value of their Social Security payments. Added to this struggle was the spiraling cost of medical care in the 1960s. The elderly as a group spent more than three times that of other groups on medical care. Another factor was the rise in property taxes, which hit the elderly disproportionately hard because of their generally fixed incomes. A final factor encouraging political activism among the elderly was the abuse of the elderly in nursing homes. Nursing homes were increasing rapidly in the 1960s and 1970s. The elderly were not alone in feeling outraged at the scandals plaguing the industry. Politicians quickly joined consumer figures such as Ralph Nader in pushing for legislation for nursing home reform.

Politicization of the elderly followed from the disappointed expectation of a secure old age promised by the enactment of the Social Security program. Added to this was the status anxiety of many newly retired elderly in a society in which status and hence in large part a sense of self-worth came from one's job. This anxiety was presumably reinforced by the increasing isolation of older folk from their families and to some extent from society at large. Finally there was the role of ageism. The pronounced youth orientation of American society caused distaste or even dread of growing old. These ideas intertwined to support the growth of vigorous interest groups geared to dynamic lobbying for the elderly.

The organized elderly enjoyed several advantages over other interest groups with regard to their political influence. First, the elderly automatically engendered a certain amount of sympathy. People saw their parents or grandparents with problems and then themselves later on confronting the same problems. Thus the elderly were difficult to oppose with virulence and had to be always handled with diplomacy. Second, they had strong alliances with powerful national groups such as the AFL-CIO and the National Retired Teachers Association.

By the 1960s several important mass membership interest groups of the elderly had emerged at the national level. The best known was, of course, the American Association of Retired Persons (AARP). It had become a household name with nine million members by the 1970s. The AARP grew out of the National Retired Teachers Association (NRTA), which was founded in 1947 in California by a retired principal, Dr. Ethel Andrus. Organized originally to press for improved teachers' pensions, the NRTA soon recognized the need among retired teachers for affordable life insurance. The Continental Casualty Company, a major underwriter in the field, agreed to sell inexpensive life insurance to retired teachers in New York state. It turned out to be a very popular aspect of the NRTA creating a demand for similar insurance benefits for retired persons who were not teachers. The AARP was established in 1958 to include retirees who were not teachers. It had its own board of directors and regional affiliates even though at first it used the same staff and offices as the NRTA.

From the start the AARP tended to be closely identified with retirees who had been professionals: the middle and upper middle class in membership and outlook. It expanded its material benefits to retirees by adding discount plans for travel, pharmacy purchases, and training services. These benefits not only attracted a wide membership but also supplied steady revenues to the organization giving it a stable financial base. With the close association with the insurance industry there tended to be a bias in favor of the business point of view. But in the 1970s a deliberate effort succeeded on the part of the leadership in changing the organization's image to one of political nonpartisanship. It thereby broadened its political influence.

On the other hand, the National Council of Senior Citizens (NCSC) began with a heavy labor orientation. It grew out of the retired workers' organizations set up by the AFL-CIO. The Democratic National Committee, which was impressed with the results of the seniors for Kennedy movement in the 1960 election, provided financial assistance in the early years as did the unions. It began very modestly with slender resources and focused exclusively on the issue of Medicare. Vocal and vigorous in its support, the NCSC proved helpful in the passage of the Medicare bill. In 1965 it broadened its political activity and took on other issues. By the 1970s it had about three million members including some who did not belong to any labor union. However, while attempting to expand its membership to include nonunion retirees, it remained heavily labor based.

Another large organization of the elderly was the National Association of Retired Federal Employees. It was narrowly focused and narrowly based in membership. It was founded in 1921 at the time of the enactment of the Federal Employees Pension Act and struggled to push for larger benefits for federal retirees. It was active in the passage of the 1959 Federal Employees Health Benefits Law and the 1962 amendments to the federal pension act, which provided cost-of-living increases. Not nearly as successful as the two major mass membership organizations, the AARP and the NCSC, it was small by comparison, with only about 182,000 members in the 1970s. It remained primarily concerned with the immediate issues of federal policy regarding federal retirees and did not address larger issues of the elderly.[18]

The Gray Panthers was another organization of the elderly. It was founded in 1970 by Maggie Kuhn and worked at the grassroots level. Their interests were broader than strictly those of the elderly. They advocated all ages working together for more radical rather than incremental social change. While it was the smallest of the elderly-based groups, it was very vocal.[19]

Finally, the National Council on the Aging was founded in 1950 as a committee of the National Social Welfare Assembly to focus on the needs of the elderly. It consisted of specialists in social welfare agencies and remained a small, professional organization with only about nineteen hundred members in the 1970s. Early on it had joined with a movement in New York state that encouraged the formation of senior centers. Backed by the National Council on the Aging, the senior centers spread well beyond New York. The centers put the organization in touch with hundreds of thousands of the elderly. The National Council on the Aging took no position on broad issues, but the senior centers were an active grassroots means for the elderly themselves to gather information and exchange ideas.

These major organizations were supplemented at the national level by a number of trade associations that lobbied in the national political arena for federal funds and to influence legislation regulating their industries. They included the American Association of Homes for the Aging, the American Nursing Home Association, the National Council of Health Care Services, and the National Association of State Units on Aging. Besides these groups with a self-interest bias were several professional organizations without a direct profit motive, such as the American Gerontological Society and the National Caucus on the Black Aged. The American Gerontological Society had been founded in the 1950s and had about two thousand members by the 1970s. The National Caucus on the Black Aged was a small group of about 150 professionals in the 1970s.[20]

The large mass membership organizations comprising the elderly themselves differed in two significant ways from their earlier small, short-lived counterparts. First, their structures were bureaucratized so that their survival did not depend on a charismatic leader, such as Dr. Townsend. Furthermore, honorary positions of leadership were filled by the elderly while relatively younger persons filled positions of daily management.[21]

Second, the financial base of these later organizations was much more solid. They did not depend on membership dues alone for most of their finances; early on both the AARP and the NCSC got significant revenues from services they sold their members for a fee. Unions also provided about 40 percent of the budget of the NCSC by 1970. The NCOA was financed largely by grants from private foundations such as the Ford Foundation and later on by federal grants.[22]

After establishing the right of the elderly to a government pension, the federal government in the period 1940–60 took the approach of incremental expansion of benefits. More groups of workers were added under the Social Security program, and the amount of the benefits increased due to the sustained effort of a group of policy experts in the bureaucracy. The sustained economic expansion after World War II, of course, made these improvements possible. There was also a bipartisan recognition by people of both political persuasions that the expansion of the Social Security system meant that they would have less worry about the future financial situation of their parents and indeed ultimately themselves.

The most important change in the Social Security program was the enactment of Medicare and Medicaid in 1965. Medicare was designed to cover a large part of the costs of hospitalization, doctors' fees, diagnostic tests, and the cost of rental of medical equipment for those enrolled under Social Security. Medicaid was created to provide medical coverage for the very poor including the elderly. Furthermore, in 1965 the Older Americans Act created an Administration on Aging in the Department of Health, Education, and Welfare. Federal funds were directed to services and programs for the elderly. All of these major advances were part of the Great Society envisaged by President Lyndon Johnson. Unfortunately his war on poverty was aborted by the change in the social and political environment due to the Vietnam War.

However, so strong was the social movement for the rights of the elderly that it was supported by both political parties. President Richard Nixon, elected in 1968, presided over a very significant expansion of Social Security benefits in 1972. Not only were the benefits increased but the automatic cost-of-living increase, which was tied to the Consumer Price Index, was established in 1975. Also in 1972 the Supplemental Security Income (SSI) program was enacted to ensure a minimum income level for the elderly poor. In 1978 Congress passed an act prohibiting age discrimination in employment.[23]

Thus by the late 1970s most of the major victories for the rights of the elderly had been achieved. Thereafter a mild backlash emerged among some politicians and segments of the public. The feeling was that the elderly had gotten enough benefits and to push for more would be greedy. As a result, care was then taken to broaden the message of the elderly advocate groups, such as AARP, to insist that they were fighting for all age groups.[24]

In sum, the rights of the elderly were at first propounded and advocated by groups of experts of various backgrounds in the 1920s and 1930s. The elderly organized themselves into fairly small organizations but these came late to the Social Security struggle and were not of central importance. Furthermore, after the passage of Social Security, they died out. The battle for more rights for the elderly reverted to the efforts of the expert groups, which now included government agencies and congressional committees. By the 1960s and 1970s powerful interest groups of the elderly themselves emerged as extremely effective lobbyists for elderly issues. These mass membership organizations were financially well based and professionally run. Their efforts were central to the advancement of the elderly cause. Thus the social movement in support of the rights of the elderly evolved to include a variety of different types of groups that succeeded in arousing broad public support.

# Why Become a Citizen?
## The Strategic Ideas of Immigrants in the Social Movement of Naturalization

## Reed Ueda

Historians have shown that advocates of Americanization in the early twentieth century envisioned naturalization as a key to the successful assimilation of the immigrant, yet they have much to understand about how immigrants of that time viewed the role of naturalization in their lives.[1] Scholars have pointed out the relative "lack of interest in becoming a part of American society" exhibited by some immigrants as an attitudinal factor impeding naturalization.[2] They have shown how transient immigration, which tended to reflect this attitude, affected the decision to naturalize.[3] While the possibility of return migration appears to have inhibited naturalization, expulsive forces in the homeland making return unattractive or dangerous strengthened interest in gaining American citizenship.[4] There is also evidence that education promoted naturalization, thus suggesting that the greater the capacity to understand the benefits of naturalization and to grasp the political significance of citizenship the more likely was the decision to naturalize.[5] This study explores the existence of additional issues the immigrants pondered in making their decision to naturalize. These were long-term plans for family life and changing American policies affording admission to the country.

To reveal the strategic thinking of immigrants, it is necessary to focus on the linkages of naturalization with national origin, the demography of immigration, family history, and federal policies governing the admission and naturalization of aliens. To provide an empirical base to analyze these factors, a sample of individual naturalization case histories was constructed out of the records of the United States First District Court of Boston in 1930.[6]

Four specific ethnic-group subsamples of naturalized citizens were constructed for the Italians, the Jews, the Irish, and the British by using the ethno-racial categories for immigrant peoples devised by the United States Bureau of Immigration at the turn of the century.[7] The remainder of the sample was assembled into two general or aggregate ethnic subsamples: Other North-West European Immigrants (for the remaining sample members who were naturalized Scandinavians, Germans, and other applicants from northern and western Europe) and Other South-East European Immigrants (for the remainder of the sample who were naturalized Poles, Greeks, and other applicants from southern and eastern Europe). These ethnic categories served in this study to represent the variable influence of ethnicity on naturalization.

As adult aliens who achieved naturalized citizenship, the applicants of 1930 had to fulfill several requirements. They had to reside at least five years in the United States. They were required to demonstrate rudimentary oral proficiency in English and a basic knowledge of American history and civics. They needed to show evidence of good character to be vouchsafed by two witnesses. They had to begin the process for naturalization by filing a "declaration of intention" to become an American citizen no less than two years and no more than seven years before the petition for naturalization.[8]

The majority of the new citizens of the 1930 sample were between 31 and 50 years of age; the largest plurality were between 31 and 40 years of age (table 1). Regional origins correlated with the timing of naturalization in the life cycle of an immigrant. Those immigrants from southern and eastern Europe who gained citizenship had the highest concentration in this midlife age bracket. About 74 percent of the Italians and Jews and 80 percent of the Other South-East Europeans were naturalized between the ages of 31 and 50. By comparison, 50 percent of the Irish, 65 percent of the British, and 65 percent of Other North-West Europeans were in this age category. Correspondingly, the northern and western European groups displayed a slightly higher tendency to achieve citizenship when they were 30 years of age or younger. The general pattern of age distribution among the newly naturalized shows that immigrants from northern and western Europe were frequently younger than those from southern and eastern Europe when they acquired citizenship. For those from English-speaking countries, naturalization at a younger age may have been related to the advantage of familiarity with English. Another factor encouraging earlier naturalization for immigrants from northern and western Europe may have been higher levels of schooling received in more economically advanced and democratically organized societies.

Let us now consider the relation of naturalization to social structure. Table 2 shows the occupational distribution of naturalized citizens accord-

| Age | 18-30 | 31-40 | 41-50 | 51 or older | Total |
|---|---|---|---|---|---|
| Italians |  |  |  |  |  |
| N | 48 | 103 | 89 | 17 | 257 |
| % | 18.7 | 40.1 | 34.6 | 6.6 |  |
|  |  |  |  |  |  |
| Jews |  |  |  |  |  |
| N | 21 | 42 | 28 | 4 | 95 |
| % | 22.1 | 44.2 | 29.5 | 4.2 |  |
|  |  |  |  |  |  |
| Irish |  |  |  |  |  |
| N | 131 | 91 | 70 | 31 | 323 |
| % | 40.6 | 28.2 | 21.7 | 9.6 |  |
|  |  |  |  |  |  |
| British |  |  |  |  |  |
| N | 55 | 105 | 62 | 32 | 254 |
| % | 21.7 | 41.3 | 24.4 | 12.6 |  |
|  |  |  |  |  |  |
| Other NW Eur |  |  |  |  |  |
| N | 36 | 52 | 34 | 11 | 133 |
| % | 27.1 | 39.1 | 25.6 | 8.3 |  |
|  |  |  |  |  |  |
| Other SE Eur |  |  |  |  |  |
| N | 25 | 80 | 56 | 7 | 168 |
| % | 14.9 | 47.6 | 33.3 | 4.2 |  |

Table 1 Age of immigrants in year of naturalization

ing to four general categories. For all ethnic subsamples, the majority of naturalized persons occupied blue-collar jobs at the time of naturalization. Becoming an American citizen was primarily a working-class experience.

The Irish, the Italians, and Other North-West European Immigrants exhibited the highest frequency of blue-collar employment. Approximately nine out of ten new citizens in these subsamples were working people. The Jews, the British, and the other South-East European Immigrants, in contrast, had notably higher rates of white-collar employment. One out of three Jews, one out of five Britons, over one of four Other South-East European Immigrants were white-collar workers.

The patterns of employment approximately corresponded to the differential rates of occupational mobility among ethnic groups and age cohorts in the Boston area. In his extensive study of occupational mobility patterns in Boston in the twentieth century, Stephan Thernstrom determined that the Jews and Protestants of British origin attained the highest rate of mobility into white-collar occupations.[9] The Jews and the British in this study—the

| | white collar (%) | skilled (%) | low manual (%) | house- wife (%) | total |
|---|---|---|---|---|---|
| Italian | 12.2 | 20.0 | 65.9 | 2.0 | 255 |
| Jews | 31.2 | 34.4 | 14.0 | 20.4 | 93 |
| Irish | 12.7 | 12.0 | 69.6 | 5.7 | 316 |
| British | 20.8 | 26.9 | 24.7 | 13.8 | 283 |
| Other NW Eur | 10.9 | 31.0 | 24.1 | 8.6 | 174 |
| Other SE Eur | 28.8 | 23.3 | 42.3 | 5.5 | 163 |

Table 2 Occupation at year of citizenship

subsamples of naturalized citizens that correspond to Thernstrom's subsamples—exhibited the white-collar occupational mobility described by Thernstrom. Conversely, the Italian and Irish naturalized citizens corresponded to the Catholic subsamples in Thernstrom's study that showed a high persistence in blue-collar work.

In the sample of naturalized citizens assembled here, the comparatively large percentage of Other South-East European Immigrants in white-collar occupations, about 30 percent, appears to be an exception to the pattern of Protestant and Jewish salience in this area of employment. The explanation for this deviation might lie in the character of Other South-East European Immigrant groups in the Boston area. Many were Armenian, Albanian, and Greek, groups whose mobility patterns have been studied less systematically than those of Italians, Irish, Jews, and British immigrants. Nevertheless, evidence suggests that these groups were quite successful in gaining access to white-collar employment through education or small-business proprietorship.[10]

With the exception of the Irish, the occupational distribution of the newly naturalized in most cases reflected the end result rather than a transitional phase of the process of occupational mobility. Thernstrom's study of social mobility in Boston demonstrated that an individual usually reached the highest lifetime rank of occupation by the age of thirty. Table 1 shows that three out of every four naturalized citizens obtained citizenship after the age of thirty. Naturalized immigrants, therefore, tended to have experienced the maximum degree of occupational mobility by the

|  | Married | Single | Divorced or widowed | Total |
|---|---|---|---|---|
| Italians |  |  |  |  |
| N | 212 | 39 | 6 | 257 |
| % | 82.5 | 15.2 | 2.3 |  |
|  |  |  |  |  |
| Jews |  |  |  |  |
| N | 77 | 18 | 0 | 95 |
| % | 81.1 | 18.9 | 0 |  |
|  |  |  |  |  |
| Irish |  |  |  |  |
| N | 88 | 221 | 14 | 323 |
| % | 27.2 | 68.4 | 4.3 |  |
|  |  |  |  |  |
| British |  |  |  |  |
| N | 171 | 73 | 10 | 254 |
| % | 67.3 | 28.7 | 3.9 |  |
|  |  |  |  |  |
| Other NW Eur |  |  |  |  |
| N | 79 | 51 | 3 | 133 |
| % | 59.4 | 38.3 | 2.3 |  |
|  |  |  |  |  |
| Other SE Eur |  |  |  |  |
| N | 112 | 50 | 6 | 168 |
| % | 66.7 | 29.8 | 3.6 |  |

Table 3 Marital status of immigrants at year of naturalization

time of naturalization. In addition, there is correlative evidence reported by a contemporaneous sociological study and a recent historical study that those who naturalized were often the most educated and socioeconomically mobile immigrants.[11] Whatever attitudinal changes toward nationality, ethnic identity or political and civil rights occurred at the time of naturalization, citizenship was usually acquired by people with a workingman's economic interests and cultural horizons.

Because a high proportion of naturalized Irish citizens were under thirty years of age and single, it was more likely that naturalization served them as a promoter of individual social mobility rather than as a consolidator. In a time when alien rights were derogated with respect to citizen rights, Irish immigrants may have banked on naturalization to give them the immediate

| | Year of declaration married (N) | Year of naturalization married (N) | Increase (N) | Ratio of married new citizens to married since declaration (%) |
|---|---|---|---|---|
| Italians | 172 | 212 | 40 | 18.9 |
| Jews | 56 | 77 | 21 | 27.3 |
| Irish | 63 | 88 | 25 | 28.4 |
| British | 95 | 171 | 76 | 44.4 |
| Other NW Eur | 35 | 79 | 36 | 45.6 |
| Other SE Eur | 82 | 112 | 30 | 26.8 |

Table 4 Marital status at declaration & at naturalization of successful applicants

chance to compete with natives in economic arenas with restrictions based on citizenship.[12] By becoming a citizen early in adulthood, they could get off to a faster start in qualifying for civil service jobs, occupational licenses, craft unions, and welfare programs that excluded aliens.[13] Indeed, the opportunity to rise on the social pyramid was there, since a substantial minority of Irish immigrants who became permanent residents and citizens enjoyed property or occupational mobility before reaching middle age.[14]

Very significant variations occurred in the marital status of new citizens (table 3). Ethnicity accounted for the largest differences. Ethnic groups from southern and eastern Europe more frequently were married at the time of naturalization. Over 82 percent of Italians and 81 percent of Jews were married. On the other end of the spectrum, the Irish displayed the lowest rate of marriage at naturalization. Only 27 percent were married when they became citizens. The naturalized British and Other North-West European Immigrants had twice the marriage rate of the Irish, but they still ranked lower than immigrant groups from southern and eastern Europe.

A more subtle aspect of the connection of family formation to naturalization was the rate at which married naturalized citizens entered into marriage from the time they filed a declaration of intention to become a citizen to the award of citizenship (table 4). The lowest rate of marriage from the declaration to citizenship was found among naturalized Italians. Fewer than two out of ten married naturalized Italians entered into marriage in the interval from declaration to citizenship. Naturalized Jews also exhibited a commit-

|  | Declared before year 1st child born | Declared in birth year of 1st child or after | Total |
| --- | --- | --- | --- |
| Italians |  |  |  |
| N | 21 | 151 | 172 |
| % | 12.2 | 87.8 |  |
| Jews |  |  |  |
| N | 4 | 52 | 56 |
| % | 7.1 | 92.9 |  |
| Irish |  |  |  |
| N | 23 | 40 | 63 |
| % | 36.5 | 63.5 |  |
| British |  |  |  |
| N | 26 | 69 | 95 |
| % | 27.4 | 72.6 |  |
| Other NW Eur |  |  |  |
| N | 9 | 26 | 35 |
| % | 25.7 | 74.3 |  |
| Other SE Eur |  |  |  |
| N | 6 | 76 | 82 |
| % | 7.3 | 92.7 |  |

Table 5 The relation of the "declaration of intention" of married naturalized citizens, to the birth year of first child.

ment to marriage before the declaration of intention. Fewer than three out of ten married naturalized Jews found spouses between declaring the intention to become a citizen and naturalization. The Other South-East European Immigrants married at the time of naturalization also exhibited a low rate of marriage from declaration to citizenship. The Italians, Jews, and Other South-East European Immigrants engaged in a high rate of marriage before naturalization (table 3) and a low rate of marriage in the interval between the declaration of intention and the award of citizenship papers. The commitment to family predetermined the time at which immigrants decided they would apply for American citizenship.

The British and Other North-West European Immigrants, in contrast, married at a comparatively greater rate between declaration and citizenship.

For these groups, the commitment to family occurred more frequently after declaring the intention to become a citizen and before receiving citizenship. Thus it appears that more British and Other North-West European Immigrants envisioned the probationary period initiated by the declaration of intention as a time to find a spouse. The decision to apply for American citizenship at a future date precipitated rather than responded to a set of commitments to establish a family before naturalization.

While the large majority of naturalized Irish immigrants were single, it appears that of the minority who were married, most were also married before their declaration of intention to become citizens. If Irish immigrants were married at the time they received citizenship, like the Italians, Jews, and Other South-East European Immigrants, they often were already married by the declaration of intention.

Naturalization was also correlated to the dynamics of family evolution. It linked up with the development of the family through production of children. Married immigrants usually declared their desire to naturalize only after their first child was born (table 5). Eighty-eight percent of Italians, 93 percent of Jews, and 93 percent of Other South-East European Immigrants registered their intention to gain citizenship only after their first child was born. For these groups not only was citizenship contingent ordinarily upon a preexisting marriage, it was also contingent upon the birth of children. The Irish, the British, and Other North-West European Immigrants tended not to link so closely the start of the process of naturalization with the birth of the first-born child, but nevertheless in these groups, too, a majority of married immigrants waited until the appearance of their first child before filing the declaration of intention.

Commitment to family development (the onset of children) was another factor leading to naturalization. The birth of the first child brought a new conception of possibilities for the future. The first born made the necessity of commitment to life in this country more clear and even incumbent for a parent looking out for the welfare of his children.

The extent to which immigrants made naturalization revolve around family development must also be visualized relative to a migratory process that subserved the transfer of families. Naturalization played a key role in the process of chain migration. Table 6 enumerates married new citizens having a spouse or a child who was resident outside of the United States. Italians stand out in this tabulation as displaying by far the highest rate of having nonresident spouses and children.[15] Over two-fifths of Italian new citizens had a nonresident spouse and nearly a third had a nonresident child. The subsample of Other South-East European Immigrants exhibited the next highest percentage of ties to nonresident family members. Sixteen

|  | Citizens married | Citizens w/ nonresident child | Citizen w/ nonresident spouse |
|---|---|---|---|
| Italians |  |  |  |
| N | 212 | 65 | 86 |
| % |  | 30.7 | 40.6 |
|  |  |  |  |
| Jews |  |  |  |
| N | 77 | 1 | 4 |
| % |  | 1.3 | 5.2 |
|  |  |  |  |
| Irish |  |  |  |
| N | 88 | 2 | 1 |
| % |  | 2.3 | 1.1 |
|  |  |  |  |
| British |  |  |  |
| N | 171 | 6 | 2 |
| % |  | 3.5 | 1.1 |
|  |  |  |  |
| Other NW Eur |  |  |  |
| N | 79 | 4 | 4 |
| % |  | 5.1 | 5.1 |
|  |  |  |  |
| Other SE Eur |  |  |  |
| N | 112 | 15 | 18 |
| % |  | 13.4 | 16.1 |

Table 6 Married naturalized citizens by residence of immediate relatives.

percent had a nonresident spouse and over 13 percent had nonresident children. Among the Jewish, the Irish, the British, and the Other North-West European Immigrant subsamples, hardly any naturalized persons had nonresident spouses and children. This characteristic of these groups probably owed to the smaller role of family chain migration or return migration in their ranks. Conversely, the comparatively larger percentages of naturalized citizens with nonresident family members found among the Italians and other South-East European Immigrants stemmed from the greater prevalence of chain and return migration.[16]

A consideration of the federal laws governing immigration, however, yields a deeper insight into these patterns of naturalization. Beginning with the Immigration Act of 1921, Congress imposed discriminatory quotas on

| | Non-quota class as percent of total immigration | | | |
|---|---|---|---|---|
| | NW Europe | | SE Europe | |
| | Quota | Non-quota | Quota | Non-quota |
| 1925 | 80 | 20 | 30 | 70 |
| 1926 | 78 | 22 | 28 | 72 |
| 1927 | 53 | 47 | 23 | 77 |
| 1928 | 74 | 26 | 24 | 76 |
| 1929 | 70 | 30 | 23 | 77 |

| | Immigrants who were wives and children of U.S. citizens as percentage of annual immigration | |
|---|---|---|
| | From SE Europe | From NW Europe |
| 1925 | 27 | 1 |
| 1926 | 31 | 1 |
| 1927 | 29 | 2 |
| 1928 | 52 | 1 |
| 1929 | 56 | 2 |

| | Immigrants who were children under 16 as percentage of total immigrants, by sex | | | | | | | | | | |
|---|---|---|---|---|---|---|---|---|---|---|---|
| | Jews | | Italian | | Polish | | English | | German | | Scandinavian | |
| | M | F | M | F | M | F | M | F | M | F | M | F |
| 1925 | 26 | 21 | 24 | 20 | 24 | 20 | 19 | 20 | 16 | 19 | 11 | 18 |
| 1926 | 22 | 18 | 27 | 16 | 27 | 17 | 18 | 20 | 14 | 15 | 10 | 13 |
| 1927 | 28 | 23 | 56 | 26 | 14 | 16 | 16 | 17 | 12 | 13 | 8 | 14 |
| 1928 | 28 | 23 | 56 | 26 | 14 | 16 | 16 | 17 | 12 | 13 | 8 | 14 |
| 1929 | 36 | 24 | 53 | 27 | 20 | 17 | 17 | 17 | 12 | 12 | 10 | 13 |

Table 7  Aspects of transition to quota system.

immigration from southern and eastern European countries, but permitted the nonresident spouses and children of American citizens an unrestricted right to enter the United States as members of the numerically unlimited nonquota category of admissions. The desirability of naturalized citizenship thus increased greatly for Italians and Other South-East European Immigrants, particularly as a route to circumventing small admissions quotas to join relatives. They could use naturalized citizenship to facilitate the process of uniting a family in the United States whose members were scattered during the various stages of chain migration.[17] Indeed, as table 7 shows, in the late 1920s, immigrants from southern and eastern Europe, compared to those from northern and western Europe, came much more often as nonquota admissions and were more frequently wives and children of American citizens (especially among Italians and Jews).

Naturalized citizenship could facilitate family reunion back in the homeland as well. Until such time as their wives and children could join him, the immigrant husband could return for long visitations. His status as a citizen ensured that he would be able to return to his residency in the United States without fear of exclusion by changing restrictive policies. Gaining American citizenship made possible a transnational maintenance of families based on periodic reunion until such time as the decision to transplant the entire family to the United States was made.

Demographic factors specific to each group doubtlessly affected the relation of family formation to naturalization. Among Jews, the high percentage of married new citizens probably owed significantly to the pattern of nuclear family emigration from Russia. Jews characteristically left their homelands in husband and wife pairs, so most were married at the time of naturalization.[18] Among the British, a preponderance of conjugal units in their migratory flow also probably accounted for the fact that two thirds were married at the time of receiving American citizenship, notwithstanding substantial single laborer migration and return migration. Despite the fact that both Italian and Irish immigrations contained a high proportion of single adult males, Italian immigrants made acquiring American citizenship contingent upon the preestablishment of a family to the greatest degree, while the Irish the least. Possibly, what accounted for this difference was the Irish propensity to marry later in life combined with the Italian preference for earlier marriage and production of children.[19]

Italian Americans attested to the overriding role of family ties in driving the transition from transient laborer migration to permanent chain migration of families. Historian Dino Cinel found that sojourner fathers who divided their time between Italy and the United States finally decided to settle in the new land because "children and grandchildren were in America, and they missed them. . . . Some confessed the major reason for staying was the children, who simply refused to return."[20] Historian Judith E. Smith showed that wives who remained behind in Italy pushed to reunite with their husbands in America.[21] Thus when they initiated the process of naturalization, Italian immigrants frequently had a developed family.

A further look at the rules governing immigrant admissions suggests additional reasons for the differential influence of family upon naturalization. Because the immigration law of 1924 imposed restrictive quotas that effectively barred entry from countries of southern and eastern Europe, it forced a stark choice upon immigrants from that area established here: to stay permanently or to leave with little hope of reentering the United States. Thus the coming of restrictive quotas crystallized the decision to make a permanent home in America. It tended to select immigrants with families. For those who stayed, the 1924 law also provided the nonquota category of admissions, which permitted entry without any limitation to alien nonresident spouses and children of naturalized citizens, so that they could transfer their families to this country. As a result of the reduced options for return migration caused by imposition of quotas and the new opportunity for family reunification offered by the creation of nonquota admissions, immigrants from southern and eastern Europe frequently began the process of naturalization as a by-product of establishing a new family or reuniting a family separated by migration. The situation among new citizens from southern and eastern Europe, where the forming of families preceded and dictated the timing and functionalism of naturalization to a greater degree than for immigrants from northern and western Europe, was a secondary effect of the immigration acts of 1921 and 1924: the result of an instrumental and coordinated response by immigrants to new rules for admission.

The pattern of relation between chain migration and naturalization described above was most well developed among Italian immigrants. It adds another dimension to the picture of family-driven commitment to the United States described by Cinel. While Cinel demonstrated that many transient laborers were pulled by bonds with their American-born children to settle permanently in the United States, the data gleaned in this study from naturalization cases indicate that others were motivated to make an American home where they could transplant their children who lived in the old country.

In sum, what do the demographic data and admissions policy tell us generally about how immigrants viewed the prospect of acquiring American citizenship in the decade when restrictive immigration policies were established? They indicate that most immigrants saw naturalization as practicable and timely only after they had well-established occupations and were developing family life. These moves constituted social investments in American society, and as they deepened, they encouraged permanent commitment. Among all the subgroups of the sample (with the exception of the Irish), the majority decided to obtain American citizenship only after marrying. Furthermore, of these, the majority applied only after the birth of their first child. These immigrants believed the growth of a family entailed that they establish themselves fully in a new nation by becoming citizens. Naturalization was a voluntary social movement driven by rational calculation of the interest not only of individuals but of the family unit, not only for the present but for the future as well.

# The International Human Rights Movement and the Human Rights Idea

## Louis Henkin

Concern for human rights has permeated international politics in the second half of the twentieth century. Philosophical and jurisprudential writings have explored "rights," "human rights," "the human rights idea." The literatures of politics, law, and sociology are heavily punctuated with references to the international human rights movement.

It is open to question whether the international human rights movement is properly seen as a "social movement." The term "international human rights movement" is used loosely, journalistically, to encompass all that has occurred to convert a seventeenth-century idea into a staple of international diplomacy, into national and international norms, laws, and institutions. The movement includes all the actions taken (and all the persons and entities who have taken them) to promote the idea of human rights and enshrine it into law, to encourage respect for human rights in every society, and to mobilize international concern and activity to that end. The individuals in the movement include officials of governments and of international organizations, scholars, public citizens, ordinary citizens. The entities include governments, as well as nongovernmental organizations (NGOs), national and international. The movement has had no definable character, no organization, no identifiable leadership.

## The Human Rights Idea

The human rights idea represents moral principles in political theory. It declares that every human being in every society has claims upon his or her society to agreed immunities, privileges, and benefits, which society is to recognize, respect, and ensure. It implies an obligation upon society to adopt laws and establish institutions to make it likely that the rights will be enjoyed in fact and that violations will be prevented, deterred, terminated, remedied, compensated. The idea of human rights differs from older conceptions of "justice," "the right," "the good," in that its focus is on the individual as a "rights-holder" entitled to benefits, and to remedies to promote and realize them, rather than on the duties of society or of one's neighbor of which the individual may be the beneficiary.

Some elements of the idea of human rights are implicit in the term. That human rights are "rights" implies entitlement in some moral or legal order, as of right, not as a matter of grace or charity. That they are "human" implies that they are universal, belonging to all human beings, everywhere, presumably at all times. They are inherent in a human being's humanity, and do not derive from or depend on a grant from some political authority; they run with one's humanity and cannot be alienated, lost, or forfeited. That the rights are "human" excludes claims by nonhuman entities: animals, even trees, may have rights in some moral order, but they are not *human* rights.

The human rights idea is commonly traced to English and European political philosophers, notably to John Locke and to the authors of the Enlightenment, and to Immanuel Kant. In their conception, human rights are "natural," deriving from one's birth as a human being. In its famous articulation in the American Declaration of Independence, all human beings, equally, are endowed by their creator with certain inalienable rights, among them life, liberty, and the pursuit of happiness. To secure their rights, individuals agree to form a society and to institute government.

## The Human Rights Idea and "Human Rights" Movements

The idea of human rights was reflected in bills of rights attached to constitutions, beginning with the constitutions of the several states of the United States, then the U.S. Constitution of 1789 as amended in 1791, and the French Declaration of the Rights of Man and of the Citizen (1791). In each instance, the articulation and implementation of the idea were promoted by some kind of movement. In the early constitutional history of the United States, the idea of individual rights was common currency, "in the air," part of the common intellectual heritage, promulgated by political leaders such as George Mason and Thomas Jefferson in Virginia and by their counterparts during the early days of the French Revolution, and influenced by writers such as Thomas Paine. The original U.S. Constitution did not contain a bill of rights because none was thought to be necessary, but the idea of rights was reflected in several provisions in the Constitution, for example that the privilege of the writ of habeas corpus shall not be suspended or that bills of attainder and ex post facto laws were prohibited. The lack of a bill of rights was invoked by many who opposed ratification of the U.S. Constitution (a "movement"?), and the proponents of ratification promised that a bill of rights would be incorporated into the new Constitution.

At various periods during U.S. history, particular movements, political or social, supported extending the idea of rights and adding to its content. The abolitionist movement invoked the idea of human rights to help establish freedom from slavery and then the right to the equal protection of the laws. The early women's movement sought to promote gender equality and led to the adoption of the women's suffrage amendment (the Nineteenth Amendment). In the second half of the twentieth century, the civil rights movement strove for the equal protection of the laws and for enlarged conceptions of liberty. Movements devoted to separation of church and state led to enlarged interpretation of the constitutional prohibition of the establishment of religion and of the constitutional right to free exercise of religion. Different movements and different kinds of movements (e.g., the labor movement) led to the New Deal and the "welfare state," to the development of various forms of social security as entitlements, subsequently denominated economic and social rights.

## The International Human Rights Movement

National and transnational movements promoting rights and benefits burgeoned and flourished in England, in Europe, in the Americas, during the nineteenth century and the first half of the twentieth century. The international political system early took small steps towards adoption of the human rights idea when it developed an international standard of justice binding on states in their relation to foreign nationals. In the nineteenth century, states agreed to the abolition of slavery and the slave trade and to make war less inhumane, promoted treaties for the protection of minorities, established the International Labour Office (under the auspices of the League of Nations) to promote enlightened standards for labor and social conditions.

The international human rights movement was born during and in the aftermath of the Second World War. At its beginning, the international human rights movement consisted of those individuals and organizations that, horrified by the horrors of Hitler, sought to promote international concern for the fate of all human beings everywhere. Singly and by various forms of cooperation, individuals and nongovernmental organizations urged governments to include the idea of human rights, and measures for its realization, in the arrangements planned for the postwar world order.

The movement produced early fruits at Nuremberg where the Allies indicted Nazi leaders for "crimes against humanity." It enshrined the human rights idea in the UN Charter, which declared the promotion of human rights one of the purposes of the United Nations. The movement achieved the Universal Declaration of Human Rights, an authoritative articulation of the human rights idea and of its content; it produced the Convention on the Prevention and Punishment of the Crime of Genocide, the first postwar international human rights treaty.

The universal declaration was a giant step in enlarging the idea of human rights. National bills of rights, such as that of the United States, began with civil rights and were enlarged to include political rights. Later, national social security systems burgeoned, but they were not necessarily and everywhere seen as "rights." The universal declaration recognized economic, social, and cultural rights equally with civil and political rights.

The universal declaration was just that, not an international treaty. It called on states to recognize rights and to promote them in their own societies through their own polities. The universal declaration inspired political and social movements and nongovernmental organizations within virtually every country as well as transnational and international movements.

The universal declaration was transformed into two legally binding international covenants, one on civil and political rights and one on economic, social, and cultural rights. And the human rights movement—governments, international officials, nongovernmental organizations, citizens—set about to promote ratification and compliance. During the same years the same movement promoted regional agreements in Europe, the Americas, later in Africa. Segments of the larger movement devoted themselves to promoting conventions on particular rights—notably on the elimination of racial discrimination, of discrimination against women, and on the rights of the child—all of which were pressed by particular movements within the larger human rights movement. The Convention against Apartheid resulted from a larger "movement," mobilized by third world governments and nongovernmental forces within virtually all countries. Third world states have sought to spread the human rights mantle over new "generations" of rights: the right of peoples to self-determination, a right to development, a right to peace, a right to a healthful environment.

The international human rights movement remains the colloquial description for the individuals, organizations and other entities responsible for this remarkable achievement, and continuing to work at it, they have "lobbied" governments and officials, enlisted the information media, supported education and scholarship—to promote the human rights idea; to develop guarantees for human rights and remedies for their violation in national and international law; to monitor compliance and to promote institutions that will do so; and to press for sanctions and other remedies for noncompliance. At the end of the twentieth century, the international human rights movement can claim to have helped establish human rights as the idea of our times and to have put in place a network of laws, institutions and other "mechanisms" to give the idea reality.

## The Human Rights Movement after the Cold War

The end of the Cold War and the demise of communism have had important effects on the idea of human rights and on the human rights movement. The communist world had not dared to reject the idea of human rights, but insisted that rights were subservient to socialism. The communist world insisted also that its brand is the only legitimate brand, and the only authentic expression, of democracy and of the internationally recognized right to universal suffrage and popular sovereignty. The end of communism eliminated the socialist alternative to individual human rights and established parliamentary democracy as authentic democracy. (It established as well the right to property and freedom of private enterprise.)

The changed world order inevitably affected the character of the international human rights movement. Once-communist governments now joined the mainstream. Nongovernmental organizations and individuals were not divided by ideological and geographic barriers. They were freer to promote and help protect human rights, to lobby, to monitor, to support new institutions such as a United Nations High Commissioner for Human Rights, international criminal courts such as the war crimes tribunals for the former Yugoslavia and for Rwanda, and soon a permanent international criminal court.

The human rights idea continues to face major challenges. Recurrently, and especially since 1994, it has met resistance flying the banner of "cultural relativism," and particularly of "Asian values." Few now dare challenge the idea of human rights, but some insist that human rights are cultural and contextual, and may mean something different in different cultures and at different times. But resistance to the universality of the idea has not prevailed. Some philosophers and some political figures have resisted extending the idea of rights beyond libertarian and political rights to include welfare rights, but that view too has not prevailed.

The realization of the human rights idea continues to depend on the international human rights movement, on constituencies within and across borders. In more and more countries, domestic human rights movements, spearheaded by courageous individuals organized in nongovernmental organizations and supported by international NGOs, aided by the press and electronic media and by some governments, continue to keep the human rights idea as the idea of our time and the human rights movement as one of the most successful movements of our time.

# The Role of Ideas in the African-American Civil Rights Movement
## The Problem of the Color-Blind Constitution

## Hugh Davis Graham

The drive for equal rights by African Americans during the 1960s restored ideas to a prominent role in explaining social movements. Prior to the 1960s, social movements had been chiefly understood as a volatile form of collective behavior driven by group anxieties. To a generation of scholars who shared the experience of worldwide depression and fascist aggression, social movement theory explained the irrational, antidemocratic psychology of the mob. The African-American civil rights movement of the 1950s and 1960s, however, by appealing to the principles of liberal constitutionalism and Christian brotherhood, challenged the assumptions underpinning the received scholarship on social movements.

In response, revisionist scholars built a new explanation. The disciplined battalions of civil disobedience, led by Martin Luther King, were engaged in rational political protest. Their vision of a "beloved community" was based on traditional democratic and Christian ideals. The chief political weapon of "the Movement" was an appeal to the moral imperative of a color-blind Constitution. Black protest against segregation had historically appealed to Justice John Marshall Harlan's dissenting claim in *Plessy v. Ferguson* (1896) that the Fourteenth Amendment's guarantee of equal protection of the law made the American Constitution "color-blind."[1] Thurgood Marshall, counsel for the NAACP in *Brown v. Board of Education,* argued that "the only thing the Court is dealing with is whether race can be used." "What we want from the Court," Marshall explained, is "the striking down of race."[2]

During the presidency of Lyndon Johnson the African-American rights movement climaxed in a textbook case of political success. The breakthrough legislation of 1964–68 established the liberal principle of nondiscrimination as national policy in public facilities and accommodations, education, employment, and housing. In response to the social protest movements of the 1960s against racial segregation, sex discrimination, war, environmental pollution, and an expanding list of social evils, sympathetic social scientists crafted new theories of resource mobilization (RM). Because galvanizing ideas were important instruments of mobilization, concepts such as constitutional color- or sex-blindness were recognized as an essential component of social movements. Mobilization theory, with its emphasis on rational political action and its respect for coherent philosophical ideals, nicely accounted for the disciplined and successful attack on racial segregation in the South during 1955–65. The surprising outburst of black urban rioting in the North and West during 1965–68 provided a stiffer challenge to a theory based on political calculus. By most accounts, however, the storm over the riot commissions ended in an interpretive victory for social scientists applying RM theory, who generally deplored the destruction but defended the black rioters as rational political protesters.[3]

If the revised social movement theory accounted well for the victory of nondiscrimination policy during the mid-1960s and at least accounted adequately for the black rioting of the late 1960s, it offered little explanation for a third surprising development: the displacement of nondiscrimination or color-blind policy during the Nixon administration by affirmative action requirements keyed to minority preferences. If ideas were important as independent variables in the development of social movements, how can we account for the rapid adoption of policies, particularly race-conscious remedies, that contradict the core idea of constitutional color-blindness that animated the social movement and shaped its legislative reforms?

## The Rediscovery of Ideas in Social Movement Theory in the 1960s

On the eve of Martin Luther King's campaign of civil disobedience against segregation in Birmingham in 1963, the predominant view of social movements was exemplified by Neil Smelser's *Theory of Collective Behavior* (1963). Grounded in the social psychology of anomie and alienation, collective behavior theory fell within the "breakdown" tradition of Emile Durkheim. It held that large structural changes in society, such as industrialization and urbanization, produced social dislocations that eroded traditional social norms and led to social disorganization.[4] The theory traced its historical lineage to Durkheim's anomie, and its social psychology focused on the anxieties of the uprooted. At the level of individuals, rapid social dislocation produced such deviant and anomic behavior as crime, mental illness, and suicide. Its concomitant social product was group insecurity and irrational tensions that could explode in collective violence.

In political sociology during the 1940s and 1950s, the collective behavior approach took the form of "mass society" theory, which reflected contemporary fears of totalitarian regimes of the right and left.[5] In such a theoretical schema, ideas were dependent variables, their role relegated largely to the realm of political propaganda and scapegoating rhetoric, appealing to the underlying psychological insecurities that drove social movements. During the 1960s the breakdown theories of collective behavior and mass society were attacked by social critics who were sympathetic to the reformist-to-radical demands of the civil rights, feminist, student, and antiwar protestors. The critics objected to the implicitly conservative indictment of breakdown theory that the demonstrators were uprooted marginalists who were releasing the anxieties of alienation. To critics sympathetic to the insurgent, reformist spirit of the 1960s, breakdown explanations legitimated violence as an appropriate instrument of social control for agents of the state, but not as an appropriate instrument of social protest. Breakdown theory, critics charged, was a top-down rationalization by governing elites; it defended the normative institutions of the established social order against irrational attacks from marginal outsiders.[6]

Arrayed against the breakdown theories was the RM model. According to its proponents, insurgent social movements more commonly attract individuals afflicted by genuine social grievances than uprooted masses.[7] The goals of such movements were rational, purposeful, and objective rather than arational, irrational, or anomic. Because the insurgents were out-group challengers—racial and ethnic minority groups, labor unions, suffering farmers, persecuted religious groups, the urban poor—their grievances and disaffections were permanent and recurring, not rare responses to unusually rapid social change. Thus socioeconomic shifts affected them indirectly by changing their potential for mobilizing noninstitutional resources (such as work stoppages or mass demonstrations) against the institutional resources of the authorities (such as government budgets, courts, police forces). Their mobilizations were driven less by psychological imperatives or anomie than by rational perceptions of injustice.[8]

## Five Attributes of Social Movements

Mobilization theorists, needing a definition that would set social movements apart from spontaneous but short-lived explosions of protest at one end of the spectrum of collective action, and at the other end from the mature interest groups of civil society, have identified five common characteristics. The African-American civil rights movement of 1955–65 provides a now classic example of the requisite attributes. The first requirement, essential as a precondition of social-movement insurgency, is a *group consciousness* anchored in shared injustice. To black southerners in the 1950s, the humiliations of Jim Crow, an old burden, were sharpened by the heightened expectations of reform following the *Brown* decision. Second-wave feminism emerged so rapidly in the 1960s not because exploitation of American women was increasing, but because feminist leaders effectively fostered consciousness-raising strategies that publicized the long-standing gap between male and female opportunity and achievement.

Group resentment, then, is a necessary but not a sufficient condition to launch a social movement. Profound group resentments, rooted in the cruelest injustice, can remain latent, as did African-American protest in most of the South during the first half of the twentieth century. Thus a second, triggering requirement is *spontaneous insurgency*. In the modern, twentieth-century examples, this has commonly taken the form of physical defiance—sit-down strikes by labor union organizers in the 1930s, the bus boycott in Montgomery, Alabama, in 1955, the wave of sit-ins to desegregate southern lunch counters in 1960, the racially integrated "freedom rides" to desegregate interstate transportation facilities in the Deep South in 1961. The ingredient of spontaneity, suggesting a spark igniting a tinderbox, gives social movements their most distinctive attribute. It sets them apart, for example, from activist organizations such as the NAACP, the National Urban League, the League of Women Voters, or the Mexican American Legal Defense and Education Fund—organizations of civil society that share many of the goals and attributes of social movements, but that were not born as spontaneous social-movement organizations themselves.

The third element is *charismatic leadership* to articulate and symbolize group grievances. The social-movement requirements for communal grievance and spontaneous protest appear to favor charismatic, locally authentic, community leaders over national elites with proven organizational skills. Such preferences can limit movement effectiveness, as for example when local leaders lack skill in articulating ideas (Rosa Parks of the Montgomery

Movement, Cesar Chavez of the Chicano farm workers union), or demonstrate ability yet withdraw from leadership roles (Robert Moses of Freedom Summer in Mississippi, Mario Savio of the Berkeley Free Speech Movement), or narrow the scope of their leadership by adopting extremist demands (Stokely Carmichael and "Black Power" in Mississippi, Mark Rudd at Columbia University in 1968, Huey Newton and the Black Panthers). The most effective American movement leaders, however, established their bona fides as charismatic community leaders in spontaneous and early insurgencies and subsequently rose to national prominence by articulating a vision of fundamental change. In the 1960s, this would include the leaders of the two most significant social movements in the postwar era: Martin Luther King and Betty Friedan, the galvanizing leader of second-wave feminism.

A fourth component of social movements is a *structure* or *organization* that will give it some institutional continuity. This provides the staying power necessary to distinguish the movement from ephemeral outbursts, such as vigilante mobs, agrarian insurrections, worker rebellions, or urban riots. The Montgomery Improvement Association (MIA) and the Southern Christian Leadership Council (SCLC), for example, enjoyed the considerable institutional advantage of the established black church. The feminist leaders of the 1960s, being affluent and well-educated, instinctively created enduring organizations, such as the National Organization of Women and local equivalents. On the other hand the rapidly changing leaders of the Student Nonviolent Coordinating Committee (SNCC) and Students for a Democratic Society (SDS), being more radical and to some degree anarchistic, and working from within to organize impoverished communities, produced fragile and poorly financed organizations that quickly crumbled.

Fifth, and most important for this essay, social movements require a movement *ideology*. It must offer group members a vision of a just future. This need not be a comprehensive or inclusive or even coherent ideology, and given the marginal and volatile nature of many social movements, it may envision a single-interest or utopian future. Major animating ideas of past American social movements have included a white-dominated caste system, coinage inflation, a single tax on the value of land, the prohibition of alcohol, immigration restriction, the subordination of non-Protestant religious groups, and group withdrawal from the larger society. But the most significant and lasting social movements in American history have tended to enlarge the national political community rather than withdraw from it. This was crucial to King's dream of the "Beloved Community," of black and white together in Christian fellowship, bound by a color-blind Constitution. In such a future, children would be judged, King said, not by the color of their skin but by the "content of their character."

## The Racial Reforms of 1964–68:
## Six Principles of American Liberalism

The ideas that animated the African-American civil rights movement of the 1960s, though regarded as radical by Goldwater conservatives, were well rooted in the core doctrines of American liberalism. At the movement's heart lay the liberal principle of racial nondiscrimination. Between 1964 and 1968 Congress passed three major reforms of race-relations law. In 1964 the Civil Rights Act outlawed discrimination on account of race in employment and public accommodations; one year later the Voting Rights Act banned racial discrimination in registration and voting; and in 1968 the Open Housing Act banned racial discrimination in private housing. The first two laws, in particular, forced changes in American society that were radical and rapid. The bedrock 1964 law destroyed the legal and economic foundation of Jim Crow segregation in the South, and the 1965 law empowered a formerly defenseless majority of African Americans who lived in the South to bargain politically with their ballots for protection and benefits.[9]

The great civil rights reform of the mid-1960s was a climax, long delayed by the hypocrisy of American racism, of the precepts of classical liberalism. It rested on six principles, and in at least five of them it enjoyed philosophical coherence and historical legitimacy. One foundation principle was *individualism*. Rights inhered in individuals, not in tribes or clans or races, or in corporatist groups—royalty, aristocracy, capital, labor, the professions, churches, ethnic organizations. A liberal constitutional order would abide no racial distinctions in the law. A second principle was *universalism*. An inherently global value drawn from the Enlightenment and natural law doctrines, universalism in practice was qualified by the legal reality of national boundaries. By consequence the fundamental rights of American citizens, once discovered and proclaimed, were everywhere and for everyone the same.

A third principle was *timelessness*. The equal rights of mankind were inherent in the human condition and were socially discovered through the unfolding of history. Because our fundamental rights were not socially constructed, they were not socially variable (except perhaps in time of war). Once such immutable equal rights were proclaimed for Americans in the Constitution, the Bill of Rights, and subsequent amendments, they became permanent. It was conceded that many ancillary rights claims, derived from statutes and administrative regulations, were properly variable (age limits for driving or voting, residency requirements, education and medical care, spousal and parental obligations). But fundamental rights could not be temporary. Fourth, in the liberal tradition rights were best protected *negatively* by prohibitions against violations. The statutes of legislators and the decrees of judges banned invidious discrimination; they commanded "Thou Shalt Not." They thereby avoided many dangers of ambiguity, such as the controversy over racial "quotas" in the 1970s and beyond. Fifth, the essential guarantees of equal rights were *procedural*. They required equal treatment, not equal results. Equal opportunity meant freedom to demonstrate merit, not an entitlement to equal achievement. Procedural equality likewise avoided the snares of ambiguity, but at the risk of blindness to substantive inequality—as when the rich and poor were equally prohibited from sleeping under the public bridges.

A final principle of postwar liberal reform was modern, not classical. This was *centralization*. Like the New Deal, the civil rights laws of the 1960s required enforcement from Washington because federalism had failed for too many generations to honor the first five principles. The states' rights tradition in the South had always defended white supremacy. As late as 1960, 60 percent of the nation's black citizens lived in the South under the humiliations of a racial caste system, and only 28.7 percent of the South's voting-age blacks were registered. Thus the reforms of the 1960s in their core policies provided for national enforcement of individual, universal, and timeless rights (as of 1964–68) through Washington-based negative procedures.[10]

The legislative victories of the mid-sixties for nondiscrimination policy were followed by two surprising developments. First, the week after President Johnson signed the Voting Rights Act of 1965, a riot broke out in the black Watts section of Los Angeles. Between 1965 and 1968 black rioting destroyed large sections of more than 300 American cities, most of them outside the South, where racial discrimination had historically been most widespread and oppressive. Second, beginning in 1969 federal agencies and courts introduced affirmative action policies that by requiring minority preferences in employment, education, and government benefits, appeared to clash with the nondiscrimination provisions of the new laws they were implementing.

## The Successes and Failures of Nondiscrimination Policy

It is important to recognize that during the initial implementing phase of the civil rights reforms of 1964–68, the race-neutral policing of discrimination produced striking results in some areas. Indeed, two core provisions were enforced by bans on discrimination that worked spectacularly. The first, desegregating public accommodations under Title II of the 1964 Civil Rights Act, had triggered a fierce defense of property rights by conservatives and was backed by the federal government's weakest enforcement club: lawsuits brought by private individuals and the U.S. attorney general. This approach had characterized voting-rights enforcement under the Civil Rights Act of 1957, and it had proven slow, expensive, and ineffective. Yet in 1964 Title II toppled Jim Crow overnight. The South's commercial establishment, weary of the turmoil over segregation, had quietly welcomed its abandonment.[11]

The second success for nondiscrimination, the Voting Rights Act of 1965, contained an automatic statistical trigger that removed procedural and institutional barriers between disfranchised southern blacks (most of them Democrats) and enforcement officials in the Justice Department (most of them also Democrats). As a consequence more than 930,000 new black voters were added to the registration rolls in the South by 1970. During the 1970s the historical novelty of mass enfranchisement for southern blacks (and working-class whites as well) replaced the old one-party politics of racial demagoguery with a competitive two-party system and sent to the southern statehouses racially liberal Democrats such as Reubin Askew of Florida, Jimmy Carter of Georgia, Bill Clinton of Arkansas, James Hunt of North Carolina, and Richard Riley of South Carolina.[12]

In two other areas, school and housing desegregation, nondiscrimination worked poorly. In the first, Congress was careful in the Civil Rights Act to specify that "'desegregation' shall not mean the assignment of students to public schools in order to overcome racial imbalance." Shortly thereafter, however, the Supreme Court, in a series of decisions running from *Green v. County Board of New Kent County* (1968) to *Swann v. Charlotte-Mecklenburg Board of Education* (1971), rejected nondiscrimination in school assignments as insufficient to "undo" the effects of past discrimination.[13] Trumping a statute with the Constitution's equal-protection clause, the Supreme Court ordered widespread school busing to correct racial imbalance in the South. Color-blindness in assigning pupils and teachers to schools was rendered obsolete (or even unconstitutional) by the federal courts after 1968, at least in the formerly segregated states. Also in 1968, color-blindness became national policy in housing. But discrimination in housing was weakly policed from Washington. Congress in 1968 refused to give significant enforcement authority over the private housing market to agency bureaucrats in Washington.[14]

The enforcement results for job discrimination were more mixed. Success was dramatic in the South, where strict nondiscrimination destroyed the omnipresent barriers of segregated jobs and unions and soon opened hundreds of thousands of jobs and promotions to African Americans. Outside the South, however, the heightened expectations of the civil rights movement had not been met with such a visible payoff. The wave of urban violence following the Watts riot of 1965 coincided with the rhetoric of Black Power, antiwar turmoil, and political assassinations and frightened the nation's policy establishment.[15] In the judgment of the Kerner Commission report, America was becoming "two nations, separate, and unequal."[16] The search for a faster and more positive job payoff than nondiscrimination, especially outside the South, led federal officials and civil rights leaders to search for more radical methods.

## Institutional and Intellectual Sources of Affirmative Action

During the Nixon presidency three new and institutionally distinct streams of thought and behavior converged to shift the focus of civil rights policy from nondiscrimination to minority preference. The first was bureaucratic. It followed a traditional pattern in the politics of regulation that students of public administration called "clientele capture." During the Johnson administration a new layer of bureaucracy was added to the federal government to enforce the new provisions in civil rights policy. The legislation of 1964–68 made civil rights enforcement a rapid growth field. In 1969 the rapidly expanding civil rights bureaucracies included the Civil Rights Division in the Justice Department, created in 1957; one new independent regulatory board, the Equal Employment Opportunity Commission (EEOC), created by the Civil Rights Act of 1964; and twenty-seven new contract-compliance offices established in the line agencies. The last was modeled after the Office of Federal Contract Compliance in the Labor Department and the Office of Civil Rights in the Department of Health, Education, and Welfare.

To the array of compliance offices, created throughout the subpresidency in response to President Johnson's executive order of 1965, the Nixon administration in 1969 added the Office of Minority Business Enterprise in the Department of Commerce and a Voting Rights Section in the Justice Department. The new offices helped agency heads meet equal-employment hiring and promotion goals for minorities and women in senior civil service ranks. Affirmative-action policies enforced by the new regulatory agencies for civil rights in the private sector and in state and local government were designed to accelerate benefits for protected-class designees.

The second source of pressure for more aggressive affirmative-action enforcement was theoretical. During the late 1960s intellectuals in the civil rights movement abandoned their historic creed of nondiscrimination with remarkable dispatch and equanimity. They did so because nondiscrimination policies, while effective in the South, were slow to change the distribution of jobs and income in the industrial cities of the North and West, where the rioting was concentrated. Consequently the intellectual leaders in the civil rights coalition constructed a new body of theory that would justify and indeed morally require the displacement of color-blind policies by minority preferences. The theoreticians of affirmative action, most of them based outside of government, were affiliated with universities (especially law schools), foundations (most prominently the Ford Foundation), think tanks (Joint Center for Political and Economic Studies), public interest law firms (the American Civil Liberties Union) and single-interest lobbying groups (Minority Business Enterprise Legal Defense and Education Fund).[17] The theoreticians of affirmative action turned to a novel social force to justify the new doctrine of affirmative action: *history itself.*

In June 1965 Lyndon Johnson told the graduating class at Howard University: "But freedom is not enough. You do not wipe away the scars of centuries by saying: 'Now you are free to go where you want, do as you desire, choose the leaders you please.'"

"You do not take a person who for years has been hobbled by chains and liberate him, bring him up to the starting line of a race and then say, 'You are free to compete with all the others,' and still justly believe you have been completely fair."[18]

History, then—the scars of centuries—had hobbled racial minorities with chains. The crippling legacy of history took the modern form of "institutional racism." The theory held that generations of racist thought and behavior had shaped institutional cultures and standards so profoundly that discriminatory results were perpetuated even in the subsequent absence of racial prejudice or discriminatory intent by individuals.[19] Whereas discriminatory behavior was relatively easy to identify but its prejudicial intent was difficult to prove, institutional racism was subtle and difficult to identify in action but was easy to demonstrate by its consequences. The results of institutionalized bias were measurable by the statistical disparity between minority potential in the applicant pool (for jobs, promotions, appointments, awards, school admissions) and minority presence on the institutional rolls. Evidence of discriminatory intent, though required by the traditional code of color-blindness that had shaped the Civil Rights Act, was held to be largely irrelevant. Compensatory justice was thus results-centered. What counted was not discriminatory intent but "disparate impact," the technical term for proportionately unequal results.

The third new stream of thought and behavior favoring affirmative action was judicial. Approval from the federal bench was essential to protect the new minority preference policies in the enforcement agencies from conservative charges that they violated the Civil Rights Act itself. Here the pathbreaking shift from nondiscrimination to positive obligations in civil rights enforcement followed the drama of school desegregation. The federal courts, embarrassed by a decade of tokenism following *Brown v. Board of Education* and encouraged by support from Congress and the executive branch in the Civil Rights Act, began in 1966 to demand from southern school officials not mere race-neutral behavior but "the organized undoing of the effects of past discrimination."[20] To redress the damage inflicted on an entire race down through the generations, the Supreme Court approved increasingly detailed school policies that stipulated the racial assignment of pupils, teachers, administrative staff, and the color-conscious construction of school budgets—judicial interventions that were similar to the minority hiring requirements adopted by the federal enforcement agencies after 1968.

When a contractor lawsuit charged that the government's minority hiring requirements for federally assisted construction projects violated the Civil Rights Act by requiring racial preferences in employment, federal courts in 1970 and 1971 upheld the "color-conscious" hiring requirements as a legitimate remedy under the president's contract-compliance program to compensate for past discrimination. When a North Carolina power company after 1964 instituted tougher but race-neutral employment and promotion standards and tests that weeded out far more blacks than whites, the Supreme Court in *Griggs v. Duke Power Company* (1971) ruled that the history of Jim Crow schooling in North Carolina had made the tests unfair even though the Civil Rights Act had specifically approved their use. In *Griggs* the Supreme Court, holding that the regulatory rulings of the EEOC expressed the intent of Congress, formally upheld the disparate impact theory of civil rights enforcement.[21] According to the disparate or adverse impact model, discrimination may be inferred from statistical underrepresentation of a protected class, thus relieving plaintiffs of the burdens of identifying specific acts of discrimination or proving harmful intent. By 1972, when President Nixon signed amendments to the Civil Rights Act that brought all state and local governments, including their school systems, under the affirmative-action regulation of the EEOC, American civil rights policy had assumed a mature form that would not fundamentally change even during the conservative Republican administrations of Ronald Reagan and George Bush.

## The Paradoxical Career of Affirmative Action

John David Skrentny has pointed out the striking ironies surrounding the development of affirmative action.[22] It arose not from minority leaders in the civil rights coalition, but from white elites in government agencies and the federal courts. It was launched not by liberal Democrats as part of President Johnson's Great Society program, but by Republican elites in the Nixon administration. During the 1970s and 1980s affirmative action matured and expanded as a comprehensive regime requiring a complex variety of minority preference policies at all levels of government and the private economy, yet public opinion has never supported it. The strange career of affirmative action demonstrates a central paradox: as affirmative-action programs spread and grew politically stronger in the 1970s and 1980s, building powerful coalitions in Congress, in federal agencies, and in city halls throughout America, its claims to legitimacy in the public eye grew weaker.

"Affirmative action" was a phrase routinely included in the president's executive order on civil rights enforcement since 1961. During the Kennedy and Johnson administrations it was interpreted as requiring employers to make unspecified outreach efforts in recruiting minority workers. The surprising leadership of the Nixon administration in establishing minority preference policies under the rubric of affirmative action opened a window of opportunity to the civil rights coalition that was expertly exploited. By 1972, when Nixon crushed McGovern and yet Congress remained firmly in Democratic hands, the legal underpinnings of disparate impact remedies were reasonably secure.[23]

The growth of affirmative-action regulation since 1972 testifies to the adroit political leadership of the civil rights coalition in Congress, the federal bureaucracy, state house, and city hall—the "inside the beltway" world of lobbyists, committee staff, and agency entrepreneurs that nourishes the bargaining routines of interest-group liberalism in America. Legislative benchmarks of the expanding array of affirmative-action programs since 1972 include bilingual education requirements for non-native speakers of English in 1975; minority contract set-asides in federal procurement for "black Americans, American Indians, Spanish-Americans, Oriental Americans, Eskimos, and Aleuts" in 1977; a statutory basis for the Small Business Administration's 8(a) program of assistance for the economic and socially disadvantaged in 1978. At the end of the 1970s, three Supreme Court decisions upheld the constitutionality of racial or minority preferences: in college admissions (*Bakke,* 1978), in private sector employment (*Weber,* 1979), and in contract set-asides for designated minority groups (*Fullilove,* 1980).[24]

This momentum continued in the 1980s, despite the conservative sweep of the Reagan administration. In 1982, Congress extended the disparate-impact or equal-results model to voting rights and electoral districting. Congress with the cooperation of the Reagan administration also established minority contract set-aside quotas (commonly 5 percent) for the major federal contracting departments—Transportation in 1982, Defense in 1985. In 1988 Congress strengthened civil rights regulation by federal agencies, overriding Reagan's veto. In 1991, President Bush signed a complex civil rights statute, one similar to a bill he had vetoed in 1990 as a "quota bill," that made sexual harassment a federal crime and made available to women large damage awards previously available only to African Americans. As conservative Republicans, Presidents Reagan and Bush appointed conservatives to the federal courts and curbed regulation by civil rights enforcement agencies. But overall the record of government behavior since the Nixon presidency shows expansion and consolidation for the affirmative-action regime. In the decade following the Supreme Court's approval in 1980 of the minority contract set-aside program in *Fullilove,* for example, more than 230 American city, county, and state governments established similar set-aside programs.

Outside the beltways, however, in the broader world of public opinion, opposition to affirmative action intensified. Most Americans, moved by the integrationist, color-blind vision of Dr. King and persuaded by the race-neutral language of the Civil Rights Act of 1964, remained hostile to the notion of racial preferences in public policy. Throughout the 1970s national polls showed persistent support for "ability" standards in jobs and education over "preferential treatment" among both black and white respondents.[25] In the 1980s, African-American support for affirmative-action policies strengthened, especially among middle-class blacks, who benefitted from affirmative action programs and resented attacks upon them.[26] Polls of Latinos showed the greatest ambivalence, combining traditional respect for meritocratic standards, including resistance to the segregating effects of bilingual education programs, with support for Latino political leaders, most of them Democrats and affirmative action champions.[27]

Among whites and Asians, however, opposition to minority preferences grew stronger in the 1990s. Significantly, white women, who comprise 40 percent of the U.S. voting population and who have benefitted greatly from nondiscrimination policy since the 1960s and relatively little from gender preferences under affirmative action, agreed with the opinion of white men.[28] The economic downturn of the early 1990s, which helped send Democrat Bill Clinton to the White House in 1992 in a three-way contest, increased job insecurity and fanned voter resentment against group preferences in employment, especially among blue-collar white workers. Opposition to affirmative action was intensified by large-scale immigration, both legal and illegal. Following the immigration reform law of 1965, more than twenty million immigrants entered the United States.

Because three-fourths of them came from Latin American or Asian countries, they were presumptively protected as minorities in the federal government's affirmative action programs. In California, hard-hit by defense cutbacks and massive immigration, voters in 1996 passed Proposition 209, an initiative banning affirmative-action preferences throughout state government. The previous year the University of California Regents voted to ban affirmative-action preferences in admissions, employment, and contracting from the nine-campus university. And increasingly in the 1990s, a conservative majority on the Supreme Court has sharply narrowed the scope of minority preference policies in affirmative-action programs.[29] The result of these trends has been not victory by one side or the other in the 1990s, but rather a hostile stalemate.

## The African-American Dilemma: Disavowing Triumphant Color-Blindness

In the four decades since the *Brown* decision of 1954, ideas have played three roles in the African-American civil rights movement. First, the traditional liberal concept of a color-blind Constitution was essential in building the successful political coalition that enacted the civil rights reforms of 1964–68. Conservatives were generally discredited in the 1960s for opposing the reform legislation, and American liberalism enjoyed its finest postwar hour. Second, the new and more radical concept of compensatory justice played an ancillary role, rationalizing affirmative-action remedies that were adopted for more pressing practical reasons. The black civil rights organizations rallied quickly to the new doctrine, as did the broader civil rights coalition, especially Hispanic rights organizations, feminist groups, and the academic community. Third, the dissonance between the color-blind principle and race-conscious rationales brought negative long-term consequences for the liberal reform tradition, especially the Democratic Party. Despite the crucial role of the Nixon administration in institutionalizing affirmative-action programs, they served constituencies, especially African-American and Hispanic groups, whose organizations and leaders were overwhelmingly Democratic.

Proponents of affirmative action since 1970 have mounted an impressive array of arguments and evidence to support the moral claims of compensatory rather than color-blind justice. Among the strongest are arguments about the cumulative nature of history itself, specifically the tendency of institutions to privilege traditional elites, with the consequence that race-neutral policies freeze in inherited disadvantages.[30] Yet such arguments have failed to supplant the deeply rooted conviction held by most Americans that it is unfair to penalize a citizen for attributes he or she was born with—that citizens accused of doing no wrongdoing should not be penalized for the alleged offenses of their ancestors. Even though the Supreme Court has never ruled that the Constitution is color-blind, most Americans understood *Brown v. Board of Education* in this way, and most understood the breakthrough civil rights laws of 1964–68 to mean what they said—that is was unlawful to discriminate against a person on account of race. Proponents of affirmative action have remained especially vulnerable because the black civil rights movement's martyred spiritual leader, Dr. King, was murdered just prior to the rise of affirmative action, and thus his speeches and writings provide canonical text supporting constitutional color-blindness.

In most American reform movements, public opinion is persuaded to replace older traditions and values with new ones. The new political consensus developed during the 1930–68 era, the New Deal political order, included among other things the legitimacy of organized labor, national regulation of labor standards, a mandatory national social security system, global collective security, racial and ethnic nondiscrimination in public policy and economic life, equal rights for women. Even affirmative action of the original, Kennedy-Johnson model, with outreach programs including targeted recruiting, internships, summer training, and financial incentives for minorities, has won the support of most Americans.[31] But the group preferences of hard affirmative action, following so close on the heels of the triumph of liberal color-blindness in the mid-sixties, were unacceptable to most Americans. The switch from color-blindness to color-consciousness at the end of the 1960s required too great a leap, and too quickly. None of the other major social movements of the 1960s—the student rights, antiwar, consumer rights, feminist, workplace safety, and environmental movements—asked supporters to accept such a radical shift in movement ideology.

Politically, the collapse of the New Deal political order predates affirmative action, but was accelerated in the 1970s by controversy over the new minority preference policies, which critics then called "reverse discrimination." Following the race riots, campus protest, and antiwar violence of 1965–68, 57 percent of American voters supported either Nixon or George Wallace. But the Janus-faced civil rights policies of President Nixon, administratively accelerating the process of school desegregation and affirmative action while publically denouncing "forced busing" and "racial quotas," helped seal the demise of the New Deal political order. Most painful for the political left in America, affirmative action became a symbol used by Republicans to discredit the Democratic party as a captive of its left-wing constituencies—radical black-power and Chicano groups, feminists seeking abortion on demand, welfare rights organizations feeding on the dole, radical lifestyle groups threatening traditional family values.[32]

Affirmative action, associated closely with the demands of multiculturalism and the politics of identity, hastened the shift of left-wing politics in America from economic redistribution to the group-based claims of African-Americans, Chicanos, feminists, American Indian insurgents, gay and lesbian rights groups. This shift fragmented the New Deal coalition, its class-based solidarity already weakened by declining union membership and Republican appeal to southern whites and northern urban ethnics. It thus helped keep the presidency (and therefore federal court nominations) in Republican hands for most of the quarter century following the exit of Lyndon Johnson.

American society responded to the social upheaval of the 1960s by polarizing, sharply but unevenly. Majority opinion shifted toward conservative positions on the failings of Big Government, high taxes, and the increasingly divisive cultural issues—crime and punishment, religion and the schools, abortion, drugs, welfare dependency. The political parties, captured by their activists, polarized accordingly—Democrats to the left, Republicans to the right. This disadvantaged Democrats greatly in national electoral competition. But the split over affirmative action, one of the era's most divisive cultural issues, has not corresponded with party alignments. Suburban Republicans, with high levels of income and education, were conservative on economic issues but commonly supported progressive positions on cultural issues (abortion, school prayers, sex education, censorship) while blue-collar white Democrats tended to be liberal on economic policy but traditional on cultural issues.[33]

Although proponents of affirmative action were remarkably successful over the years in expanding their program base in government and the private economy, they lost the battle of public opinion. And most damaging to their efforts in this contest was not the opposition of conservatives, which was to be expected. Rather, it was a fatal cleavage among liberals themselves. Recent survey research, using experimental interview techniques where multiple factors are varied to probe the range of respondent opinion, shows that Americans who describe themselves as both liberals and Democrats are equally split over whether remedies for black disadvantage should take account of race or be color-blind.[34]

The rise of affirmative action did not merely sharpen divisions between the left and the right in America. It split the liberals right down the middle. The seeds of this failure lay in the surprising, unique policy turnabout of the Nixon administration, which offered the civil rights

145

coalition an unanticipated opportunity for rapid policy change through the inside channels of administrative and judicial directives. But as a price; the liberal creed of a color-blind Constitution had to be disavowed by the very forces that had carried its banner to triumph under Lyndon Johnson. It was a unique burden, born of unique circumstances, and apparently impossible to overcome.

# Sentiments, Ideas, and Animals
## Rights Talk and Animal Protection

## James M. Jasper

For several hundred years sympathy for nonhuman species has grown at an accelerating rate in the Western world, culminating in today's animal rights movement. One of the most energetic protests in Reagan's America, this protest effort can hardly be understood through the lens of self-interest, since activists and their beneficiaries, far from overlapping, are not even members of the same species. This level of compassionate altruism can only be understood through the ideas and moral visions of the protectors. Only a major shift in worldview could lead to such an extensive and radical effort to change age-old relationships between humans and other species.[1]

Although the effects may be clearest in a movement such as animal rights, all social movements are based, at their deepest level, on inchoate moral intuitions—"structures of feeling," in Raymond Williams's apt phrase. A given cluster of intuitions may be held by a majority or a minority in a society. A small number of intellectuals articulate these sentiments in explicit ideas and ideologies, which moral entrepreneurs can then deploy in recruiting participants. The best ideas are normally those that act as symbolic lightning rods, resonating in numerous ways with common underlying sentiments. If the organizers can stir up sufficient outrage, anger, or fear, they may ignite a protest movement. Such dynamics have typically been overlooked in social scientific research, on the assumption that in the long run people follow their own (usually material) interests or on the restrictive definition of social movements as efforts by outsiders to gain access to the political system.[2] The time has come to recognize that people also pursue changes simply because they feel these are morally just.

A single cluster of moral intuitions forms the basis both of the humane tradition in animal protection, which arose in the mid-nineteenth century and has persisted since, and of the more radical animal rights movement, which arose in the 1970s. But the formal articulations of these underlying sentiments differed, leading to contrasting tactics and goals in the two movements. Even today, there are other ideologies and languages of critique that could have taken the animal protection movement in a different direction. Specifically, the current focus on the rights of individual animals could instead have been a more environmental concern for ecosystems and species.

## Sentiments of Compassion

Throughout most of their history, humans have treated animals in two simultaneous ways: as resources to be exploited at will, but also as pets to be treated with love and care. They have tenderly nurtured their lambs, then slaughtered them. They have doted on their pet dogs, while stuffing cats into burlap sacks and setting them afire at carnivals. This balance between two attitudes, one instrumental and the other sentimental, has shifted in the countries of the industrializing West during the past several hundred years, with sentimental feelings toward animals gaining hegemony.

New ideas about nonhuman species have roots in sixteenth- and seventeenth-century Europe, when there emerged a distinct middle class whose experiences were shaped by towns rather than by agriculture. This new commercial milieu accelerated what Norbert Elias called the "civilizing process" through which Europeans learned concern for the sensibilities of others; no longer did they spit on the floor, blow their noses on their sleeves, or eat out of common bowls.[3] One result of this growing awareness of unique individual identities and emotional needs was that children were no longer seen as small adults, but as beings to be cherished and protected. In a process of "sentimentalization," love and affection rather than economic need came to be the glue holding the family together.[4] In the paintings of the sixteenth and seventeenth centuries, families and interior spaces began to replace the crowd scenes and public places of artists like Peter Brueghel.

Pets became part of the new bourgeois family and home, often appearing in family portraits. By the early eighteenth century, many people were giving their pets human names, burying them and writing epitaphs for them, and occasionally leaving them legacies. Except for cart and carriage horses, town dwellers lost more and more instrumental contacts with animals. They hunted less, had fewer fields to plow, and raised fewer animals to slaughter (the longest lasting exception being a few chickens). Their main contact with animals was now with their pet dogs. As a result they were less likely to see animals primarily as resources, existing to serve economic ends. Animals could still fulfill important emotional needs for humans, however, providing love and loyalty. In a long process extending from the sixteenth century to the present, compassion replaced cruelty as the acceptable stance toward animals.[5]

Beginning in the eighteenth century scientific developments also contributed to a revaluation of animals. Naturalists developed classifications based on similarities between humans and animals. Geologists studied the age of the earth and speculated about the evolution of complex species. The Comte de Buffon and others searched for the missing link between humans and apes. The capstone of this process was Charles Darwin's 1871 publication of *The Descent of Man,* which supported the growing belief that humans and animals were descended from common ancestors, with all the similarities that implied. Darwin wrote *The Expression of the Emotions in Man and Animals* to demonstrate the common physiological source of emotions across species, insisting that human mental capacities were superior in degree but not in kind from those of animals.[6]

This rethinking of animals accelerated in nineteenth-century Britain and the United States, spreading across social class boundaries. With nature neutralized for many by industrialization and the growth of cities, reduced to a suburban garden and a pretty landscape painting, people could romanticize it as innocent and good, ignoring its cruelty and violence. Animals, accordingly, were seen not simply as like humans in their emotional capacities, but as superior. They were never duplicitous or unkind. They were innocent and helpless, perfect objects for compassion.

## Nineteenth-Century Articulations

This sentimental attitude toward animals was common enough by the nineteenth century in Britain and the United States to inspire political efforts to protect animals. Victorians articulated their feelings by linking kind treatment of animals to a range of other moral virtues. Kindness toward dogs and horses (affection for cats lagged) was a training ground for kindness to other humans, as the multiple meanings of "humane" imply. Victorian elites were particularly critical of lower-class amusements, such as bullbaiting, but also of the cruel treatment that carriage horse drivers gave their animals (the only instrumental uses of animals they still saw regularly). Animal protection was merely one aspect of the moral improvement of mankind, part of a cluster of middle-class causes that included child protection, moral reform, and temperance. Reformers hoped that, "by the discouragement of cruelty and insensibility of heart, in the treatment of inferior creatures, human beings will be rendered more susceptible of kind impressions towards each other, their moral temper will be improved, and consequently, social happiness and genuine philanthropy must, infallibly, be strengthened and enlarged."[7]

The animal protection movement of the nineteenth century developed to pursue this vision. In 1822, the British parliament passed a bill protecting draft and farm animals from unnecessary cruelty, and the Society for the Prevention of Cruelty to Animals (SPCA) was formed to help enforce it. The movement focused on ending cruelty largely through education of children and the lower classes; the drivers who whipped their horses were the main target of SPCA enforcement efforts until horse-drawn transportation began to disappear in the twentieth century. The movement was explicit in its efforts to impose middle-class morals on the working class.

The humane movement arrived in America after Henry Bergh, son of a wealthy New York shipbuilder, observed especially cruel treatment of carriage horses during a diplomatic assignment to Saint Petersburg in 1863–64. Returning to America via London, where he attended a meeting of the SPCA, he decided to devote himself to defense of the "friendless dumb brute. " He formed an American SPCA in New York and by 1900 no fewer than seven hundred similar groups had been formed nationally. Their paternal attitude toward animals as defenseless objects of compassion was aptly captured in the title of the Massachusetts SPCA publication, *Our Dumb Animals.* Capable of devotion and emotional warmth, but lacking thoughts or awareness of their own, the best situation for pets was to be cared for in loving human families. As in London, the groups saw themselves as a "humane and civilizing charity," devoted to preventing pain to animals, but also to disseminating the values associated with the upper classes.

In the United States and Britain, humane societies had uneasy relations with antivivisectionists. The British RSPCA ("Royal" was added at Queen Victoria's approval) briefly attacked vivisection, but this strategy was controversial among its members and it dropped the cause after mild restrictive legislation was passed in 1876. In both countries antivivisectionists—often from the lower classes—were attacking one of the important idols of the era, scientific progress, and they found little support among upper-class humanitarian groups. In its nineteenth-century articulation, animal protection did not extend to laboratories, which were coming to be associated (by the end of the century) with the same process of moral improvement that animal protection supposedly fostered. Despite a brief flirtation, animal protection and antivivisection remained separate causes until their new articulations in the 1970s and 1980s.

## Recent Articulations

In recent years, the moral intuitions supporting animal protection have, if anything, grown stronger. Urbanization and industrialization have continued, with only 3 percent of contemporary Americans working in agriculture. Pet owning has continued to expand so that 60 percent of American households now have pets. The personification of these animals continues, as people often project onto their animals suspiciously human tastes. They buy their dogs mink stoles, bottled water, and vegetarian, low-cholesterol food. Pets receive orthodonture, plastic surgery, pacemakers, even CAT scans. Humans treat their "companion animals" as full members of the family: talking to them, carrying their photos, celebrating their birthdays, and even sharing their beds.

There has been one additional twist since the days of Henry Bergh, however. Extensive scientific research on animal communication and cognition has filtered into public awareness. We watch a gorilla named Koko use primitive forms of sign language to interact with human researchers. We listen to tapes of haunting and complex whale songs. We read about the ways that birds use different song patterns for different purposes. We now appreciate animals for their intelligence as well as their loyalty, and our sympathy has expanded to incorporate "intelligent" species such as whales and dolphins as well as cuddly, loving ones such as dogs and cats. Animals are no longer "dumb brutes." The natural sciences have blurred the boundaries between humans and other species even further.[8]

The biggest difference between the recent movement and its nineteenth-century precursor, though, is in the explicit ideas derived from the compassionate sentiments. Beginning in the early 1970s, philosophers articulated several kinds of claims for the protection of animals. In his 1975 book *Animal Liberation*, Peter Singer provided a utilitarian argument, carefully avoiding the concept of rights.[9] Because animals are capable of feeling pain, humans have a moral obligation to weigh animals' pain against humans' pleasure derived from their use. The dreadful lives of animals in "factory farms," for instance, should outweigh human pleasures in meat eating. Animals may be used in experiments, but only if the likely benefits are high and only if humans are also considered as potential subjects. Severely retarded humans, the argument goes, may be capable of less pleasure in their lives than many intelligent nonhuman mammals. To automatically give every human priority over every nonhuman, no matter what their comparative potential for pleasure and pain, is "speciesism," a mistake parallel to racism and sexism. Singer thus provided an epithet, a rational argument, and extensive evidence of animal suffering in laboratories and farms. He implicated modern societies' central institutions in the abuse of animals, transcending the humane movement's focus on aberrant cases of individual cruelty.

In a 1983 book *The Case for Animal Rights,* Tom Regan went further than Singer, arguing that animals had natural rights similar to those of humans and therefore should not be used as a resource at all, no matter what the possible benefits to others. Even though animals are not themselves moral actors, they have inherent worth as living creatures, "subjects" in control of their lives. In his words, "It is not an act of kindness to treat animals respectfully. It is not 'the sentimental interests' of moral agents that grounds our duties of justice to children, the retarded, the senile, or other moral patients, including animals. It is respect for their inherent value."[10] Developing a true "rights" position, Regan claimed that "they, like us, have a value of their own, logically independently of their utility for others and of their being the object of anyone else's interests" (p. 384). Inherent worth does not come in degrees; an animal either has it or does not.

Singer and Regan both made antivivisection central to their programs. By grounding animal protection in the characteristics of animals rather than in human capacities for sympathy, they cast doubt on the freedom of scientists to do what they wish with animals. They criticized as "instrumentalism" the reduction of living beings, whether humans or animals, to the status of tools for researchers. In contrast to the uneasy nineteenth-century relationship between animal protection and antivivisection, the two now became inextricable.

Not only scientific research but every human interaction with animals—even well-intentioned ones—could now come under scrutiny. Some clearly involved suffering, such as trapping and hunting, modern methods of raising chickens or veal calves, and the Draize test, in which substances are tested in the eyes of white rabbits. Others were offensive primarily because they did not seem "natural": zoos, carnivals, and other displays of animals; vivisection with anesthetics; even horseback riding and the keeping of pets. Pet owning, the ideal of the humane movement, was attacked as a form of fascism, necessarily involving dominations.[11]

The rights discourse, not the utilitarian one, prevailed in the contemporary animal protection movement, lending it its name. Regan's *The Case for Animal Rights* is a dense philosophical treatise that few in the movement have read. In contrast, Singer's *Animal Liberation,* easy if gruesome reading, has been extremely influential in attracting converts to animal rights—but for its evidence of abuse not for its philosophical arguments. Indeed protectors avoid Singer's utilitarian language in favor of rights talk. They routinely refer to Singer to buttress their arguments for animal rights, even though he avoids the language of rights and, according to Regan, does not even provide coherent philosophical support for the rights of animals. Activists commonly attribute Regan's arguments about rights to Singer. In the United States, at least, people feel more comfortable with political arguments phrased in terms of individual rights.

The rights discourse proved effective for building the contemporary animal rights movement. In the United States, activists founded hundreds of groups in the early 1980s, and membership in these groups soared, especially in the late 1980s. As many as one million people joined explicit animal rights groups, in addition to the millions supporting traditional humane organizations. The new groups are a diverse lot. At the more radical end of the spectrum groups such as the Animal Liberation Front (ALF), which began in Britain but was soon imported to the United States, favor sabotage and laboratory break-ins—which have not only "liberated" animals but also yielded notorious videotapes showing experimenters in an unfavorable light. Even activists within the movement debate whether such tactics help or hurt the movement's public image. Staying with legal tactics, People for the Ethical Treatment of Animals (PETA), the United States' largest animal rights group with several hundred thousand paying members, deploys many tactics, especially those involving media attention. For example, it sponsored a "barf-in" at the headquarters of cosmetics giant l'Oreal; protectors pretended to vomit into a large papier-mâché toilet because animal testing "made them sick." Older organizations, like the Humane Society of the United States, founded in 1954, have also grown more radical under the influence of new groups and ideas, although they continue their traditional practices of lobbying and education. Diverse groups pursue diverse goals using diverse tactics.

## Rights Talk

Appeals to rights have become a reflex in American society at least since the Civil Rights Act of 1964. Groups have organized to defend the rights of fetuses, children, prisoners, future generations, and animals. People claim the right to life, the right to die, the right to privacy, and the right to know. All these claims are represented as bedrock moral imperatives: compelling, unassailable, and beyond negotiation. Every group claims "oppression" if it is prevented from doing what it wishes—even when that desire is owning guns or distributing pornography. In the United States moral claims are inevitably framed in the language of rights, even when the rhetoric of rights is simply a strategic means to present particular interests as compelling moral claims.

All claims to rights must be grounded in higher, immutable principles of nature, of religion, or of traditional values. But what are the sources of these principles? In a world increasingly recognized as socially constructed, it is no longer possible to say convincingly, "We hold these truths to be self-evident." Religion is no longer universally accepted as a source of justice or truth. Nor does science any longer seem sufficient to legitimate moral claims, since scientific evidence is increasingly perceived as malleable and available for conflicting points of view. At least, most philosophers agree that rights claims cannot be proven. In fact, new rights claims are grounded in changing social practices and concrete situations and in the intuitions and articulated beliefs associated with them. When social and economic conditions change, they generate new standards of behavior. Long-standing practices may then come under attack, and such attacks are usually framed in the language of rights. Rights claims are, in effect, a moral barometer, reflecting public anxieties and social cleavages that develop in the social conditions of a given place and time. They may not be philosophically provable, but they are plausible to large numbers of people.

Thus it was natural for animal protectionists to turn to rights talk in the United States in the 1970s and 1980s. It fits the sentimental individualism derived from the image of pets as family members. The language of rights leads in turn to a radical extension of protection efforts to ever more species (since there are no obvious boundaries for deciding which species have rights and which do not) and to more urgent tactics. Yet animal protectionists in other countries have not embraced the cry of rights so thoroughly (Regan is American, Singer Australian). Are other frameworks possible?

## Alternative Formulations

The individualistic rights formulation was hardly the only way that animal protection claims could have been articulated. Several philosophers have pointed out problems with Regan's rights ideology.[12] In particular, there is no single trait or ability one can point to as making an animal worthy of rights: the ability to feel pain, to communicate, to plan one's life, to have a self-image? All of these are important, and all come in varying degrees. The more that a species or individual has, the more worthy of rights it is (and humans score highest on most measures).[13] But there is no absolute boundary, only more and less. Singer draws the line between a mollusk and a crustacean, on the basis of ability to feel pain. Regan can only appeal to our lack of certainty to give the benefit of the doubt to frogs and other species whose mental lives are opaque to us.

British philosopher Mary Midgley outlined an alternative in a brilliant but seldom read book called *Animals and Why They Matter* in 1983.[14] Dismissing "rights" as "the really desperate word," better as a political slogan than a philosophical principle, she said that the challenge for animal protectionists was redrawing the group boundary (which the concept of rights does not help us do), not deciding what rights to grant those within it. "Speciesism" is not really parallel to racism, since knowing the race of a human is irrelevant for how you will treat her or him, while knowing the species of a nonhuman is absolutely crucial for how to treat it. The best rationale for helping animals, she concluded, may be old-fashioned compassion. That we are different from other species does not prevent us from sympathizing with them, especially since humans and domesticated species have lived together for thousands of years, becoming mutually dependent in every possible way. Love for animals is perfectly appropriate. Midgley thus avoided Regan's need to speculate on the mental life of animals or to identify with them.

Midgley's position involves a more critical anthropomorphism than most activists demonstrate, admitting that there are similarities but also important differences between species. We are encouraged to discover what the differences are, so that we can learn how to treat each species properly. Rather than personifying animals, she encourages us to appreciate their diversity. "Critical anthropomorphism" of this kind could even link scientists and animal protectionists in common cause.

Midgley's formulation also provides a way to distinguish between the treatment of domestic and wild animals. Domesticated animals are part of a "mixed community" with humans; because they are already under our control, we bear considerable responsibility for their good treatment. We have bred them for thousands of generations to be our companions. But wild animals live by their own rules. For them, the best we can do is to refrain from destroying their habitats.

This opening to environmentalism is significant, for it provides an alternative vision of the treatment of animals in the wild. As the environmental movement developed during the 1970s, it elaborated a pantheistic view of the sacred integrity of nature and the fragile balance of plant, animal, and human life—an idea reaching its extreme in the "Gaia hypothesis" that the earth itself is a kind of organism capable of healing and self-regulation.[15] In this ecological vision, plants and animals had inherent value independent of their utility, simply because they were part of this system. Their value did not rest on their rights as individuals, but on their contribution to habitats, ecosystems, and balances between species.[16]

Animal rights groups, in contrast, believe that all animals deserve equal rights regardless of their place in nature. Aside from a tendency to focus on cute or humanlike animals (furry, intelligent, with humanesque facial features) for purposes of fund-raising, the movement literature draws few distinctions between species. It does not distinguish between animals that are "renewable" and those that are endangered; equally egregious are experiments on artificially bred mice and those on monkeys captured in the wild. Similarly, in targeting fur coats, the animal rights activists do not distinguish animals trapped in the wild from those raised on ranches. An ecologist, in contrast, would emphasize such distinctions. Those concerned with preserving species, after all, may destroy individual animals that threaten the survival of a herd; the ecological balance of certain communities may require the killing of animals. Many environmentalists criticize animal rights activists for treating wild animals as though they were domestic, whereas different rules should apply to the two categories. If animals were granted rights to live full lives without interference, then humans could justify meddling in the wilderness to protect animals from many predators. The deer's right to life can be violated as easily by a mountain lion as by a human hunter, after all. The concept of rights for animals becomes absurd at this point. The contrast between saving individual animals and saving species has precluded much cooperation between the two protest movements.[17]

Another problem with the current rights framing is that, given present laboratory technologies, the rights of animals occasionally do conflict with life-and-death human issues. The urgency of the AIDS epidemic, for example, would seem to demand that every avenue of research be explored; absolute rights for animals might well slow progress. This recognition that there may be tradeoffs between life-giving discoveries and the rights of animals is a popular source of resistance to the movement. Midgley's compassionate stance, like Singer's utilitarian one, would allow the sacrifice of animals in cases, like these, where there are clear or very likely benefits.

## Conclusion

There are many complex steps from moral intuitions to protest activities, especially a compelling ideological articulation and organizers to act upon it. The complexity of the links, however, hardly proves that the ideas and intuitions are not important in rousing political action. Even when these moral visions are not camouflage for material interests, they are effective. Protest has many motivations and symbolic sources, despite the efforts of social scientists to reduce it to elegantly simple models. Ideas and moral visions matter.

Intuitions and ideas not only help create protest, but direct its choice of targets and tactics. Some ideological formulations may lead to tactical errors. Is the individualism of rights talk, for example, a dead end? A misguided way to articulate sincere and persistent moral sentiments? Will the animal rights movement suffer because it is clear to many people that, when expressed as absolute moral rights, the rights of humans and those of nonhumans may indeed occasionally clash? Alternative formulations, I have argued, are available. A regrouping of the movement could allow a new articulation, one based on compassion for domestic animals and an ecological approach to wild ones. It will be interesting to see how persistent current formulations prove to be.

# Fear and Redemption in the Environment Movement

## Donald Worster

The Age of Ecology opened on the New Mexican desert, near the town of Alamogordo, on July 16, 1945, with a dazzling fireball of light and a swelling mushroom cloud of radioactive gases.[1] As the world's first atomic bomb went off and the color of the early morning sky changed abruptly from pale blue to blinding white, physicist and project leader J. Robert Oppenheimer felt at first a surge of elated reverence. Then a somber phrase from the *Bhagavad-Gita* flashed into his mind: "I am become Death, the shatterer of worlds." In later years, although Oppenheimer could still describe the making of bombs as "technically sweet," his worry about the consequences of that achievement increased. Other atomic scientists, including Albert Einstein, Hans Bethe, and Leo Szilard, became even more anxiously determined to control the awesome weapon that their research had made possible, a determination eventually shared by many ordinary Americans, Japanese, and others around the world. It was increasingly feared that the bomb—however justifiable its invention to meet the challenge of fascism—had put into humankind's hands a more dreadful power than we might be prepared to handle. For the first time, there existed a technological force that seemed capable of destroying much of the life on the planet. As Oppenheimer warned, humans, through the work of the scientist, now knew sin. The implied question was whether they also knew the way to redemption.[2]

Clearly, Francis Bacon's seventeenth-century dream of extending man's empire over nature, "to the effecting of all things possible," a dream that had propelled much of modern technology and science, had sudden-

158

ly taken a macabre, even suicidal, turn. The bomb cast doubt on the entire project of the domination of nature that had been at the heart of modern history. It raised doubts about the moral legitimacy of science, about the tumultuous pace of technology, and about the Enlightenment dream of replacing religious faith with human rationality as a guide both to material welfare and to virtue. That the bomb, a product of European and North American physicists, was first used against Asians, not the Germans for whom it had been designed, confirmed for many that western civilization had little respect for other races and cultures. None of those doubts and complaints was new, but the development of the atomic bomb gave them an urgency they had never had before. Doubts about the dark side of the Enlightenment legacy spread not only among scientists but also among philosophers, poets, historians, and political leaders.

The fundamental challenge raised by the bomb was whether there was sufficient capacity for moral restraint in human beings, enough to trust themselves with so much power. Other modern technologies, from the railroad to the airplane, had also stirred up controversy, but none of it had significantly slowed their use or development. There was little precedent, at least in modern Euro-American civilization, for instituting strong collective checks on any technological innovation. But the discovery and splitting of the atom was unprecedented too; not at all like laying rails to California, it involved sophisticated knowledge of the very structure of matter. The exploitation of that knowledge seemed more transcendent, an exercise of divine power. Humans were now playing God. Or, many wondered, were they playing the role of Lucifer, the corrupt angel who rebelled and tried to overthrow the heavenly throne? However theologians might debate the spiritual meaning of the new technology, ultimately the issues must be faced by the new class exercising power, the scientists and technicians, and by the public who had supported them in their uninhibited quest for knowledge. Was either party prepared to exercise restraint over the pursuit of knowledge and its applications? Could either manage to impose effective control over this newest and most deadly military innovation where none had succeeded before? If not, then Bacon's ambition must lead to widespread death and destruction, not only among human beings but within the whole living creation.

The quest for redemption was not slow in finding its voice. Under the threat of the atomic bomb a new moral consciousness called environmentalism began to take form, whose purpose paradoxically was to use insights from the science of ecology to restrain the use of modern science-based power over nature. Environmentalism as a modern political movement began, appropriately, in the United States, where the nuclear era was launched, and where, in the summer of 1946, while the afterglow of American victory in the war was still in the air, scientists first began to study the environmental effects of man-made radiation. The government planned to test its fourth and fifth bombs (bombs two and three had been dropped on Hiroshima and Nagasaki) in the Marshall Islands, almost 3,000 miles south of Hawaii. Here lay the Bikini atoll, a necklace of small coral islands surrounding a blue lagoon that had escaped the ravages of war. The U.S. military chose the site for Operation Crossroads in which they would set off a series of underwater explosions to study the atomic bomb's environmental effects. All the atoll residents were removed to other islands, and in their place came 42,000 military personnel, who would monitor the experiment. Would the blast open a crack into the subterranean rock, touching off earthquakes all over the world? Would a tidal wave roll from Bikini all the way to Los Angeles? Would the ocean catch on fire? Many worried about the potentially catastrophic environmental effects of this strange new power that had already leveled whole cities, vaporized civilians in their tracks, and left hundreds of thousands of maimed survivors. On July 1 a bomb exploded in the lagoon, lifting millions of tons of water, mud, and ship wreckage into a white column over a mile high, then collapsed back into the ocean, churning up a maelstrom of violence, filling the scoured-out basin with radioactive sludge, while the mushroom cloud of gases and steam continued to mount. A crew in rubber gloves and gas masks shoved a boat into the lagoon to study the impact. They found a live pig blown out of one of the target vessels and floating in the churning water, but there was no tidal wave nor any crack into an abyss. The beaches of Bikini were littered with pieces of rope and canvas, scraps of twisted metal, boards and tires, scums of oil, rusty beer cans, dead fish, and palm fronds, but there were no human casualties. According to relieved officials, the damage was containable and the radioactivity was quickly dissipating. Nonetheless, the government sent in a team of biologists to study what had happened to the radioactive isotopes released in the explosion. Over the next few years they prowled the sands with Geiger counters, dove into the lagoon waters, and collected fish to study the effects of radiation on them. In what was the first ecological study of the atomic era they wanted to see how the entire food chain had been affected. What they discovered was that, contrary to first impressions, there remained a significant residual radioactivity in the food chain for at least five years after the explosion. Tuna in the surrounding sea carried the residuum in their fatty tissues, and so would anyone who ate them.[3]

The atoll remained a favored site for weapons testing, including the first American hydrogen fusion bomb, detonated off Namu Island in

February 1954. Eighty-five miles away the unsuspecting crew of a Japanese fishing trawler, the *Fukuryu Maru,* was exposed to the H-bomb fallout, and even farther off was a group of Marshall Islanders, who like the fishermen suffered vomiting, burning skin, suppurating lesions, and other radiation-induced sicknesses, some of which lingered for the rest of their lives. Their suffering made them international news, but all of these victims were still rather out of American focus.

Less remote and more immediately threatening than the events in the South Pacific was what had begun to take place in the deserts of the American West. Fearful of spies stealing American military secrets (the Russians were now testing their own bombs) and nervous about the high cost of overseas operations, the military moved most of its atomic testing program home to a desolate site north of Las Vegas, the Nevada Proving Grounds, where the first domestic bomb series, code-named Ranger, began in 1951. Here in the southwestern desert nuclear technology came once more to make grisly progress. The government built a "Doom Town" of suburban-type houses, filled with life-sized mannequins sitting in easy chairs, to determine the potential effects of atomic warfare on its citizens; the fireball from a blast seared not only the dummies and their furniture and automobiles but also the native vegetation of creosote bush and cactus, leaving only bare sand. Hot debris fell repeatedly over the Great Basin throughout the fifties, poisoning flocks of sheep, exposing their herders to damaging radiation, along with other rural residents all over Nevada and Utah, the fallout blowing on eastward toward Denver, Chicago, and Washington.[4]

The devastation of Bikini atoll, the poisoning of the domestic and foreign atmosphere with the radioactive isotope, strontium 90, and the threat of irreversible genetic damage, along with leukemia, struck public consciousness with an impact that no previous human impact on the earth had ever had. This was no distant problem or an easily ignored issue; the bomb posed a danger to the health and survival of all Americans, a threat coming from their own military defenders against enemy forces. By the mid-fifties national magazines were filled with stories about bigger and bigger bombs, each of them with the force of millions of tons of TNT, and about their impact on land and air. The National Academy of Sciences released a report on radioactive fallout in 1956, offering only limited reassurance. Atmospheric testing of weapons, the report said, had so far not raised worldwide radiation to levels significantly greater than those resulting from natural background radioactivity, and citizens would get a stronger dose of radiation from dental and medical use of X-rays than from bombs. On the other hand, it admitted that even the lowest levels of radiation could have serious effects. And the drive underway to harness the fission process to provide cheap electrical energy, which might put nuclear power plants in the environs of every American city, posed a still larger threat. According to the scientists, the development of peacetime nuclear reactors could produce enough strontium 90 by the end of the century that the dispersal of a mere one percent of it would seriously contaminate the entire earth. The disposal of nuclear wastes from those reactors would demand the most careful monitoring.[5]

That was the picture as it looked a mere decade after the Bikini tests. Not until 1958, however, did the ecological effects of atomic fallout become of more widespread concern to American scientists. In that year the Committee for Nuclear Information was organized in St. Louis with the aim of stripping all secrecy from the government's weapons program and warning citizens of the dangers in further nuclear testing and nuclear power development. One of its members was the plant physiologist Barry Commoner, who would become a prominent leader in a new environmental movement.[6] Other scientists began to join this campaign of information and protest, and increasingly they were from the biological side of science. Their campaign against the radiation threat to the planet set a precedent for scientists taking up political issues, mobilizing public opinion, and out of guilt as much as responsibility, calling for a new ethic toward nature. The bomb tested at Alamogordo had, by the late 1950s, begun to set off a powerful moral reaction.

The writer and scientist Rachel Carson was not a leader in that early political movement among scientists. For a while she shunned politics and controversy. But as she listened to the debate going on, she became increasingly worried, and soon she joined the reaction. When she made her commitment to speak out, she came armed with facts and eloquence, animated by an intense conviction that the world had entered a more dangerous era than any before and that scientists could no longer do their science as usual. No American individual became more important than she in that awakening of ethical concern. Through her writings, particularly her book *Silent Spring* (published in 1962), she taught the public how to think about the new vulnerability of nature, and she was the first to warn them of a whole new generation of toxic substances: not only radioactive isotopes but also pesticides made of chlorinated hydrocarbons that were polluting the earth. Translated into more than two dozen languages, her work inspired a global environmental consciousness.

Carson was born in 1907 and grew up on what was then the rural outskirts of Pittsburgh. With the aid of a scholarship she attended the Pennsylvania College for Women (now Chatham College), then went on to Johns Hopkins University for an M.A. degree in genetics. Her most important scientific training, though, came in summers spent at Woods Hole Marine Biological Laboratory on Cape Cod, where she discovered the ecology of the sea. She felt drawn to it emotionally as well as scientifically and devoted most of her life to its study and enjoyment. What she found in the sea was a vast, so far untouched realm in which living organisms had evolved in an environment quite unlike the land surface. The sea seemed an unspoiled part of nature, whereas the North American continent had, by her lifetime, been explored, settled, and manipulated extensively. Had Carson lived during earlier days, she might have longed to go westward and alone into the wilderness. Instead, this small, shy woman became a marine biologist prowling the wild oceanic world of the East Coast, peering into tide pools, wading at night onto mudflats with bucket and flashlight in hand, diving into deeper waters with a snorkel or pressurized helmet. No one would do more than she to direct American thinking to the vast ocean environment, which comprises three-fourths of the planet's surface.

The decade of the thirties was not a propitious one for a woman seeking a career in the natural sciences. She became her mother's sole financial support and, in 1936, found it necessary to accept a job as junior aquatic biologist with the Bureau of Fisheries, then in the Department of Commerce, later absorbed into the Fish and Wildlife Service of the Department of the Interior. Until 1952 that government agency was her professional home, and she worked her way up to become its chief editor of publications. She resigned when her own writings gave her sufficient income to be independent. Her first book was *Under the Sea Wind* (1941), but it was her second, *The Sea around Us* (1951), that brought her fame and a small fortune; it was on the best-seller lists for more than eighty weeks and won the National Book Award. A third title, *The Edge of the Sea*, appeared in 1955. By that point Carson had found a new career as a free-lance science writer, searching for meaning, beauty, even inspiration in the stories of the sea.

World War II left an unintended but destructive legacy for nature in many ways other than the atomic bomb. Carson's own government agency had been mobilized to learn more about the marine environment and help devise means to exploit it for food, navigation, and defense. In a second edition of *The Sea around Us*, published in 1961, Carson acknowledged how much had been changed by the new war-generated technology. Americans and Russians were dumping radioactive wastes in the ocean, and fallout from the testing of bombs was settling over the waters. The effects of those substances on the whole chain of living organisms, from the smallest diatoms to the largest marine mammals, and on humans themselves, could not be foretold. "Although man's record as a steward of the natural resources of the earth has been a discouraging one," she wrote, "there has been a certain comfort in the belief that the sea, at least, was inviolate, beyond man's ability to change and to despoil. But this belief, unfortunately, has proved to be naive." The fate of Bikini atoll made that clear.[7]

Carson subsequently turned her attention to other deadly poisons falling from the sky, particularly the persistent pesticides like DDT (dicholoro-diphenyl-trichloroethane) that had also come out of the war years and were spreading through terrestrial food chains and draining into the sea, affecting even penguins at the South Pole. After years of gathering all the scientific data she could find on the ecological consequences of pesticides, she brought out *Silent Spring,* a measured but severe indictment of modern agriculture, the chemical industry, and applied entomology. The message of the book, still controversial, was that humans were endangering their own lives through an arrogant, manipulative attitude toward other forms of life: "Along with the possibility of the extinction of mankind by nuclear war, the central problem of our age has . . . become the contamination of man's total environment with such substances of incredible potential for harm—substances that accumulate in the tissues of plants and animals and even penetrate the germ cells to shatter or alter the very material of heredity upon which the shape of the future depends." Carson assembled enough facts to show why the more persistent chemicals must be restricted, but her deeper message was the need for ethical change, away from a spirit of conquest and toward a respect for all forms of life and an acknowledgment of our dependence on them. "The 'control of nature,'" she wrote, "is a phrase conceived in arrogance, born of the Neanderthal age of biology and philosophy, when it was supposed that nature exists for the convenience of man. . . . It is our alarming misfortune that so primitive a science has armed itself with the most modern and terrible weapons, and that in turning them against the insects it has also turned them against the earth."[8]

Recent feminist scholars have argued that Carson's moral critique of the conquest of nature emerged out of a "women's culture" that had long emphasized cooperation and nurturance instead of the pursuit of conquest and wealth.[9] Certainly, Carson drew on many women for support during what became a storm of reaction, much of it belittling to her as a woman. But the major intellectual influences on her life that she acknowledged most were men like Albert Schweitzer and Henry Bigelow, and millions of men as well as women looked on her as the prophet of a new ethic toward nature. When she died of cancer at age 56, she had organized no political movement nor seen that new environmental ethic become common; however, she had helped make ecology a familiar word and environmentalism a growing international cause.[10]

In the earlier part of this century the word "environment" referred mainly to the external social influences working on the individual (as opposed to genetic endowment), and environmentalism referred to the belief that the "physical, biological, psychological or cultural environment" was a crucial factor shaping "the structure or behavior of animals, including man."[11] But increasingly as the heredity versus environment battle lost saliency after World War II, environment came to mean the *natural* influences surrounding people, including flora, fauna, climate, water, and soil. Human beings, it was understood, were not passive victims of their surroundings; they interacted with them and could have a large-scale impact. An environmentalist, consequently, became anyone who was concerned with the preservation of those biophysical surroundings from pollution, depletion, or degradation. For generations technological development had carried the promise of transforming the natural world—even replacing it with "second nature," a work of artifice and intelligence. Environmentalists now countered that humans, no matter how impressive their technology, needed to protect that natural world from their own actions in order to survive or even to live well. Nature is not a realm set apart from humans like another country that one visits from time to time, but instead is a vast, intricate community, a system of connections and interchanges highly vulnerable to disturbance, a world on which humans must inescapably depend and cannot be replaced.

The new environmentalism, to be sure, did not appear suddenly on the scene with no precedents or intellectual preparation. Rachel Carson expressed indebtedness to such nineteenth-century figures as Henry David Thoreau and John Muir, who had celebrated nature in a wild state and sought to reestablish a direct personal relationship with the nonhuman. Both men pursued private strategies for getting outside the cocoon of civilization and into the woods or mountains. But in a nation of over 200 million people, with a far denser web of artifice obscuring the natural order, that kind of private quest had become difficult. Environmentalism was, therefore, not a private relationship of individual to nature, nor a kind of retreat into nature, but a decidedly public engagement—a strategy pursued in the courtroom and legislative chamber to defend a relationship found even in the heart of the largest megalopolis.

Other precedents included the resource conservation movement, which gained momentum in the early twentieth century under the leadership of Gifford Pinchot, chief forester during the Theodore Roosevelt administration. But that movement had aimed at preserving national parks and wildlife refuges, setting up a national forest system under sustained-yield management, and protecting the nation's soils and minerals. Typically, conservation had been a movement to put the government in charge of overseeing and even of perpetually owning the land. Activists like Pinchot understood that American society could not endure without a permanent supply of natural resources, and they feared that a short-sighted consumption might threaten the nation's security. On the other hand, conservationists tended to look on nature as a series of discrete places needing defense or problems needing solution—a Yosemite Valley, a pine forest, an eroded farm on the Great Plains. When environmentalism emerged, it maintained some of that same commitment to the older program of land and wildlife conservation; for example, it supported the Wilderness Act of 1964 along with the Endangered Species Act of 1973. But at the same time the core of the movement shifted to embrace a new, broader concern about health—health of the organism, health of the global ecosystem—as more and more citizens sensed that the human-nature umbilical itself was under attack and that defending it required a more comprehensive way of thinking.[12]

The emergence of the new viewpoint owed much to a relatively obscure group of thinkers who preceded the rise of environmentalism in the 1960s and 1970s, most of them academics in such fields as ecology and geography. They were the first to reconceptualize "the environment" as a set of complex, interactive relationships between humans and the rest of nature. Many of them thought about those relationships on a more international scale, transcending dramatically the more limited national consciousness of the conservationists. Their ideas often came from abroad: for example, from the Austrian geologist Edward Suess, inventor of the concept of the biosphere; from French and German geographers, who had long debated the question of nature as a limiting factor on human activity; and from a succession of English naturalists, including Charles Darwin, Charles Elton, and Arthur Tansley.[13] A key American figure in this emerging body of thought was the Midwesterner wildlife scientist Aldo Leopold, who introduced many readers to the science of ecology through his 1949 book of outdoor essays, *A Sand County Almanac*. By the fifties those influences had all come together in a new integrative, interdisciplinary point of view that united the natural and social sciences, a view that might be called human ecology. That view must be put alongside the atomic bomb and its use and misuse as immediate spawning ground for modern environmentalism. Avoiding the extremes of, on the one hand, environmental determinism, which had tried to reduce cultures to their physical circumstances, and on the other hand, of a technological optimism that was blind to all side-effects, the new view taught that human life must be lived within a set of constraints, both biophysical and moral.

Examples of that emergent human ecology run all through the late forties and the fifties. Among anthropologists of the period Betty Meggers and Julian Steward, one working in Amazonia, the other in the desert Southwest, laid the foundations for "cultural ecology." Among geographers Carl Sauer was the crucial figure—a broad-ranging scholar who produced a number of influential studies of people living in close contact with nature. Two important books published simultaneously in 1948, *Our Plundered Planet,* by Fairfield Osborn, and *Road to Ruin,* by William Vogt, both offered a planetary perspective on man's growing effect on his surroundings. Then in 1955 several of those same scholars, and many more from many disciplines and many countries, came together in Princeton, New Jersey, for a symposium on the state of the human-nature relation, dedicated to the memory of the nineteenth-century American conservationist, George Perkins Marsh. As much as any single event, that Princeton gathering prepared the intellectual ground for the environmental movement.[14]

Take, for example, the contribution by Paul Sears, botanist and chairman of the conservation program at Yale University. Sears reviewed the global impact of human population growth, the intensification of agricultural land-use, water and air pollution in industrial areas, noting along the way that the United States, with less than a tenth of the world's population was consuming more than half of the mineral production. "Man is dependent," he argued, "upon other organisms both for the immediate means of survival and for maintaining habitat conditions under which survival is possible.[15] Neither Sears nor the other 1956 conference-goers called themselves environmentalists, but their focus on the place of humans in the global environment and their general concern about the state of that environment would both help to give environmentalism a set of defining ideas.

What environmentalism added to those fertile ideas of human ecology was a sense of urgency, bordering at times on apocalyptic fear, that the atomic bomb had ignited. The global environment was everywhere in a state of "crisis." The specter haunting scientists like Carson was widespread, wholesale death—the death of birds, of ecosystems, of nature itself, and, because of our dependence on nature, the possible death of humans as well. Though environmentalists sometimes tried to temper their gloom with a more hopeful and politically acceptable emphasis on a "green future" in which cities, economies, and productive technologies would all be reembedded in the tangled web of life, they had trouble convincing themselves that public attitudes were changing fast enough to avert disaster. In his widely admired and influential Reith lectures delivered in 1969 over the BBC, one of Britain's most prominent environmentalists, Frank Fraser Darling, though admitting that Carson's "emotional overtones" made him uncomfortable, also admitted that he could not be an optimist and that he was troubled by the constant necessity, for political reasons, of "expressing faith which at bottom I do not feel."

In 1968, a half-dozen years after *Silent Spring* appeared, the California biologist Paul Ehrlich heard yet another bomb ticking, ready to usher in chaos and mass death: the "population explosion," which in that year had reached over three billion and was increasing at a global average of more than 2 percent a year—and in many poorer countries at a rate of 3 percent or more. Thus, it was not technology alone, but human biology that now had become a factor in the rush to Armageddon. Once more the wraith of Thomas Malthus materialized, warning of approaching limits to human population and human consumption, a prediction echoed in such books as *The Limits to Growth, Blueprint for Survival,* and *Small Is Beautiful,* all of which expressed the fear that complex industrial civilization as a whole might be breaking down. In their view, an economy expanding at a constant geometric ratio, using ever more energy, land, minerals, and water, must eventually run up against the limits of the earth. Looked at as a set of interdependencies rather than as a storehouse of commodities, the environment was not merely a set of discrete things to be used, depleted, and replaced by substitutes. Here the environmentalists confronted deeply seated attitudes among traditional economists, business leaders, politicians, and the public about the virtues of economic growth, attitudes underlying the modern economic system, and indeed the whole materialistic ethos of modern culture.[17]

Barry Commoner, who had been among the first scientists to move into environmental politics, kept pace with the broadening agenda, though he never became a Malthusian about population or resource scarcity. In 1963 the U.S. Senate ratified a treaty banning the atmospheric testing of nuclear weapons, effectively removing the first great cause from the environmentalist agenda, but Commoner saw that there were plenty of other dangers threatening planetary health. His Committee for Nuclear Information became the Committee for Environmental Information and publisher of a new magazine called *Environment.* He began studying the damaging effects of nitrate-based chemical fertilizers, seeping from agricultural fields into the public's water supply, on the body's ability to transport oxygen in the blood. He also began alerting the country to what he called "the most blatant example of the environmental crisis in the United States," the galloping eutrophication of 12,000–year-old Lake Erie from phosphates in household detergents. The drive to maximize corporate profit, he maintained, was the force behind the development of those new harmful products, all of which had safer but less lucrative substitutes. In his book *The Closing Circle,* published in 1971, Commoner argued that the great need was for an awakened public, led by informed scientists, to force the government to restrain the development and marketing of those technologies by corporate America.[18]

By the late sixties that call for regulating the polluters began to have a significant effect on the political process. In 1969 Congress passed the National Environmental Policy Act, which set up a new Environmental Protection Agency and required an "environmental impact statement" for any federally funded project that might cause damage to the earth. Other landmark legislation included clean water acts in 1960, 1965, and 1972 and clean air acts in 1963, 1967, and 1970. Other countries followed suit; in Britain, for instance, a Control of Pollution Act passed Parliament in 1974. By that point the list of international pollutants had expanded to include automobile emissions, solid wastes, toxic metals, oil spills, even (and most ominous of all) the heat caused by the atmospheric buildup of carbon dioxide which could lead to global warming, melting the polar ice caps and raising the sea level.[19] This discovery of nature's vulnerability came as so great a shock that, for many Britons and Americans, the only appropriate response was talk of revolution. On the more trivial side, new terms were added to the English language like "ecopolitics," "ecocatastrophe," and "ecoawareness." Beyond such new language, however, more fundamental changes in the economy, political parties, and even worldview were called for. To cite only one instance, Michael McCloskey, the executive director of the Sierra Club, concluded in 1970 that "a revolution is truly needed—in our values, outlooks and economic organization. For the crisis of our environment stems from a legacy of economic and technical premises which have been pursued in the absence of ecological knowledge. That other revolution, the industrial one that is turning sour, needs to be replaced by a revolution of new attitudes toward growth, goods, space, and living things." The "enemy" that this writer perceived and wanted defeated was more numerous and diffuse than Commoner's economic class of capitalists, the men who had been the great architects of industrial revolution. Like many other environmentalists, McCloskey was pointing not to a single class but to a whole set of *values.* Many of those values had long been associated with the rise of a bourgeois civilization—a dedication to technological progress, to unlimited production and consumption, to material self-advancement, to individualism, and to the domination of nature—but they were no longer limited to a ruling class.

Similarly, the political scientist William Ophuls insisted that it was "the basic principles of modern industrial civilization [that were] incompatible with ecological scarcity and . . . the whole ideology of modernity growing out of the Enlightenment, especially such central tenets as individualism, may no longer be viable." Time, in other words, had run out on an entire culture. Nature's economy had been pushed to the breaking point, and "ecology" was to be the rallying cry for nothing less than a broad cultural revolution.[20]

If the overthrow or drastic reform of modern industrial civilization had become the most radical aim of the ecology movement, it was ironic to find the movement's strongest support coming from the middle classes of western societies. That fact was well and often noted, sometimes with indignation, by the would-be middle classes of the world. Many of the latter asked whether the message of ecology was a sermon on the virtues of poverty to be heeded only by those who were still have-nots. Could middle-class environmentalists, they questioned, bring off a revolution against their own economic self-interest, or did they really mean after all merely to enact a few modest, liberal, pragmatic reforms that would leave the base of industrial culture intact? Was it even conceivable, two hundred years after Watts's steam engine, to abandon the achievements of the industrial revolution, or had the force of history left us with no alternative but more industrialism, not less? What would an alternative social order to industrialism, one founded on the science of ecology, look like—and would the middle class, or humanity in general, really accept such a world? Perhaps most significantly, would the billions of people still living in relative or absolute scarcity want to live there?

The culmination of those events and ponderings came on April 22, 1970, when citizens around the United States, and many abroad, observed the first Earth Day, an annual day henceforth to be set aside for sober reflection on the world's deteriorating environmental condition. The idea of such a day originated with Senator Gaylord Nelson of Wisconsin, but the main organizer was a 25–year-old antiwar activist, Sam Brown, who held distinctly apocalyptic views about the fate of the earth. He now tried to apply the tactics of student protests against the Vietnam War and race discrimination to the environmental crisis. Some observers thought there was less urgency in the new cause; burning a credit card somehow did not seem as radical as burning a draft card. A *Newsweek* reporter wrote, "Despite the desperate sickness of the environment, despite the turnout of millions of at least partially awakened Americans, the whole demonstration seemed to lack the necessary passion."[21] Perhaps, if that was so, most Americans had not yet been scared enough. They had not yet absorbed all the fear and anxiety that was driving many scientists and a growing number of environmentalists.

There was still plenty of fierce passion in the busiest figure of Earth Day 1970, Barry Commoner, who managed to address audiences on four different campuses in the space of a few hours. Commoner had a few eminent companions on the day's lecture circuits, including Paul Ehrlich, Rene Dubos, Ralph Nader, Benjamin Spock, and even the beat poet Allen Ginsberg. At least one prominent figure, however, took a novel approach to the issues agitating students: Secretary of the Interior Walter Hickel traveled to the University of Alaska to speak, and there he announced that he would approve the construction of an 800–mile pipeline from the North Slope of that state to supply America's vast fleet of automobiles with a new supply of gasoline. In contrast, most Earth Day speakers called on the public to drive less, conserve more, and they questioned the automobile as they questioned a way of life based on maximizing the consumption of oil and other natural resources, on promoting private wealth and national prestige as the highest social goals.

President Richard Nixon, though no environmentalist himself and everywhere rebuffed in angling for a campus speaking opportunity, nonetheless called on citizens to make their peace with Mother Nature. Easy words from a man who was still waging a war in Southeast Asia, but the shift in official language coming out of Washington was nonetheless striking. The old imperialistic slogan that Carson had protested, "the conquest of nature," had suddenly gone hollow all over the country, even if many of the forces behind the words remained as strong as ever. In a mere quarter of a century the nation had raced from Alamogordo to Earth Day. A period that had begun with the demonstration of an awesome weapon to defend American freedom and empire, along with the consumer way of life, against evil regimes had rapidly arrived at the point where that same way of life had itself become the greatest danger. The danger to American life now lay within, requiring a new kind of defense.

In the aftermath of Earth Day environmentalists began to seek more and more alliances with other groups demanding cultural change—with feminists, some of whom insisted that women were more attuned to grasping ecological interdependencies than men; with ethical radicals who wanted to extend rights to animals, trees, and the rest of nature; and with advocates for the poor and powerless at home and abroad, who demanded protection from environmental damage and toxic dumping done by the rich and powerful. In 1972, when environmentalists from all over the world, official and nonofficial, assembled in Stockholm, Sweden, to survey the global situation, they faced the formidable task of learning to work together, across all the deep, historic barriers of class, language, ideology, and religion that separated them, in order to meet the new global problems of nuclear proliferation, overpopulation, overconsumption, industrial pollution, and resource exhaustion.

The first Earth Day and the Stockholm event, the first of a series of international environmental conferences, suggested to the American media that the decade of the seventies would become the "Age of Ecology." If the phrase suggested that everyone in the nation or world had accepted the message of ecologists like Carson and her political allies, then it was surely a joke. Even among the small circle of international scientists, there was no consensus on how bad the environmental crisis was, or even whether there was a crisis at all. Nonetheless, a new phase of civilization did seem to be appearing even if in a fitful, halting, and confused way. The covers of news magazines were now graced by a starkly beautiful image of Earth that had never been possible before: a photograph taken from an American spaceship showing a gleaming sphere dappled with green and brown continents, with wide expanses of deep-blue water and swirling white clouds. Earth, all nations could now see, was a single unique sphere of life surrounded by blackness. That lonely planet had in the postwar years become a small and fragile entity, more fragile than at any other time in human experience. Its thin film of life—humanity's sole means of survival—was far thinner and far more vulnerable than anyone had ever imagined. And that perception had now engendered a worldwide movement of political reform.

# The Future of
# the Global Environment

## Giulio Pontecorvo

> But man has such a predilection for systems and abstract
> deductions that he is ready to distort the truth intention-
> ally, he is ready to deny the evidence of his senses only to
> justify his logic.[1]

## Introduction: Time Horizons, Complexity, and Uncertainty

Soothsayers and their crystal balls are not all created equal. One may with
some reasonable degree of accuracy predict the course of a country's gross
domestic product (GDP) for the next six months or even a year. But when
we shift to geologic time horizons, the environment of the planet is so complex a phenomenon and the level of our uncertainty and lack of knowledge
about fundamental forces, both natural and human, is so high as to preclude us from making anything but relatively weak probability statements
about the future.[2] The more authoritative or definitive anyone's statements
about what was or what will be on a planetary scale, the more likely the air
is to be redolent with the scent of snake oil.

However uncertain the future may be, some taxonomy is still needed
to assist us in analyzing the future of the global environment. The first
step in this classification is to separate long-run (geologic time) events
from proximate ones, events that are likely to occur in the next half century or so. This distinction allows us to identify changes in the environment either with natural forces or with the impact of human activity. The

relationship between long-run natural forces and human activity can only be hinted at here (see n. 5).

This paper will first look briefly at the role of natural events affecting the global environment and then, in more detail, discuss two global problems: (1) population size, growth and its linkages to the level of income; and (2) global warming.

Today we are faced with a high level of uncertainty about the underlying forces that currently shape and have shaped the environment of the planet. Perhaps a reasonable analogy to our present level of knowledge about planetary environmental forces is that we are in a position similar to that of Leonardo, who in the fifteenth century could visualize the possibility of an airship but lacked the technology, ancillary knowledge, infrastructure, and materials required to make one, much less fly it.

Keeping this warning about the gaps in our knowledge and the uncertainty we face in mind, we will first probe the existing state of knowledge about developments over the geologic time horizon and then see what picture emerges of the past history of the environment of the planet. Let us further divide the historical evolution of the planet into two sets of forces: one, physical and chemical, another, biological. This division is a useful intellectual construct, but it is at best only partially accurate, because biological evolution is not independent of the other forces. The division does, however, allow us to distinguish between and comment on exogenous and endogenous events, a distinction that will be useful when we come to evaluate today's environmental concerns.

The environment of the planet is often referred to as fragile, a synonym for easily subject to change, but it is also possible to think of it as tough. Prior to the advent of any human impact on the environment, the planet was able to withstand countless exogenous and endogenous shocks. The earth came into being by the accretion of material (exogenous shocks) during the formation of the solar system. It has been buffeted by this process ever since. Currently the most debated exogenous event among the several mass extinctions of life in geologic time is the hypothesis that provides a rationale (the planetary impact of a large celestial object) for the demise of the dinosaurs at the end of the Cretaceous period sixty million years ago. If this hypothesis is correct, this event created a major environmental shift (cooling of the planet). The environment of the planet recovered from this shock. Our primitive mammalian ancestors who had lived among the dinosaurs for millions of years also survived the shock, but the dinosaurs did not.

Endogenously, geologically the planet is active; the continents drift, collide, and separate, earthquakes are ubiquitous, volcanism has a major impact on the atmosphere and land formation, key ocean currents shift, the surface is subject to periodic glaciation, etc. More generally, the physical/chemical environment of the planet is and always has been in flux. We only partially understand these processes and as yet have little ability to forecast, influence, and/or control these fundamental changes.[3]

Another way of looking at this evolutionary history is to imagine a planet that has over time experienced a variety of environmental regimes. Since many environmental regimes have existed, none of these regimes is "optimal" except to the life forms that happen to be dominant when a particular environmental regime is in place. Thus, in the broadest sense, Homo sapiens' current concern about the environment reduces to our attempting to keep in place one regime, a set of environmental conditions in preference to all the other environmental regimes that are potentially possible, many of which existed in the past. Note also that our current preference for the existing environment has important implications for the distribution of income and wealth among the people of the earth. This last point is a central political issue in our current struggle to preserve what is.

The biological history of the earth is equally complex. Scientists have provided a reexamination of a basic premise of evolutionary theory.[4] The new premise in contrast to a previous view of evolution as a continuous process is that biological change, biological evolution, is without teleology. Whether our arrival at our present state of consciousness of ourselves and of the world around us is a result of purely stochastic biological and physical/chemical conditions or of a set of fortunate coincidences is not yet known. But in either case there is very strong evidence against the idea of an evolutionary process that begins with the simplest life forms and marches continuously towards a pinnacle, Homo sapiens.[5]

This view of biological evolution and of the dramatic physical/chemical history of the planet suggests that there are many different paths that could have been taken by the evolution of life on earth or that may be taken in the future. To say this differently, given the complexity of the planet's physical/chemical and biological history, it would have been difficult if not impossible for a skilled observer from outer space to forecast at any time in the geologic past the current environment of the planet and the existence of humanity.

This idea of possible alternative paths that might have been taken by life on earth suggests a caveat; today we cannot tell which of the environmental policy alternatives that confront us is optimal, i.e., most likely to sustain the status quo or something close to it. If this is so, then flexibility and reversibility are desirable elements in all our thinking about the future and in our environmental policy decisions.

## Current Environmental Problems

When we reduce our time horizon from a geologic to a human scale, we can consider current environmental concerns. However, it is desirable to keep in mind that many of today's concerns are transitory and that, in the rush to right an obvious wrong, only partial solutions are considered, i.e., only the immediate issue is considered and not the full range of the impact of any environmental change. In economic terms, particularly at the policy level, we use partial equilibrium models not general equilibrium ones to assess and evaluate environmental problems.

For example, for many years the northwest Atlantic baby seal population had been subject to a particularly brutal kind of slaughter to obtain their skins. The practice was held up to public scrutiny. The government of Canada was subjected to pressure and the practice was stopped. However, this was done without consideration of the population dynamics of the seal herds, and once harvesting was stopped the seal populations increased. Since seals, among other organisms, eat capelin and cod, and capelin is a key food for northern cod, protection of the seals has impacted in some way (unknown) on the cod stocks.

Today, these northern Newfoundland cod stocks are in such desperate shape that the government of Canada has declared a moratorium on cod fishing within the EEZ (Extended Economic Zone) off Newfoundland. This action has unemployed almost 20,000 fishermen in Newfoundland and adversely affected the economic well-being of their families and local businesses. This example, one of many, suggests that specific environmental issues should not be considered sui generis but that they should be evaluated as part of a general equilibrium problem and that, as far as possible, the full range of consequences should be evaluated before any policy action is taken.

It is useful for the purposes of this paper to divide current environmental problems along the following lines:

This paper is limited to consideration of two global problems, and while there are legitimate questions about "overlap" (e.g., sea level rise has local impact), the distinction between global and regional or local is useful because it provides a basis for focusing our analysis on the key questions. Local and regional problems are more tractable and have smaller implications for humanity, and mistakes in policy are less costly to the entire human family (table 1).

Global problems include the size and rate of growth in the human population, global warming/sea level change, biodiversity, and the condition of the ozone layer. This categorization is general in that each problem covers a set of issues, e.g., biodiversity includes the problem of tropical

|                     | Global                                        | Local/Regional                                                              |
| ------------------- | --------------------------------------------- | --------------------------------------------------------------------------- |
| Theoretical Aspect  | Human population dynamics                      | Preconceived attitudes towards women and family planning                    |
|                     | General atmospheric models                    | Local sources of pollution                                                  |
| Applied Aspect      | Family planning programs                      | Technology available for reducing the number of births. Jobs for women      |
|                     | Impact of climatic change on agriculture, etc. | Localized famine                                                            |

Table 1 Current Environmental Problems: A Possible Classification

rain forests.[6] In this paper we limit our discussion to two global problems: the population problem and global warming. The other global issues are of course substantive in themselves. However, what is said here about the scientific uncertainty and economic, political, and social dimensions of the population and warming issues also applies to the other global issues we confront today and to those that may emerge in the future.

If we exclude "natural" environmental change over which we have very little if any control, the human population problem is the most important environmental problem confronting us. It represents the demand side of the current environmental crises, ceteris paribus, more people, more environmental stress. As Pogo so aptly put it, "we have met the enemy and he is us." The demands on the environment for sustenance and for maintaining living standards by the human population are responsible for environmental change throughout the world. The demand for arable land by Brazilian farmers encroaches on the rain forest. A similar demand in Africa threatens the wildlife habitat. The need for lumber for housing endangers species in the Pacific Northwest, and the demand for fish protein threatens the stocks of fish in the sea and so forth.

These demand side pressures on the environment can be alleviated, in varying degree, by changing production functions, by creating substitute products, and by establishing rigorous and expensive regulatory procedures. *But if population growth is unchecked all attempts at conservation will eventually collapse before the relentless pressure of the short-run human need to survive or to maintain the existing standard of living.*[7]

This last observation should lead into an extended discussion of "sustainability." However, the constraints on this brief paper preclude an extended digression on intergenerational equity. Suffice it to say that the sustained use of the resource endowment of the planet requires both a process of substitution among inputs in the production of GDP and technological advances that increase the efficiency of their use, a continuous metamorphosis of the capital stock on which the world's economy rests. How well we will protect the interests of future generations is uncertain, but here we stress only the need for reducing the rate of increase in the demand for the output from these resources.[8]

The impact of human beings on the planetary environment lies in the combination of the size of the world's population and the level of income this population enjoys. Thus, the population problem is a combination of the reproductive strategy that has evolved with our species (and our capacity and willingness to modify it) and the rate of growth of the world's economy (gross product). More formally we may specify the demand placed by human beings on the resource endowment of the planet, now and in the future, as the product of the number of people times the level of income. We may express this as follows: demand for environment services (DE) = number of people (P) times technology (T) (T = the production techniques used to produce GDP worldwide) or $DE = P \times T$.[9]

The equation is useful because it emphasizes that both the number of people and technology (techniques used to produce our standard of living) exert demands on the environment. Therefore, even if the world had zero or negative population growth, the stress on the environment could increase if global income rose and/or rose fast enough to offset the decline in human numbers. The equation also makes clear the two necessary conditions that we must address in order to reduce the stress imposed by the number of human beings and their human activity on the environment:

1. Every effort must be made to reduce the rate of population growth worldwide to zero and then to a negative value, i.e., the numbers of people on the earth should be reduced.
2. Given a constantly changing technology set, every effort that is cost effective, at each point in time, should be employed to change the techniques of production so that the creation of goods and services and their recycling will place the smallest possible demand on the environment. This latter condition is

continuous. As technology changes and productivity of capital and labor grows over time, a constant effort must be made to seek the least environmentally damaging alternative modes of production.

If we move from the obvious impact of the numbers of people and the level of income on the environment to population policy, we move into more difficult terrain. The importance of the population problem, the projected increase in human numbers from today's five billion individuals to ten billion in the next century, is broadly recognized by both individuals and governments. However, the determinants of human fertility remain elusive and vary from society (culture) to society. Since birth control first became a political issue in the early years of this century the question of how to achieve results, i.e., to reduce the rate of growth of the world's population, has gone through a number of phases or changes. Today recent work on this difficult problem provides us with a more complete analytical framework in which to think about the problem and work toward a solution.[10]

Poverty, inadequate or unavailable artificial means to prevent births, the position or role of women in society, vacillating government policies toward family planning, opposition from fundamentalists, the degraded condition of the environment and the associated resource base, the need for children, and the lack of interest or concern by public interest groups all are elements that in different cultures contribute in different ways to the level of fertility and population growth. Here let us emphasize three of these elements, the role of women, the technology of birth control, and the policies of governments and nongovernmental, environmental organizations (NGOs).

In developed western nations the political articulation of "feminism" may be viewed as an effort primarily by educated women to raise the value of the marginal product (economic value) of female labor in the market place, thereby, among other objectives, reducing the number of births. In the less developed world, which has the largest part of the world's population, women tend to be both uneducated and not employed outside the home. The evidence presented by Dasgupta (pp. 1888–89) suggests that the latter, providing employment for women outside the home, is the most important single social change required to reduce the birth rate. Unfortunately while internationally developed policies involving social change, specifically reduction of gender bias, and the gainful employment of women can be put forward as desirable goals for all societies, implementation of these goals is dependent on national and local political entities.

The two things that can be done on a global scale are investment in improving the technology of birth control, i.e., reducing cost, improving effectiveness and ease of use (a low-cost, high-return activity), and a consistent effort by western governments and NGOs to put population control at the top of their political and economic agendas and to further these agendas by worldwide educational efforts.

Calculation of the value of reduced numbers of people may be made, as indicated below, in purely economic terms, but the political and social dimensions of reduced numbers of people should not be ignored. Historically, individuals left Europe from 1500 on for the New World, in part, for the greater economic opportunity, social flexibility, and political freedom offered by a land with abundant resources and relatively few people, and therefore, a looser social structure. In a low population density environment, the marginal value of each individual may rise. On the other hand, extensive crowding of people together apparently has significant implications for social structures, the form and efficacy of governance, and individual human behavior.[11]

However, despite the obvious benefits from population control, the current state of the population problem is an excellent illustration of many of the difficulties involved in dealing with global environmental issues. The central role of population in all environmental problems is widely recognized. Compared with other global issues, e.g., global warming, biodiversity, ozone depletion, and the management of commercial fisheries, etc., the level of scientific uncertainty about a change in human reproductive strategy is relatively low, i.e., the medical implications of existing birth control techniques are reasonably well understood.

The professionals in the field emphasize the need for further research on new and improved low-cost birth control techniques. The investment required to achieve the new lower cost techniques is, by world standards, modest. Yet for the most part the private environmental groups focus their attention on marine mammals, "endangered species," preservation of wilderness areas, etc. If these private environmental groups would make population control their first priority, it would have a significant impact on the political aspects of the problem.

For political reasons which include fear of voter hostility and pressure from religious lobbies, government response in most developed states has ranged from being hesitant to being in a state of complete paralysis. This despite the understanding by world leaders that population growth is one of the key forces making for human hunger and political instability in the world.

Pharmaceutical companies which could reap significant profits by the manufacturing and distributing of more effective birth control techniques are prevented from doing so by the threat of economic boycott of the other products they make. The population problem presents the dilemma of our knowing what needs to be done without being able to do it. This case makes clear the difficulty in forecasting the state of the future environment of the planet. Today we are in a position where we could do more at low cost about the "P" term in $DE = P \times T$ and thereby reduce the stress on the environment. In an optimistic mood, one can assert that ultimately we will. But the question is when and to what degree?

Slow and hesitant steps will ultimately bring results, but is this sufficient to prevent significant damage to the global environment when the world's population is expected to increase from five to ten billion persons in the next half century? A bolder, more aggressive attack on the problem will produce large dividends in reducing stress on the environment and improve the chances for political stability, but unfortunately, our crystal ball cannot tell us which course the world will follow in the next half century.

The "T" term in our basic equation includes a variety of forces. Today, it represents the existing modes of production and the environmental stress produced, e.g., tons of carbon dioxide released into the atmosphere. In the future, it allows for modification of existing modes of production, such as the use of scrubbers in smokestacks that reduce the stress on the environment but may create in themselves a new set of problems. In this case changes in production will represent a trade-off between a reduction in the standard of living for a reduction in the stress on the environment—a choice that is difficult since it will involve political risks to those who opt to implement it.

The second option is to develop new technologies that are both efficient, in that they do not reduce the standard of living, and effective in eliminating or substantially reducing environmental stress, e.g., electric automobiles, solar and fusion power, etc. However, we have no reason to expect any quick technological fixes. These new technologies will take time to evolve, and we don't know if they will be energy efficient. For example, if all automobiles were electric and electric power generation was still primarily based on fossil fuels, would the power required to run the automobile fleet present a larger or smaller environmental problem than exists today?

Let us leave exotic technologies and return to the use of today's modes of production and see what they imply for global warming.[12] It is generally agreed, in an area where there is significant uncertainty and, therefore, significant disagreement on many issues, that the current heat budget—inflow vs. outflow of heat forcing radiative factors—of the planet will result in rising global temperature in the foreseeable future. There is also some but not complete agreement that the cause of the increase is an increase in the emission of so-called greenhouse gases, of which carbon dioxide is the most abundant.[13]

Starting from this point two questions arise: What can be done to reduce the quantity of carbon dioxide released into the atmosphere and therefore presumably to reduce the rate of increase in the global temperature? And what, if any, are the implications of warming for human society? Recall that on the geologic timescale the planet has gone through many periods of warming and cooling—the most recent period of cooling involving the last period of glaciation.

The problem of global warming as we conceptualize it today involves condensing this global process into a reduced form—a brief time interval during which we assume that human intervention, by increasing the supply of carbon dioxide and the other gases in the atmosphere, has caused global warming. And we assume further that if we change the degree of intervention, a different result will be achieved. This argument abstracts from any basic planetary forces that may be at work influencing what happens in ways we do not understand, e.g., how much carbon may be absorbed by the oceans, etc. The crystal ball gets cloudier. However, the elementary facts are clear: we have significantly increased the supply of carbon dioxide in the atmosphere, the planet is getting warmer, and it is within our power to reduce the carbon dioxide emissions. The question is, Should we do so, and, if we act to do so, what is the most efficient way to achieve a desired level of emission?[14]

The first part of the question has in fact been answered. The message from the "Earth Summit," the United Nations Conference on Environment and Development (UNCED) in Brazil in June 1992, made clear that reduction of greenhouse gases was a clear priority of the international body politic (although it was left to each nation as to how and to what degree it should proceed to reduce emissions). This basic decision to reduce emissions leaves us with the question of how to proceed. The answer is in part technical, but in much larger part it is economic and political; and it is in the economic and political arena that considerable progress is possible. Economists have argued for many years that incentives and appropriate taxes are more effective regulatory tools than mandated (command) reductions in emissions.[15] Economists have traditionally pointed out the importance of incentives in guiding economic behavior. This welfare argument rests on the assumption that markets and markets incentives are more, "efficient," i.e., that an existing level of output can be achieved at lower cost by the use of incentive and market forces rather than by command and control regulations.

Timing of the initial application of this general economic principle to problems of the environment is not clear. The issue was raised in an article by Thomas Crocker in 1966 and in a book by Dales in 1968.[16] Subsequently the idea was debated at several Organization for Economic Cooperation and Development (OECD) meetings in the early 1970s, and in 1983 New Zealand adopted a system of ITQs, (individual tradable quotas) for a new fishery. This approach has produced a large literature on "tradable quotas" but as yet the applications of the principle to either fisheries or point source air pollution have not been broad enough or continued over sufficient time to produce measurable changes in economic efficiency. However, this view has gained the upper hand, and in the United States a limited system of trading emissions quotas began in 1993.

In general, these economic incentive systems work as follows: For a given set of production units (e.g., public utility power plants) that cause pollution emissions at some level, say one million tons of carbon dioxide per unit of time, the authority mandates a fixed reduction to say 60 percent of the current level. Then each firm (plant) receives a quota to pollute equal to its share of the now allowable total emissions of 600,000 tons. Since some plants are more efficient, use newer and better technology, etc., they will not use their entire quota, which they may then sell to a less efficient plant. In this way the aggregate level of pollution, emission of carbon dioxide, is reduced, plants are encouraged to invest in the best equipment, and less efficient plants are not forced to rush into costly investment right away. If the authorities continue to reduce the total allowable level of pollution, the system ultimately leads to the minimum level of emissions that any future technology will yield.

Since it is partial not general, this system is not optimal.[17] However, it has the great advantage that it has been accepted—albeit grudgingly—by most of the environmental interest groups, the industry (certain public utilities), the financial community, and politicians. Supply side systems of this kind, combined with some level of taxation (carbon tax) to reduce demand, point to the possibility of significant reduction in the emission of greenhouse gases without too much economic dislocation, dislocation of the type that would occur by just mandating reduction in emissions for all emitting units regardless of their technological efficiency.

The remaining question is this: What is the time horizon over which this approach can have any significant impact on the warming process? Keep in mind that the assumption is that global warming results from a cumulative process and that reduction in emissions at the margin today will not stabilize the warming process for many years. An associated problem is that regardless of any policy changes that lower the level of emissions, significant warming will presumably still take place over roughly the next half century. What are the implications of global warming for human society?[18]

Here we have few guidelines as to what will occur. Some careful work has been done on world agriculture, but not in other areas; for instance, there is no similar analysis on the impact of global warming on the composition and growth rate of the biomass in the oceans. The available analysis of the impact of warming on agriculture focuses on the distribution of output world wide.[19] These results are extremely pessimistic, as they suggest the greatest impact on existing agricultural practices are in the tropical areas of the world where most of the world population lives. This will result in an increase in the proportion of the population at risk from hunger. These results by Rosenzweig et al. hold under different assumptions about the amount of warming, the rate of population growth, the rate of economic growth, and the degree of freedom of trade in basic food grains worldwide.

The distribution problem, in this instance, the greater loss of agricultural output in the more densely populated poorer countries, is a major political obstacle to any improvement in worldwide environmental management. Consider the following scenario: The developed states act to reduce the emission of greenhouse gases by changing technology and imposing use taxes that reduce the rate of growth in their standard of living. Despite this effort, the cumulative effects of emissions continue to warm the planet. This in turn results in ever increasing poverty and hunger in the third world. This results in increasing political instability in the LDCs (less developed countries) and the need for intervention to prevent hunger and stabilize the political situation, (e.g., Somalia, the Sudan, etc.). The cost of this intervention process is a further tax on the developed states.

Therefore, we need to consider how far the nations of the developed world will go in having their standards of living reduced to achieve political stability and to prevent starvation. At the moment there is neither a broad recognition of this possible scenario nor any suggestion of how to deal with it on the political agenda of the developed states.

## Conclusions and Policy Options

Any attempt to understand and influence the future of the global environment is confronted by a complex general equilibrium problem. There is uncertainty about the contours of the problem. While carbon dioxide is the most abundant greenhouse gas, others such as methane and water vapor, may play a key role in the warming process. And this uncertainty extends to the parameters of the other global problems—loss of biodiversity, depletion of the ozone layer, etc. We do not understand or more precisely, cannot measure the linkages between these global problems. For example, if the rate of population growth should fall to zero today, we would not be able to measure accurately the effect this change would have on the emission of greenhouse gases. That measurement would turn on the effects the change in the population growth rate would have on the rate of economic growth and on the technology that might be used in that growth. This would allow a number of possible scenarios to be written about the impact of the initial disturbance on the system.

Below the level of the general set of relationships between human beings, the background or geologic time environment, and today's environmental conditions lies another set of problems that have great significance for human society but are also cloaked in uncertainty. Based on what we know, any significant increase in global warming generated largely by the developed states of the northern hemisphere will have more than proportionate adverse effects on the population of the southern hemisphere. In other words, lurking in any environmental change are important distribution problems. This suggests that any change in climate will impact (in a materialistic sense in the distribution of the world's income) different people differently—according to their location on the face of the earth, how they make their living, the social structure of their society, etc.

In light of the uncertainty generated by the complexity of the problems and by the limits to our understanding, what positions can we take that will move this complex natural/human system in a positive direction? On the side of nature, we can, I believe, rule out with two exceptions most changes. Changes in the environment that take place gradually over thousands of years are changes that human society can adjust to. The onset of another period of glaciation, while extremely costly and destructive, could be accommodated over an extended time horizon. Any change that proceeds gradually over a 50–100 year time space allows economic forces to adjust to the new conditions. If the time horizon of the average investment is 10 years or less, clearly capital market forces will bring about reinvestment that will over time accommodate long-run environmental changes.

One of the two exceptions is the small but positive (greater than zero) probability of a collision between the earth and a sizable interstellar body. Of greater likelihood is the problem posed by the level of volcanism. Note that the eruption of one volcano in the Philippines in 1991 had an impact on the climate of the northern hemisphere (cooling). Any increase in volcanism is important and is a subject that should receive significant investment in science to gain greater understanding of the phenomenon and the ability to predict its occurrence. If in the short run there are only two primary sources of natural disturbance that have global significance, what can we do about human activity that will have a positive effect on the current environment?

Our crystal ball lights up and says that in the short run reduction in the rate of growth of human numbers will have the greatest impact on the environment. The technology to control this problem is at hand or can be obtained by modest investments, and the importance of employment for women will become widely recognized. It is up to humanity with its variety of institutions, governments, and nongovernmental organizations, to act on this problem. This will require governments to have the foresight and political courage required to deal with fundamentalist forces, and it will require nongovernment organizations to focus primarily on the population problem rather than on oil spills and spotted owls.

However, even if humanity revises its reproductive strategy, a strategy that has evolved over the last seven million–odd years, it will take more than half a century to stabilize the population at some level between five and ten billion people. As noted above, there is a time lag between the initiation of a policy, reduction in greenhouse gas emissions, and the stabilization of the chemical composition of the atmosphere. The extended time horizons required to achieve results present a policy problem. Since these time horizons extend well beyond the time in office of any elected leader, no political leader will be able to claim the benefits of greenhouse gas–reducing policies. Furthermore since these global problems are not perfectly defined as to benefits and costs, they are subject to tinkering and adjustment by governments as they move through time.[20] Therefore, consistency is a necessary condition for success in global environmental regulation. The goals adopted and the means to achieve them should be a continuing commitment by the entire body politic in the key nations. The need for this kind of commitment may be contrasted with the kind of public outcry that takes place if one beach is contaminated by an oil spill or by the presence of medical waste or when one creature on the endangered list becomes threatened.

The vision in our crystal ball, while clouded and imperfect, suggests the following "optimistic" view of the future. The population question (the demand side of environmental problems) will get increasing recognition, and the world's population will stabilize at less than ten billion persons and then begin to decline. Continuing efforts will be made to reduce the impact of the supply of contaminants (controlling emissions of greenhouse gases, etc.), and there will be a continuing willingness on the part of the developed states to respond to the world hunger problem. These efforts should lead to some kind of a stabilized environmental structure for the planet and a relatively stable world economy by the end of the twenty-second century.

The pessimists may write their own scenario.

# Notes

## Editors' Introduction

1. The International Commission on the History of Social Movements and Social Structures, headquartered in Paris, is an affiliate of the International Congress of Historical Sciences, the official coordinating body for historians and professional historical associations worldwide. The essays included in this volume were written for a research project sponsored by the commission. Two other volumes have grown out of earlier research projects sponsored by the commission. See Stuart Bruchey, ed., *Small Business in American Life* (New York: Columbia University Press, 1980); Joel Colton and Bruchey, eds., *Technology, the Economy, and Society: The American Experience* (New York: Columbia University Press, 1987).

2. Few historians today need to be convinced of the importance of these facets of culture—particularly memory—in the construction and representation of reality. The vast body of scholarship on historical memory produced over the past decade testifies mightily to this point. On the role of music in social movements, see Ron Eyerman and Andrew Jamison, *Music and Social Movements: Mobilizing Traditions in the Twentieth Century* (Cambridge and New York: Cambridge University Press, 1998).

3. *Second Treatise of Government,* in John Locke, *Two Treatises of Government,* ed. Thomas I. Cook (New York: Hafner, 1947), pp. 184, 191–92.

4. "The Defence of the Funding System," July 1795, in *The Papers of Alexander Hamilton,* ed. Harold C. Syrett, 26 vols. (New York: Columbia University Press, 1961–73), 19:47.

5. *The Works of John Adams, Second President of the United States . . .,* ed. Charles Francis Adams, 10 vols. (Boston: Charles C. Little and James Brown, 1851), 6:280. On the concern over property rights more generally in early modern America, see Stuart Bruchey, "The Impact of Concern for the Security of Property Rights on the Legal System of the Early American Republic," *Wisconsin Law Review* (1980): 1135–58.

6. The Madison quote is from an unsigned essay called "Property," which appeared in Philip Freneau's rabidly Republican *National Gazette* on March 29, 1792. The essay is reprinted in *The Papers of James Madison,* Congressional Series, ed. William T. Hutchinson et al., 17 vols. (Chicago and Charlottesville: University of Chicago Press and University Press of Virginia, 1962–91), 14:266–68. The other quote is from *Trop v. Dulles,* 356 U.S. 86, 102 (1958) (Warren, C. J.).

7. The literature on the origins, attributes, and social concomitants of capitalism is truly vast. For excellent introductions to the issues involved, see Robert L.

Heilbroner, *The Nature and Logic of Capitalism* (New York: W. W. Norton, 1985); Peter L. Berger, *The Capitalist Revolution: Fifty Propositions about Prosperity, Equality, and Liberty* (New York: Basic Books, 1986). For a broad overview of early capitalism and some of its effects, see Fernand Braudel, *Civilization and Capitalism 15th–18th Century*, 3 vols., trans. Sîan Reynolds (New York: Harper and Row, 1981–84).

8. These manifestations are, of course, commonly associated with the so-called liberal tradition of the West. Even after centuries of debate, scholarship on liberalism, both pro and con, continues to flourish. For recent defenses, see Stephen Macedo, *Liberal Virtues* (Oxford: Clarendon Press, 1990); David Johnston, *The Idea of a Liberal Theory: A Critique and Reconstruction* (Princeton: Princeton University Press, 1994). For more critical views of liberalism, particularly of the "hyperindividualism" said to be characteristic of liberalism today, see Mary Ann Glendon, *Rights Talk: The Impoverishment of Political Discourse* (New York: Free Press, 1991); Michael Piore, *Beyond Individualism* (Cambridge: Harvard University Press, 1995); Michael J. Sandel, *Democracy's Discontent: America in Search of a Public Philosophy* (Cambridge: Belknap Press of Harvard University Press, 1996). For recent balanced reassessments, see Jack Crittenden, *Beyond Individualism: Reconstituting the Liberal Self* (New York and Oxford: Oxford University Press, 1992); Sidney Tarrow, *Power in Movement: Social Movements, Collective Action and Politics* (Cambridge and New York: Cambridge University Press, 1994); John Gray, *Liberalism*, 2d ed. (Minneapolis: University of Minnesota Press, 1995); Ellen Frankel Paul, Fred D. Miller, Jr., and Jeffrey Paul, eds., *The Communitarian Challenge to Liberalism* (New York and Cambridge: Cambridge University Press, 1996); Patrick Neal, *Liberalism and Its Discontents* (New York: New York University Press, 1997).

It should be noted, of course, that liberalism in the West is an "umbrella" category sufficiently broad to cover contemporary theorists as diverse as John Rawls and Robert Nozick, both of whom legitimately can be called liberals. In this essay we follow this latitudinarian tradition and use the terms "liberal" and "liberalism" to distinguish mainstream Western value orientations in this period from those characteristic, let us say, in early modern Asia or Africa. We are less concerned to draw fine distinctions among related Western subtraditions derived primarily from natural rights philosophy, Christianity, civic humanism, etc. On the breadth of the liberal tradition, see Gray, *Liberalism*, pp. xi–xiii especially.

9. See Thomas L. Haskell, "Capitalism and the Origins of the Humanitarian Sensibility," *American Historical Review* 90 (April and June 1985): 339–61 and 547–66.

10. For introductions to the theoretical literature on social movements, see Rudolf Heberle, "Types and Functions of Social Movements," in *The International Encyclopedia of the Social Sciences*, ed. David L. Sills, 18 vols. (New York: Free Press, 1968–79), 14:438–44; Joseph R. Gusfield, "The Study of Social Movements," in *The International Encyclopedia of the Social Sciences*, 14:445–52; Aldon D. Morris and Carol McClurg Mueller, eds., *Frontiers in Social Movement Theory* (New Haven: Yale University Press, 1992); Robert D. Benford, "Social Movements," in the *Encyclopedia of Sociology*, ed. Edgar F. Borgatta and Marie L. Borgatta, 4 vols. (New York: Macmillan, 1992), 4:1880–87; Anthony Oberschall, *Social Movements: Ideologies, Interests, and Identities* (New Brunswick, N.J.: Transaction, 1993); Doug McAdam and David A. Snow, "Social Movements: Conceptual and Theoretical Issues," in *Social*

*Movements: Readings on Their Emergence, Mobilization, and Dynamics,* ed. McAdam and Snow (Los Angeles: Roxbury, 1997), pp. xviii–xxvi; James M. Jasper, *The Art of Moral Protest: Culture, Biography, and Creativity in Social Movements* (Chicago: University of Chicago Press, 1997), pp. 1–99 and passim.

11. On pro-slavery ideology in the nineteenth century, see the work of Eugene D. Genovese and Elizabeth Fox-Genovese.

12. On the shifting emphasis and constituencies of American liberalism, see Gary Gerstle, "The Protean Character of American Liberalism," *American Historical Review* 99 (October 1994): 1043–73.

13. This conclusion seems inescapable in a society that is home to "rights" groups ranging from NAAFA—the National Association to Advance Fat Acceptance—to NAMBLA—the National Man/Boy Love Association.

14. Francis Fukuyama, *The End of History and the Last Man* (New York: Free Press, 1992).

15. For an interesting recent account of one such cult, see Paul E. Johnson and Sean Wilentz, *The Kingdom of Matthias: A Story of Sex and Salvation in 19th-Century America* (New York: Oxford University Press, 1994).

16. See Lacy K. Ford, "Democracy in the United States: From Revolution to Civil War," in this volume, p. 29.

17. Ibid., p. 29.

18. See Mark A. Noll, "The Enlightenment and Evangelical Intellectual Life in the Nineteenth Century," in this volume, p. 49.

19. Ibid., p. 48. Also see Theodore Dwight Bozeman, *Protestants in an Age of Science: The Baconian Ideal and Antebellum American Religious Thought* (Chapel Hill: University of North Carolina Press, 1977), pp. 3–31 especially.

20. See Louis Henkin, "The International Human Rights Movement and the Human Rights Idea," in this volume, pp. 125.

21. For a devastating critique of contemporary "rights talk" in the United States, see Glendon, *Rights Talk: The Impoverishment of Political Discourse.*

## Responsibility, Convention, and the Role of Ideas in History

Parts of this essay draw on three previous essays of mine on humanitarianism and antislavery that first appeared in the *American Historical Review* between 1985 and 1987. Those essays now appear together with vigorously critical rejoinders by David Brion Davis and John Ashworth in *The Antislavery Debate: Capitalism and Abolitionism as a Problem in Historical Interpretation,* ed. Thomas Bender (Berkeley: University of California Press, 1992). Reviews of the Bender volume include Seymour Drescher, review of *The Antislavery Debate, History and Theory* 32 (1993): 311–29, and Morton J. Horwitz, "Reconstructing Historical Theory from the Debris of the Cold War," *Yale Law Journal* 102 (1993): 1287–92. An important comment on and extension of the argument appears in David Eltis, "Europeans and the Rise and Fall of African Slavery in the Americas: An Interpretation," *American Historical Review* 98 (December 1993): 1399–423. Another essay by Seymour Drescher, "The Long Goodbye: Dutch Capitalism and Antislavery in Comparative Perspective," *American Historical Review* 99 (February 1994): 44–69, is also relevant. I have received valuable advice about this essay—often taking the form of vigorous dissent from its conclusions—from Don Morrison, David Nirenberg, Larry Temkin, and Martin Wiener. What I say here has undoubtedly been influenced by all these critics and commentators, but of course they bear no responsibility for my views, and this essay is not meant as a response to any of them.

1. Quentin Skinner, "Meaning and Understanding in the History of Ideas," in *Meaning and Context: Quentin Skinner and His Critics,* ed. James Tully (Princeton: Princeton University Press, 1988), p. 67. This influential essay originally appeared in *History and Theory* 8 (1969): 3–53.

2. For an intriguing effort to convert this art of "reading between the lines" into a science of presuppositions—and call it "metaphysics"—see R. G. Collingwood, *An Essay on Metaphysics* (London: Oxford University Press, 1940), chaps. 4–7. The most revealing presuppositions of all are those that underwrite common sense. As Louis Mink, a careful reader of Collingwood, put it, "Nothing is more wonderful than common sense. The common sense of an age, we recognize when we compare that age with others, may well be for different times and places beyond the limits of comprehension or even of fantasy. A primary reason for this is that common sense of whatever age has presuppositions that derive not from universal human experience, but from a shared conceptual framework, which determines what shall count as experience for its communicants." Louis O. Mink, "Narrative Form as a Cognitive Instrument," in *The Writing of History: Literary Form and Human Understanding,* ed. R. H. Canary and H. Kozicki (Madison: University of Wisconsin Press, 1978), p. 129. Also published in Mink, *Historical Understanding,* ed. Brian Fay, Eugene O. Golob, and Richard T. Vann (Ithaca, N.Y.: Cornell University Press, 1987), pp. 182–203.

3. The label "history of ideas" is sometimes contrasted with "intellectual history" on the one hand and "cultural history" on the other. No such distinction is intended here. In the passage quoted at the head of the essay, Skinner uses "history of ideas" to stand indiscriminately for a variety of approaches, and for the sake of consistency I follow suit.

4. Hans-Georg Gadamer, *Truth and Method* (New York: Seabury, 1975), p. 245. The implications of Gadamer's position are spelled out in characteristically candid fashion by Stanley Fish, "Critical Self-Consciousness, or Can We Know What We're Doing?" in *Doing What Comes Naturally: Change, Rhetoric, and the Practice of Theory in Literary and Legal Studies* (Durham and London: Duke University Press, 1989), pp. 437–67.

5. Richard McKeon, "The Development and the Significance of the Concept of Responsibility," *Revue Internationale de Philosophie* 11 (1957): 6–8, 23. Relying on the *OED,* McKeon credits Alexander Hamilton with first use of the term (in *Federalist* 64) and dates it in 1787. In fact, Madison used the term in *Federalist* 63, which appeared in 1788. See Bernard Bailyn, comp., *The Debate on the Constitution* (New York: Library of America, 1993), pt. 2, p. 317.

6. Richard McKeon, "The Development and the Significance of the Concept of Responsibility," pp. 6–8, 23.

7. Skinner, "Conventions and the Understanding of Speech Acts," *Philosophical Quarterly* 20 (1970): 135, 137. Here and elsewhere, in quoting from this article, I have spelled out Skinner's shorthand notation. Thus instead of "S" and

"A," I use "Speaker" and "Audience." In place of t1 and t2 I use "time one" and "time two."

8. Ibid., p. 136.

9. Clifford Geertz, "Thick Description: Toward an Interpretive Theory of Culture," in *The Interpretation of Cultures: Selected Essays* (New York: Basic Books, 1973), pp. 5, 7, 12.

10. These obviously are far-reaching philosophical issues, but since the entire pragmatic tradition from Charles Pierce to Richard Rorty might be described as an effort to chart a middle path between the extremes of "History" and "Reason," perhaps I will be forgiven the parochialism of confining myself to a few recent North American texts: James T. Kloppenberg, *Uncertain Victory: Social Democracy and Progressivism in European and American Thought, 1870–1920* (New York: Oxford University Press, 1986); Robert B. Westbrook, *John Dewey and American Democracy* (Ithaca, N.Y., and London: Cornell University Press, 1991); Richard Rorty, *Philosophy and the Mirror of Nature* (Princeton: Princeton University Press, 1979); Richard J. Bernstein, *Beyond Objectivity and Relativism: Science, Hermeneutics and Praxis* (Philadelphia: University of Pennsylvania Press, 1988). For an uncritical embrace of contingency, see Barbara Herrnstein Smith, *Contingencies of Value: Alternative Perspectives for Critical Theory* (Cambridge: Harvard University Press, 1988). For excess in the opposite direction, see Allan Bloom, *The Closing of the American Mind: How Higher Education has Failed Democracy and Impoverished the Souls of Today's Students* (New York: Simon and Schuster, 1987). For unusually trenchant commentaries on these and related problems see David Hollinger, "How Wide the Circle of the 'We'? American Intellectuals and the Problem of the Ethnos since World War II," *American Historical Review* 98 (April 1993): 317–37; "Postethnic America," *Contentions* 2 (1992): 79–96. Also relevant is my own essay, "The Curious Persistence of Rights Talk in the 'Age of Interpretation,'" *Journal of American History* 74 (December 1987): 984–1012, also published in *The Constitution and American Life,* ed. David Thelen (Ithaca, N.Y., and London: Cornell University Press, 1988), pp. 324–52, and in Thomas L. Haskell, *Objectivity Is Not Neutrality: Explanatory Schemes in History* (Baltimore: Johns Hopkins University Press, 1998).

11. Friedrich Nietzsche, *On the Genealogy of Morals and Ecce Homo,* trans. Walter Kaufmann and R. J. Hollindale (New York: Random House, 1969), pp. 57–58. Italics in the original.

12. This is not to suggest that Nietzsche took causality at face value. On the contrary, he ultimately reduced it to "fear of the unfamiliar." For a useful discussion, see Walter Kaufmann, *Nietzsche,* 4th rev. ed. (Princeton: Princeton University Press, 1968), pp. 263–64.

13. Nietzsche, *On the Genealogy of Morals and Ecce Homo,* pp. 58–59. Italics in the original.

14. Ibid., pp. 67, 84, 59–60. Italics in the original.

15. Ibid., p. 85.

16. McKeon, "Concept of Responsibility," pp. 6–7; Nietzsche, *On the Genealogy of Morals and Ecce Homo,* pp. 95, 66, 62.

17. Max Weber, *The Protestant Ethic and the Spirit of Capitalism,* trans. Talcott Parsons (New York: Scribners, 1976), p. 154. For a fuller account of the implications of Weber's analysis for causal attribution and perceptions of responsibility, see my

essay "Persons as Uncaused Causes: John Stuart Mill, the Spirit of Capitalism, and the 'Invention' of Formalism," in *The Culture of the Market: Historical Essays,* ed. Thomas L. Haskell and Richard F. Teichgraeber III (Cambridge: Cambridge University Press, 1993), pp. 441–502. Also published in Haskell, *Objectivity Is Not Neutrality.*

18. To cite only the best known authority, and one who had no sympathy whatever with the evangelicals' project, see Edward P. Thompson, *The Making of the English Working Class* (New York: Knopf, 1963), chap. 11.

19. Roberto Calasso, *The Marriage of Cadmus and Harmony,* trans. Tim Parks (New York: Knopf, 1993), pp. 93–94. Italics in the original.

20. *Basic Writings of St. Thomas Aquinas,* ed. Anton Pegis (New York: Random House, 1945), 5:2, 121, 134.

21. Here I paraphrase Bernard Williams, *Shame and Necessity* (Berkeley: University of California Press, 1993), p. 77. His principal target is A. H. Adkins, *Merit and Responsibility: A Study in Greek Values* (Oxford: Oxford University Press, 1960).

22. Williams, *Shame and Necessity,* pp. 21, 33.

23. Ibid., p. 55.

24. Ibid., p. 56.

25. Ibid., p. 55.

26. Ibid., p. 4.

27. Ibid., pp. 123, 116.

28. Skinner stresses that the historian who tries to reconstruct the meaning of a text has not completed the job until the text is translated into terms intelligible to modern minds. Showing that the text is convention-governed is not enough. "It will be necessary, in short, if it is to be said that [the historian] has *understood* [the text] at all, that he should be capable of rendering into terms that make sense [by the standards of the present] of the meaning and force of [the author's] utterance [as understood by the author's contemporaries]." Skinner concedes that translation will sometimes prove to be impossible. Skinner, "Conventions and the Understanding of Speech Acts," pp. 136–37. Italics in the original.

29. Williams, *Shame and Necessity,* p. 117.

30. My puzzlement about Williams's distinction between "unjust" and "not just" may reflect nothing more than my inadequate socialization into a way of speaking conventional among philosophers, one that reserves the word "unjust" for remediable evils and rejects in principle the notion of natural or cosmic injustice. If so, my sole remaining difference with Williams is his failure to address the key *historical* question of why perceptions of necessity change, converting necessary evils into remediable ones. I am obliged to Larry Temkin for bringing this possibility to my attention.

31. Williams, *Shame and Necessity,* p. 7. My emphasis.

32. Ibid., pp. 124–25.

33. Bernard Williams, *Moral Luck* (Cambridge: Cambridge University Press, 1981), and Williams, *Ethics and the Limits of Philosophy* (Cambridge: Harvard University Press, 1985). In the latter volume, see especially chapter 10, "Morality, the Peculiar Institution."

34. J. L. Mackie, *The Cement of the Universe: A Study of Causation* (Oxford: Clarendon Press, 1974).

35. For a fuller development of this line of argument, see my "Capitalism and the Origins of the Humanitarian Sensibility [pts. 1 and 2]," originally published in the *American Historical Review* 90 (April and June 1985), also available in *The Antislavery Debate: Capitalism and Abolitionism as a Problem in Historical Interpretation*, ed. Thomas Bender (Berkeley: University of California Press, 1992), pp. 107–60, as well as Haskell, *Objectivity Is Not Neutrality*.

36. The point I am making about the unavoidable role of convention in judgments of responsibility parallels the illustration Geertz famously used to make his own point about the importance of "thick description" (which he, in turn, borrowed from philosopher Gilbert Ryle). A wink, Geertz observed, is much more than a twitch of the eye muscles, and any analyst who fails to grasp the difference—which resides not in the physical movement itself, but in the culturally defined meanings assigned to that event by a particular community—will be a very poor student of human affairs. In the case of the suffering earthquake victim, the corresponding error would be to lump together as if ethically indistinguishable all failures to render aid, whether by the victim's next door neighbors or by strangers living thousands of miles away. An analyst who appreciated the "thickness" of the conventions governing responsibility would not make this mistake, recognizing that not all who could, in principle, render aid are under equal obligations to do so. All of us who *could* go to the stranger's aid are, indeed, causally implicated in the prolongation of his suffering: it is undeniably true that *but for* our inaction, his suffering would be relieved. But only those of us falling within conventionally defined limits of proximity and ease of intervention will actually be vulnerable to allegations of irresponsibility. The conventions of responsibility always *and inevitably* fall short of much suffering that we could alleviate if we wanted to badly enough. Acknowledging convention's force does not prevent us from calling conventions morally wrong when they underestimate our real power to render aid.

37. Williams made a similar point when he likened the ancient attitude toward slavery to modern attitudes toward social injustices of a comparatively intractable kind: those about which we lack any remedy sufficiently familiar, "cost effective," and certain of success to justify confidence. The recent debacle of United Nations–sponsored humanitarian aid in Somalia might be taken as an example of misplaced confidence in our powers of intervention. Some would point to the absence of intervention in the Bosnian or Rwandan nightmares as examples of the opposite error. Williams's words, already quoted above, bear repeating here: "We recognise arbitrary and brutal ways in which people are handled by society, ways which are conditioned, often, by no more than exposure to luck. We have the intellectual resources to regard the situation of these people, and the systems that allow these things, as unjust, but are uncertain whether to do so, partly because we have seen the corruption and collapse of supposedly alternative systems, partly because we have no settled opinion on the question about which Aristotle tried to contrive a settled opinion, how far the existence of a worthwhile life for some people involves the imposition of suffering on others." *Shame and Necessity*, p. 125.

38. David Brion Davis, *The Problem of Slavery in Western Culture* (Ithaca, N.Y.: Cornell University Press, 1966).

39. Hans Jonas, *The Imperative of Responsibility: In Search of an Ethics for the Technological Age*, trans. Hans Jonas with the collaboration of David Herr (Chicago and London: University of Chicago Press, 1984), p. ix.

40. Alasdair MacIntyre, *After Virtue: A Study in Moral Theory,* 2d ed. (Notre Dame: University of Notre Dame Press, 1984), p. 10.

41. Jonas, *Imperative of Responsibility,* pp. 5–6.

42. Ibid., p. x.

43. Skinner, "Conventions and the Understanding of Speech Acts," pp. 137, 138.

## Democracy in the United States

1. Edmund S. Morgan, *Inventing the People: The Rise of Popular Sovereignty in England and America* (New York: W. W. Norton, 1988), pp. 237–306.

2. J. G. A. Pocock, *The Machiavellian Moment: Florentine Political Thought and the Atlantic Republican Tradition* (Princeton: Princeton University Press, 1975).

3. Gordon S. Wood, *The Creation of the American Republic 1776–1787* (Chapel Hill: University of North Carolina Press, 1969), especially pp. 162–96; Morgan, *Inventing the People,* pp. 157–73.

4. Chilton Williamson, *American Suffrage: From Property to Democracy, 1760–1860* (Princeton: Princeton University Press, 1960), pp. 117–299.

5. Merrill D. Peterson, ed., *Democracy, Liberty, and Property: The State Constitutional Conventions of the 1820's* (Indianapolis: Bobbs-Merrill, 1966), pp. 60–61.

6. Ibid. , pp. 65–66.

7. Ibid., p. 188.

8. Ibid., pp. 190–97.

9. Ibid., pp. 206–14.

10. Williamson, *American Suffrage,* pp. 224–35; William W. Freehling, *The Road to Disunion: Secessionists at Bay 1776–1854* (New York: Oxford University Press, 1990), pp. 162–77; Dickson D. Bruce, Jr., *The Rhetoric of Conservatism: The Virginia Convention of 1829–30 and the Conservative Tradition in the South* (San Marino, Calif.: Huntington Library Press, 1982.)

11. Peterson, *Democracy, Liberty, and Property,* p. 389.

12. Ibid., pp. 408–909.

13. Williamson, *American Suffrage,* pp. 242–80.

14. Leon F. Litwack, *North of Slavery: The Negro in the Free States 1790–1860* (Chicago: University of Chicago Press, 1961), pp. 74–93.

15. Peterson, *Democracy, Liberty, and Property,* pp. 217–19.

16. Ibid., p. 215.

17. Ibid., pp. 214–33.

18. Litwack, *North of Slavery,* p. 75.

19. Fletcher M. Green, "Cycles of American Democracy," *Mississippi Valley Historical Review* 48 (June 1961): 3–23.

20. Fletcher M. Green, *Constitutional Development in the South Atlantic States 1776–1860: A Study in the Evolution of Democracy* (Chapel Hill: University of North Carolina Press, 1930); Don E. Fehrenbacher, *Constitutions and Constitutionalism in the Slaveholding South* (Athens: University of Georgia Press, 1989), pp. 1–32.

21. Lacy K. Ford, Jr., *Origins of Southern Radicalism: The South Carolina Upcountry, 1800–1860* (New York: Oxford University Press, 1988), pp. 103–8.

22. Peterson, *Democracy, Liberty, and Property,* pp. 69–71.

23. Ibid., pp. 75–77.

24. Ibid., pp. 80–81.

25. Ibid., pp. 92–108.

26. Ibid., p. 289.

27. Ibid., pp. 307–31.

28. Ibid., pp. 332–37.

29. Ibid., pp. 355–56.

30. Ibid., pp. 360–64.

31. Green, *Constitutional Development,* pp. 210–24.

32. Ibid., p. 342.

33. Richard P. McCormick, *The Second American Party System: Party Formation in the Jacksonian Era* (Chapel Hill: University of North Carolina Press, 1966), especially pp. 329–56.

34. Ibid., p. 342.

35. For an overview, see Harry L. Watson, *Liberty and Power: The Politics of Jacksonian America* (New York: Hill and Wang, 1990).

36. Eric Foner, *Free Soil, Free Labor, Free Men: The Ideology of the Republican Party before the Civil War* (New York: Oxford University Press, 1971).

37. Richard N. Current et al., *The Political Thought of Abraham Lincoln* (Indianapolis: Bobbs-Merrill, 1967), p. 328.

38. See William E. Gienapp, *The Origins of the Republican Party, 1852–1856* (New York: Oxford University Press, 1987); J. Mills Thornton III, "The Ethic of Subsistence and the Origins of Southern Secession," *Tennessee Historical Quarterly* 48 (Summer 1989): 67–85.

39. Ellen Carol DuBois, *Feminism and Suffrage: The Emergence of an Independent Women's Movement in America, 1848–1869* (Ithaca, N.Y.: Cornell University Press, 1978), especially pp. 15–52.

40. Stanton quoted in DuBois, *Feminism and Suffrage,* p. 40.

41. Ibid., p. 41.

42. Louisa S. McCord, "Enfranchisement of Woman," *Southern Quarterly Review* 5 (April 1852): 322–41. This essay is reprinted in *All Clever Men, Who Make Their Way: Critical Discourse in the Old South,* ed. Michael O'Brien (Fayetteville: University of Arkansas Press, 1982), pp. 337–56.

43. Current, *Abraham Lincoln,* p. 326.

44. James M. McPherson, *Battle Cry of Freedom: The Civil War Era* (New York: Oxford University Press, 1988); J. Mills Thornton III, *Politics and Power in a Slave Society: Alabama 1800–1860* (Baton Rouge: Louisiana State University Press, 1978); Ford, *Origins of Southern Radicalism,* especially pp. 338–73.

45. Current, *Abraham Lincoln,* p. 105.

46. Ibid., pp. 293–94.

47. Eric Foner, *Reconstruction: America's Unfinished Revolution, 1863–1877* (New York: Harper and Row, 1988), pp. 251–61.

48. Ibid., pp. 444–49.

49. J. Morgan Kousser, *The Shaping of Southern Politics: Suffrage Restriction and the Establishment of the One-Party South, 1880–1910* (New Haven: Yale University Press, 1974).

## The Enlightenment and Evangelical Intellectual Life in the Nineteenth Century

For the purposes of this paper, the "nineteenth century" is construed generously to run from the Revolutionary period to the era of the First World War.

1. W. R. Ward, *The Protestant Evangelical Awakening* (New York: Cambridge University Press, 1992); Mark A. Noll, George A. Rawlyk, and David W. Bebbington, eds., *Evangelicalism: Comparative Studies on the Popular Protestantism of Great Britain, North America, and beyond, 1700–1990* (New York: Oxford University Press, 1994).

2. David W. Bebbington, *Evangelicalism in Modern Britain: A History from the 1730s to the 1980s* (London: Unwin Hyman, 1989), pp. 2–17.

3. Lawrence A. Cremin, *American Education: The National Experience, 1783–1876* (New York: Harper and Row, 1980), and Cremin, *American Education: The Metropolitan Experience, 1876–1980* (New York Harper and Row, 1988), pp. 17–126.

4. See D. G. Hart, "Faith and Learning in the Age of the University: The Academic Ministry of Daniel Coit Gilman," and Bradley J. Longfield, "'For God, for Country, and for Yale': Yale, Religion, and Higher Education between the World Wars," in *The Secularization of the Academy,* ed. George M. Marsden and Longfield (New York: Oxford University Press, 1992), pp. 107–45, 146–69.

5. James Bryce, *The American Commonwealth*, 3d ed., 2 vols. (New York: Macmillan, 1893), 2:706–7, 714–27; Andre Siegfried, *America Comes of Age: A French Analysis* (New York: Harcourt, Brace, 1927), pp. 33–37; and Philip Schaff, *America: A Sketch of Its Political, Social and Religious Character* (1855), ed. Perry G. Miller (Cambridge: Harvard University Press, 1961), pp. 104–44.

6. For some of the studies describing these matters, see Nathan O. Hatch, *The Democratization of American Christianity* (New Haven: Yale University Press, 1989); Robert M. Calhoon, *Evangelicals and Conservatives in the Early South 1740–1861* (Columbia: University of South Carolina Press, 1988); Larry E. Tise, *Proslavery: A History of the Defense of Slavery in America 1701–1840* (Athens: University of Georgia Press, 1987); Drew G. Faust, *A Sacred Circle: The Dilemma of the Intellectual in the Old South 1840–1860* (Philadelphia: University of Pennsylvania Press, 1986); Ray Allen Billington, *The Protestant Crusade 1800–1860* (New York: Macmillan, 1938); Conrad Cherry, ed., *God's New Israel: Religious Interpretations of American Destiny* (Englewood Cliffs, N.J.: Prentice Hall, 1971); and Milton B. Powell, ed., *The Voluntary Church: American Religious Life 1740–1860 Seen through the Eyes of European Visitors* (New York: Macmillan, 1967).

7. The argument in this section is expanded in Mark A. Noll, "The American Revolution and Protestant Evangelicalism," *Journal of Interdisciplinary History* 23 (Winter 1993): 615–38.

8. Henry F. May, *The Enlightenment in America* (New York: Oxford University Press, 1976). Similarly discriminating are D. H. Meyer, *The Democratic Enlightenment* (New York: G. P. Putnam's Sons, 1976); and J. R. Pole, "Enlightenment and the Politics of American Nature," in *The Enlightenment in National Context,* ed. R. Porter and M. Teich (Cambridge: Cambridge University Press, 1981), pp. 192–214.

9. Among the most helpful of many recent books are S. A. Grave, *The Scottish Philosophy of Common Sense* (Oxford: Clarendon Press, 1960); Richard B. Sher,

*Church and University in the Scottish Enlightenment: The Moderate Literati of Edinburgh* (Princeton: Princeton University Press, 1985); and Istvan Hont and Michael Ignatieff, eds., *Wealth and Virtue: The Shaping of Political Economy in the Scottish Enlightenment* (New York: Cambridge University Press, 1983). For brief but expert orientation, see Knud Haakonssen, "Scottish Common Sense Realism," in *A Companion to American Thought,* ed. Richard Wightman Fox and James T. Kloppenberg (Cambridge, Mass.: Blackwell, 1995), pp. 618–20.

10. Garry Wills, *Inventing America: Jefferson's Declaration of Independence* (Garden City, N.Y.: Doubleday, 1978); as modified by Ronald Hamowy, "Jefferson and the Scottish Enlightenment: A Critique of Garry Wills's *Inventing America,*" *William and Mary Quarterly* 36 (1979): 503–23; Roy Branson, "James Madison and the Scottish Enlightenment," *Journal of the History of Ideas* 40 (1979): 235–50; Herbert Hovenkamp, *Science and Religion in America 1800–1860* (Philadelphia: University of Pennsylvania Press, 1978); John C. Greene, *American Science in the Age of Jefferson* (Ames: Iowa State University Press, 1984), pp. 12–36, 411–12; and Terrence Martin, *The Instructed Vision: Scottish Common Sense Philosophy and the Origins of American Fiction* (Bloomington: University of Indiana Press, 1961).

11. The two most helpful general studies are Sydney E. Ahlstrom, "The Scottish Philosophy and American Theology," *Church History* 24 (1955): 257–72; and Theodore Dwight Bozeman, *Protestants in an Age of Science: The Baconian Ideal and Antebellum American Religious Thought* (Chapel Hill: University of North Carolina Press, 1977). For the colleges, see Daniel Walker Howe, *The Unitarian Conscience: Harvard Moral Philosophy 1805–1861* (Cambridge: Harvard University Press, 1970); Mark A. Noll, *Princeton and the Republic 1768–1822: The Search for a Christian Enlightenment in the Era of Samuel Stanhope Smith* (Princeton: Princeton University Press, 1989), pp. 36–43, 117–23, 188–91, 284–86; and for collegiate instruction generally, D. H. Meyer, *The Instructed Conscience: The Shaping of the American National Ethic* (Philadelphia: University of Pennsylvania Press, 1972). For the Scottish Enlightenment among southern Protestants, see E. Brooks Holifield, *The Gentlemen Theologians: American Theology in Southern Culture 1795–1860* (Durham, N.C.: Duke University Press, 1978), pp. 96–101, 110–54; and Fred J. Hood, *Reformed America: The Middle and Southern States 1783–1837* (University: University of Alabama Press, 1980), pp. 1–67, 88–112.

12. James Ward Smith, "Religion and Science in American Philosophy," in *The Shaping of American Religion,* ed. Smith and A. Leland Jamison (Princeton: Princeton University Press, 1961), pp. 414–16.

13. The argument on this repudiation in Norman Fiering, *Jonathan Edwards's Moral Thought and Its British Context* (Chapel Hill: University of North Carolina Press, 1981), has been modified slightly by Paul Ramsey, introduction, *The Works of Jonathan Edwards:* vol. 8, *Ethical Writings* (New Haven: Yale University Press, 1989), pp. 6–7, n. 5; 18, n. 3; and 29, nn. 5–6, to suggest that Edwards was not as directly addressing the Scottish moral philosophy of Francis Hutcheson as Fiering contended.

14. On the cultural importance of the Great Awakening, see Alan E. Heimert, *Religion and the American Mind from the Great Awakening to the Revolution* (Cambridge: Harvard University Press, 1966); and Rhys Isaac, *The Transformation of Virginia 1740–1790* (Chapel Hill: University of North Carolina Press, 1982), pp. 143–80.

15. John Witherspoon, "Ecclesiastical Characteristics" (1753), in *The Works of the Rev. John Witherspoon*, 4 vols. (Philadelphia: William W. Woodward, 1802), 3:229.

16. Historians have shied away from causal explanations for the rise of the Scottish philosophy in America. Perry Miller seemed to link it to the spread of revival, *The Life of the Mind in America from the Revolution to the Civil War* (New York: Harcourt, Brace, and World, 1965), pp. 3–95; and Lewis Perry simply notes that it was appealing because of "its avoidance of abstract dogma," *Intellectual Life in America: A History* (New York: Franklin Watts, 1984), p. 199. Early in this century I. Woodbridge Riley helpfully explored both "intrinsic" and "extrinsic" explanations for the rise of the Scottish philosophy, but his "extrinsic" reasons concerned mostly the intellectual usefulness of common sense realism for "educational and ecclesiastical orthodoxy," *American Philosophy: The Early Schools* (New York: Russell and Russell, 1958; orig. New York: Dodd, Mead, 1907), pp. 475–79.

17. Meyer, *The Democratic Enlightenment*, p. xxvi.

18. Hatch, *Democratization of American Christianity*, p. 6.

19. Norman Fiering, *Moral Philosophy at Seventeenth-Century Harvard: A Discipline in Transition* (Chapel Hill: University of North Carolina Press, 1981), p. 300.

20. For an overview, see Mark A. Noll, "Common Sense Traditions and American Evangelical Thought," *American Quarterly* 37 (Summer 1985): 216–38.

21. For a fine discussion of the intellectual background of the political founders, see Daniel Walker Howe, "The Political Psychology of *The Federalist*," *William and Mary Quarterly* 44 (1987): pp. 485–509.

22. Witherspoon, "Lectures on Moral Philosophy," *Works*, 3:369, 470. For Witherspoon's use of Hutcheson, see Jack Scott, ed., *An Annotated Edition of Lectures on Moral Philosophy by John Witherspoon* (Newark: University of Delaware Press, 1982), especially pp. 26–28.

23. Samuel Stanhope Smith, *An Essay on the Causes of the Variety of Complexion and Figure in the Human Species* (Philadelphia: Robert Aitkin, 1787), pp. 109–10.

24. See Hood, *Reformed America*, p. 1046, on the specific influence of Witherspoon and Smith in the South; and Robert M. Calhoon, *Evangelicals and Conservatives in the Early South 1740–1861*, p. 85: Witherspoon fashioned "a kind of secularized Calvinism that filled a real need in early national political culture."

25. Wilson Smith, *Professors and Public Ethics: Studies of Northern Moral Philosophers before the Civil War* (Ithaca, N.Y.: Cornell University Press, 1956); Howe, *Unitarian Conscience;* and Meyer, *The Instructed Conscience.*

26. Witherspoon, "Moral Philosophy," in *Works*, 3:368.

27. Wilson Smith, "William Paley's Theological Utilitarianism in America," *William and Mary Quarterly* 11 (1954): 402–24; and Bruce Kuklick, *Churchmen and Philosophers from Jonathan Edwards to John Dewey* (New Haven: Yale University Press, 1985), p. 53.

28. Sereno E. Dwight, "Memoir," in Timothy Dwight, *Theology Explained and Defended*, 4 vols. (New Haven: S. Converse, 1823), 1:22–23.

29. Bozeman, *Protestants in an Age of Science*, pp. 3–31.

30. For examples in divinity, see John Witherspoon, "Lectures on Divinity," *Works*, 4:22–75; Samuel Stanhope Smith, *A Comprehensive View of the Leading and Most Important Principles of Natural and Revealed Religion* (New Brunswick, N.J.: Deare

and Myer, 1815); Archibald Alexander, *A Brief Outline of the Evidences of the Christian Religion* (Princeton: D. A. Borrenstein, 1825); Nathaniel W. Taylor, *Lectures on the Moral Government of God*, 2 vols. (New York: Clark, Austin and Smith, 1859). For harmonizations with science, see Bozeman, *Protestants in an Age of Science*, pp. 71–159; Hovenkamp, *Science and Religion in America*.

31. Stanhope Smith, *Essay on Variety in the Human Species*, p. 3.

32. See Garry B. Nash, "The American Clergy and the French Revolution," *William and Mary Quarterly* 22 (July 1965): 402–4; and James H. Smylie, "Clerical Perspectives on Deism: Paine's *Age of Reason* in Virginia," *Eighteenth-Century Studies* 6 (1972–73): 203–20.

33. For a good discussion of "supernatural rationalism," see Kuklick, *Churchmen and Philosophers*, p. 87. On the harmonizations, see Ronald L. Numbers, *Creation by Natural Law: Laplace's Nebular Hypothesis in American Thought* (Seattle: University of Washington Press, 1977), pp. 55–66; Bozeman, *Protestants in an Age of Science*, pp. 96–97; and Hovenkamp, *Science and Religion in America*, pp. 119–46.

34. Elias Boudinot, *The Age of Revelation: Or the Age of Reason Shewn to Be an Age of Infidelity* (Philadelphia: Asbury Dickens, 1801), p. 30.

35. Dwight, *Theology Explained and Defended*, 4 vols. (New Haven, 1825), 4:55, 260–61, as quoted in George M. Marsden, "Everyone One's Own Interpreter? The Bible, Science, and Authority in Mid-Nineteenth-Century America," in *The Bible in America*, ed. Nathan O. Hatch and Mark A. Noll (New York: Oxford University Press, 1982), p. 85.

36. N. W. Taylor, undocumented quotation in William G. McLoughlin, *Revivals, Awakenings, and Reform* (Chicago: University of Chicago Press, 1978), p. 119.

37. Archibald Alexander, "Theological Lectures, Nature and Evidence of Truth" (1812ff.), in *The Princeton Theology 1812–1921*, ed. Mark A. Noll (Grand Rapids: Baker, 1983), p. 65.

38. Kuklick, *Churchmen and Philosophers*, p. 222.

39. Joseph A. Conforti, *Samuel Hopkins and the New Divinity Movement* (Grand Rapids: Eerdmans, 1981), pp. 59–75; and Glenn Paul Anderson, "Joseph Bellamy (1719–1790): The Man and His Work" (Ph.D. diss., Boston University, 1971), pp. 737–48.

40. Robert L. Ferm, *A Colonial Pastor: Jonathan Edwards the Younger 1745–1801* (Grand Rapids: Eerdmans, 1976), pp. 55, 110–26; Timothy Dwight, *Theology, Explained and Defended* (Middletown, Conn., 1818), 1:407, 507, as quoted in Conrad C. Cherry, *Nature and Religious Imagination from Edwards to Bushnell* (Philadelphia: Fortress, 1980), p. 122.

41. Taylor, *Lectures on the Moral Government of God*, 1:382.

42. E. A. Park, "New England Theology," *Bibliotheca Sacra* 9 (1852): 191–92, 210.

43. Kuklick, *Churchmen and Philosophers*, p. 53.

44. Noll, ed., *The Princeton Theology*; Edward H. Madden and James E. Hamilton, *Freedom and Grace: The Life of Asa Mahan* (Metuchen, N.J.: Scarecrow, 1982); and Richard T. Hughes and C. Leonard Allen, *Illusions of Innocence: Protestant Primitivism in America 1630–1875* (Chicago: University of Chicago Press, 1988).

45. A good discussion of Enlightenment revivalism is in C. Leonard Allen, Richard T. Hughes, and Michael R. Weed, *The Worldly Church* (Abilene: ACU Press, 1988), pp. 27–31.

46. Charles G. Finney, *Lectures on Revivals of Religion* (1835), ed. William G. McLoughlin (Cambridge: Harvard University Press, 1960), p. 33.

47. Hatch, *Democratization of American Christianity*, p. 182; the quotation is from John W. Nevin.

48. Moses Stuart, *Commentary on Romans* (1832), p. 541, as quoted in John H. Giltner, *Moses Stuart: The Father of Biblical Science in America* (Atlanta: Scholars Press, 1988), p. 115.

49. Leonard Woods, as quoted in Hovenkamp, *Science and Religion in America,* p. 61; and Kuklick, *Churchmen and Philosophers,* p. 89.

50. Robert Breckinridge, quoted in Holifield, *Gentlemen Theologians,* p. 203.

51. Hodge, *Systematic Theology* (1872–73), 3 vols. (Grand Rapids: Eerdmans, n.d.), 1:10–11.

52. Hughes and Allen, *Illusions of Innocence,* p. 143.

53. Quoted in ibid., pp. 157, 161, 156.

54. See Nathan O. Hatch, *The Sacred Cause of Liberty: Republican Thought and the Millennium in Revolutionary New England* (New Haven: Yale University Press, 1977); John F. Berens, "The Sanctification of American Nationalism," in *Providence and Patriotism in Early America 1640–1815* (Charlottesville: University Press of Virginia, 1978), pp. 112–28; and Ruth Bloch, *Visionary Republic: Millennial Themes in American Thought 1756–1800* (New York: Cambridge University Press, 1985).

55. For a trenchant expression of those differences, see Alexis de Tocqueville, *L'Ancien Regime et la revolution* (1967 ed.), pp. 252–53, as translated in Thomas L. Pangle, *The Spirit of Modern Republicanism: The Moral Vision of the American Founders and the Philosophy of Locke* (Chicago: University of Chicago Press, 1988), p. 284, n. 8: "There is no country in the world where the boldest doctrines of the *philosophes* of the eighteenth century, in matters of politics, were more fully applied than in America; it was only the anti-religious doctrines that never were able to make headway."

56. The best account of this process is George M. Marsden, *The Soul of the American University: From Protestant Establishment to Established Nonbelief* (New York: Oxford University Press, 1994).

57. On this massive subject, the following offer expert orientation and important arguments: Laurence R. Veysey, *The Emergence of the American University* (Chicago: University of Chicago Press, 1965); Burton J. Bledstein, *The Culture of Professionalism: The Middle Class and the Development of Higher Education in America* (New York: Norton, 1976); Bruce Kuklick, *The Rise of American Philosophy: Cambridge, Massachusetts, 1860–1930* (New Haven: Yale University Press, 1977); and Alexandra Oleson and John Voss, eds., *The Organization of Knowledge in Modern America 1860–1920* (Baltimore: Johns Hopkins University Press, 1979).

58. William R. Hutchison, *The Modernist Impulse in American Protestantism* (Cambridge: Harvard University Press, 1976), especially pp. 87–94 on accommodations with the new science.

59. George M. Marsden, *Fundamentalism and American Culture: The Shaping of Twentieth-Century Evangelicalism 1870–1925* (New York: Oxford University Press, 1980), especially pp. 55–62 and 212–21 on the scientism of fundamentalists.

60. On the psychological and technological modernity of fundamentalism, see Douglas Frank, *Less than Conquerors: How Evangelicals Entered the Twentieth Century*

(Grand Rapids: Eerdmans, 1986); and Martin E. Marty, *Modern American Religion:* vol. 1, *The Irony of It All 1893–1919* (Chicago: University of Chicago Press, 1986), pp. 208–47.

61. A good account of this middle group is in Grant A. Wacker, "The Holy Spirit and the Spirit of the Age in American Protestantism, 1880–1910," *Journal of American History* 72 (1985): 45–62.

62. The following paragraphs rely heavily on the analysis of Jon H. Roberts, *Darwinism and the Divine in America: Protestant Intellectuals and Organic Evolution 1859–1900* (Madison: University of Wisconsin Press, 1988); as supplemented by James R. Moore, *The Post-Darwinian Controversies: A Study of the Protestant Struggle to Come to Terms with Darwinism in Great Britain and America 1870–1900* (Cambridge: Cambridge University Press, 1979); David N. Livingstone, *Darwin's Forgotten Defenders: The Encounter between Evangelical Theology and Evolutionary Thought* (Grand Rapids and Edinburgh: Eerdmans and Scottish Academic Press, 1987); and John C. Greene, *Darwin and the Modern World View* (Baton Rouge: Louisiana State University Press, 1961).

63. See especially Numbers, *Creation by Natural Law.*

64. See George M. Marsden, "Fundamentalism as an American Phenomenon: A Comparison with English Evangelicalism," *Church History* 46 (1977): 215–32.

65. On that consensus, see John D. Woodbridge, *Biblical Authority: A Critique of the Rogers-McKim Proposal* (Grand Rapids: Zondervan, 1982), as supplemented by Jack B. Rogers and Donald K. McKim, *The Authority and Interpretation of the Bible: An Historical Approach* (San Francisco: Harper and Row, 1979). The paragraphs that follow draw on Mark A. Noll, *Between Faith and Criticism: Evangelicals, Scholarship and the Bible,* 2d ed. (Grand Rapids: Baker, 1991), and Noll, "Review Essay: The Bible in America," *Journal of Biblical Literature* 106 (1987): 493–509.

66. Charles A. Briggs, "Critical Theories of the Sacred Scriptures in Relation to Their Inspiration," *Presbyterian Review* 2 (July 1881): 558; Henry Preserved Smith, "The Critical Theories of Julius Wellhausen," *Presbyterian Review* 3 (April 1882): 386; and Briggs, "Critical Theories," p. 557.

67. A. A. Hodge and Benjamin B. Warfield, "Inspiration," *Presbyterian Review* 2 (April 1881): 237; William Henry Green, "Professor W. Robertson Smith on the Pentateuch," *Presbyterian Review* 3 (January 1882): 111; Willis J. Beecher, "The Logical Methods of Professor Kuenen," *Presbyterian Review* 3 (October 1882): 706.

68. R. A. Torrey, *What the Bible Teaches* (Chicago: Fleming H. Revell, 1898), p. 1.

69. Robert Dick Wilson, *A Scientific Investigation of the Old Testament* (Philadelphia: Sunday School Times, 1926), pp. 6–7.

70. As quoted in William J. Hynes, *Shirley Jackson Case and the Chicago School* (Chico, Calif.: Scholars Press, 1981), p. 80.

71. Hynes, *Shirley Jackson Case,* p. 119.

## Ideas behind the Women's Movement

1. Betty Friedan, *The Feminine Mystique* (New York: Norton, 1963). The quotation is the title of chapter one.

2. Wollstonecraft quotations are from *A Vindication of the Rights of Woman,* ed. Miriam Brody (London: Penguin, 1992).

3. Ibid., p. 103.

4. Dorothy Dinnerstein, *The Mermaid and the Minotaur: Sexual Arrangements and Human Malaise* (New York: Harper and Row, 1976); Sara Ruddick, *Maternal Thinking: Toward a Politics of Peace* (Boston: Beacon Press, 1989).

5. Sarah Blaffer Hrdy, *The Woman That Never Evolved* (Cambridge: Harvard University Press, 1981).

6. Grimké, "Dress of Women," in Aileen S. Kraditor, ed., *Up from the Pedestal: Selected Writings in the History of American Feminism* (Chicago: Quadrangle Books, 1968), p. 122.

7. December 1, 1855, in Kraditor, *Up from the Pedestal,* pp. 125–26.

8. Ibid.

9. December 21, 1855, in ibid., p. 130.

10. See, for example, Mott's speech to the Fourteenth Annual Meeting of the American Anti-Slavery Society, New York, May 9, 1848, in *Lucretia Mott: Her Complete Speeches and Sermons,* ed. Dana Greene (New York: Edwin Mellen Press, 1980), pp.71–79.

11. Wollstonecraft, *A Vindication,* p. 174.

12. "Discourse on Woman, " delivered in Philadelphia, December 17, 1849, in *Lucretia Mott,* ed. Greene, pp. 143–62.

13. *Bitter Milk: Women and Teaching* (Amherst: University of Massachusetts Press, 1988), p. 8.

14. Susan Gorsky, *Femininity to Feminism: Women and Literature in the Nineteenth Century* (New York: Twayne, 1992), p. 17.

15. Gena Corea, *The Mother Machine: Reproductive Technologies from Artificial Insemination to Artificial Wombs* (New York: Harper and Row, 1985).

16. Wollstonecraft, *A Vindication,* p. 164.

17. Carol Gilligan, *In a Different Voice: Psychological Theory and Women's Development* (Cambridge: Harvard University Press, 1982).

18. Ruddick, *Maternal Thinking,* pp. 38–39.

19. Mary Wollstonecraft, *Mary, a Fiction, and The Wrongs of Woman* (1788; New York: Oxford University Press, 1976).

20. Susan Bordo, *Unbearable Weight: Feminism, Western Culture, and the Body* (Berkeley: University of California Press, 1993), p. 14.

21. Ibid., p. 72.

22. Ibid., p. 76.

## Ideas of the American Labor Movement, 1880–1950

1. Werner Sombart, *Why Is There No Socialism in the United States* (1906; White Plains, N.Y.: International Arts and Sciences Press, 1976); Louis Hartz, *The Liberal Tradition in America: An Interpretation of American Political Thought since the Revolution* (1991; New York: Harcourt, Brace, 1955); Marc Karson, *American Labor Unions and Politics, 1900–1918* (Carbondale, Ill.: Southern Illinois University Press, 1958); See also John H. M. Laslett and Seymour Martin Lipset, eds., *Failure of a Dream? Essays in the History of American Socialism* (Garden City, N.Y.: Anchor Press, 1974); Eric Foner, "Why Is There No Socialism in the United States," *History Workshop* 17 (Spring 1984): 57–80; and Michael Kazin, "Daniel Bell and the Agony

and Romance of the American Left," introduction to Daniel Bell, *Marxian Socialism in the United States* (1967; Ithaca, N.Y.: Cornell University Press, 1995).

2. Samuel Gompers, *Seventy Years of Life and Labor: An Autobiography*, ed. and intro. Nick Salvatore (Ithaca, N.Y.: ILR Press, 1984); Stuart Kaufman, *Samuel Gompers and the Origins of the American Federation of Labor, 1848–1896* (Westport, Conn.: Greenwood Press, 1973); Selig Perlman, *A History of Trade Unionism in the United States* (New York: Macmillan, 1922); Selig Perlman, *A Theory of the Labor Movement* (New York: Macmillan, 1928), pp. 154–233.

3. Leon Fink, "The New Labor History and the Powers of Historical Pessimism: Consensus, Hegemony, and the Case of the Knights of Labor," *Journal of American History* 75 (June 1988): 116; Melvyn Dubofsky, *We Shall Be All: A History of the Industrial Workers of the World* (New York: Quadrangle Books, 1969); Nick Salvatore, *Eugene V. Debs: Citizen and Socialist* (Urbana: University of Illinois Press, 1982); Herbert G. Gutman, *Work, Culture, and Society in Industrializing America: Essays in American Working-Class and Social History* (New York: Knopf, 1976); Herbert G. Gutman, *Power and Culture: Essays on the American Working Class*, ed. Ira Berlin (New York: Pantheon, 1987); Alan Dawley, *Class and Community: The Industrial Revolution in Lynn* (Cambridge, Mass.: Harvard University Press, 1976); Sean Wilentz, *Chants Democratic: New York City and the Rise of the American Working Class, 1788–1850* (New York: Oxford University Press, 1984); Bruce G. Laurie, *Working People of Philadelphia, 1800–1850* (Philadelphia: Temple University Press, 1980); Leon Fink, *Workingmen's Democracy: The Knights of Labor and American Politics* (Urbana: University of Illinois Press, 1983); John H. M. Laslett, *Labor and the Left: A Study of Socialist and Radical Influences in the American Labor Movement, 1881–1924* (New York: Basic Books, 1970).

4. David Montgomery, *The Fall of the House of Labor: The Workplace, the State, and American Labor Activism, 1865–1925* (Cambridge: Cambridge University Press, 1987).

5. David Montgomery, "Workers' Control of Machine Production in the Nineteenth Century," in Montgomery, *Workers' Control in America: Studies in the History of Work, Technology, and Labor Struggles* (New York: Cambridge University Press, 1979), pp. 9–31.

6. Herbert G. Gutman, "Protestantism and the American Labor Movement: The Christian Spirit in the Gilded Age," in Gutman, *Work, Culture, and Society*, pp. 79–117; Victor Greene, *The Slavic Community on Strike* (Notre Dame: University of Nortre Dame Press, 1968); Eric Foner, "Class, Ethnicity and Radicalism in the Gilded Age: The Land League and Irish America," *Marxist Perspectives* 2 (Summer 1978): 6–55; Gary Gerstle, *Working-Class Americanism: The Politics of Labor in a Textile City* (New York: Cambridge University Press, 1989).

7. J. G. A. Pocock, *The Machiavellian Moment: Florentine Political Thought and the Atlantic Republican Tradition* (Princeton: Princeton University Press, 1975); Bernard Bailyn, *The Ideological Origins of the American Revolution* (Cambridge, Mass.: Belknap Press of Harvard University Press, 1967); Gordon S. Wood, *The Creation of the American Republic, 1776–1787* (Chapel Hill: University of North Carolina Press, 1969); Rowland Berthoff, "Independence and Attachment, Virtue and Interest: From Republican Citizen to Free Enterpriser, 1787–1837," in *Uprooted Americans: Essays to Honor Oscar Handlin*, ed. Richard L. Bushman et al. (Boston: Little, Brown, 1979), pp. 95–124; Isaac Kramnick, *Republicanism and Bourgeois Radicalism: Political Ideology in Late Eighteenth-*

*Century England and America* (Ithaca, N.Y.: Cornell University Press, 1990); Joyce Appleby, *Liberalism and Republicanism in the Historical Imagination* (Cambridge, Mass.: Harvard University Press, 1992).

8. Sean Wilentz, "Against Exceptionalism: Class Consciousness and the American Labor Movement, 1790–1920," *International Labor and Working Class History* 26 (Fall 1984): 1–24.

9. For works in this vein, see ibid., as well as the citations in n. 3.

10. Richard Oestriecher, "Terence V. Powderly, the Knights of Labor, and Artisanal Republicanism," in *Labor Leaders in America,* ed. Melvyn Dubofsky and Warren Van Tine (Urbana: University of Illinois Press, 1987), pp. 30–61; Melvyn Dubofsky and Warren Van Tine, *John L. Lewis: A Biography* (New York: Quadrangle/New York Times Book Company, 1977).

11. Linda Kerber, *Women of the Republic: Intellect and Ideology in Revolutionary America* (Chapel Hill: University of North Carolina Press, 1980); Steven Hahn, *The Roots of Southern Populism: Yeoman Farmers and the Transformation of the Georgia Upcountry, 1850–1890* (New York: Oxford University Press, 1983); Fink, *Workingmen's Democracy.*

12. David R. Roediger, *The Wages of Whiteness: Race and the Making of the American Working Class* (New York: Verso, 1991); Alexander Saxton, *The Rise and Fall of the White Republic: Class Politics and Mass Culture in Nineteenth-Century America* (New York: Verso, 1990); Gwendolyn Mink, *Old Labor and New Immigrants in American Political Development: Union, Party, and State, 1875–1920* (Ithaca, N.Y.: Cornell University Press, 1986); Matthew Jacobson, *Becoming Caucasian: The Vicissitudes of Whiteness in American Politics and Culture* (Cambridge, Mass.: Harvard University Press, 1998); Kerber, *Women of the Republic;* Michael B. Katz, *In the Shadow of the Poorhouse: A Social History of Welfare in America* (New York: Basic Books, 1986).

13. For a summary of most of these conflicts, see Jeremy Brecher, *Strike!* (Boston: South End Books, 1972). See also Robert V. Bruce, *1877: Year of Violence* (Indianapolis: Bobbs-Merrill, 1959), on 1877; Bruce C. Nelson, *Beyond the Martyrs: A Social History of Chicago's Anarchists, 1870–1900* (New Brunswick, N.J.: Rutgers University Press, 1988), on 1886; Paul Krause, *The Battle for Homestead, 1880–1892: Politics, Culture and Steel* (Pittsburgh: University of Pittsburgh Press, 1992); Almont Lindsey, *The Pullman Strike: The Story of a Unique Experiment and of a Great Labor Upheaval* (Chicago: University of Chicago Press, 1942), and Salvatore, *Eugene V. Debs,* on the Pullman strike; J. Anthony Lukas, *Big Trouble: A Murder in a Small Western Town Sets Off a Struggle for the Soul of America* (New York: Simon & Schuster, 1997), on Coeur d'Alene; Graham Adams, *Age of Industrial Violence, 1910–1915: The Activities and Findings of the United States Commission on Industrial Relations* (New York: Columbia University Press, 1966). Robert Wiebe, *The Search for Order, 1877–1920* (1967; New York: Hill and Wang, 1992), discusses the fears that these conflicts generated among middle-class and elite groups of Americans.

14. Salvatore, *Eugene V. Debs;* Lukas, *Big Trouble;* Dubofsky, *We Shall Be All;* James R. Green, *Grass-Roots Socialism: Radical Movements in the Southwest, 1895–1943* (Baton Rouge: Louisiana State University Press, 1978); Elliott Shore, *Talkin' Socialism: J. A. Wayland and the Role of the Press in American Radicalism, 1890–1912* (Lawrence: University Press of Kansas, 1988); John L. Thomas, *Alternative America:*

*Henry George, Edward Bellamy, Henry Demarest Lloyd, and the Adversary Tradition* (Cambridge, Mass.: Belknap Press of Harvard University Press, 1983); Dorothy Ross, *The Origins of American Social Science* (New York: Cambridge University Press, 1991); Ronald Steel, *Walter Lippmann and the American Century* (Boston: Little, Brown, 1990); Kathryn Kish Sklar, *Florence Kelley and the Nation's Work: The Rise of Women's Political Culture, 1830–1900* (New Haven: Yale University Press, 1995); Montgomery, *Fall of the House of Labor;* Alan Dawley, *Struggle for Justice: Social Responsibility and the Liberal State* (Cambridge, Mass.: Belknap Press of Harvard University Press, 1991); Thomas J. Knock, *To End All Wars: Woodrow Wilson and the Quest for a New World Order* (New York: Oxford University Press, 1992), pp. 15–30; James T. Kloppenberg, *Uncertain Victory: Social Democracy and Progressivism in European and American Thought, 1870–1920* (New York: Oxford University Press, 1986).

15. Salvatore, *Eugene V. Debs,* pp. 153–54.

16. Gerstle, *Working-Class Americanism,* pp. 5–15, 153–95; Maurice Isserman, *Which Side Were You On? The American Communist Party during the Second World War* (Middletown, Conn.: Wesleyan University Press, 1982).

17. Robert B. Westbrook, *John Dewey and American Democracy* (Ithaca, N.Y.: Cornell University Press, 1991); Sklar, *Florence Kelley;* Steven Fraser, *Labor Will Rule: Sidney Hillman and the Rise of American Labor* (New York: Free Press, 1991); Frederick Howe, *Confessions of a Reformer* (1925; New York: C. Scribner's Sons, 1967).

18. *Seattle Union Record,* June 21, 1921, quoted in Montgomery, *The Fall of the House of Labor,* p. 404.

19. Fraser, *Labor Will Rule,* pp. 114–77; Joseph A. McCartin, *Labor's Great War: The Struggle for Industrial Democracy and the Origins of Modern American Labor Relations, 1912–1921* (Chapel Hill: University of North Carolina Press, 1997); Gary Gerstle, "The Politics of Patriotism: Americanization and the Formation of the CIO," *Dissent* 33 (Winter 1986), 84–92; Howell John Harris, "Introduction: A Century of Industrial Democracy in America," in *Industrial Democracy in America: The Ambiguous Promise,* ed. Nelson Lichtenstein and Howell John Harris (Washington and New York: Woodrow Wilson Center Press; Cambridge University Press, 1993), 1–19; W. Jett Lauck, *Political and Industrial Democracy, 1776–1926* (New York: Funk and Wagnalls Co., 1926).

20. Joseph A. McCartin, "'An American Feeling': Workers, Managers, and the Struggle over Industrial Democracy in the World War Era," in *Industrial Democracy,* ed. Lichtenstein and Harris, p. 71; Lauck, *Political and Industrial Democracy, 1776–1926;* John L. Lewis, *The Miners' Fight for American Standards* (Indianapolis: Bell Publishing Co., 1925); Gerstle, "Politics of Patriotism," pp. 90–91.

21. Historians have been much more inclined to study the break with laissez-faire and the liberal embrace of government planning than to document and analyze the persistence of antistatism into the twentieth century; for glimpses of this latter force at work, consult John W. Chambers, *To Raise an Army: The Draft Comes to America* (New York: Free Press, 1987); Barry D. Karl, *The Uneasy State: The United States from 1915 to 1945* (Chicago: University of Chicago Press, 1983); Stephen Skowronek, *Building a New American State: The Expansion of National Administrative Capacities, 1877–1920* (New York: Cambridge University Press, 1982); James Patterson, *Congressional Conservatism and the New Deal: The Growth of the Conservative Coalition in Congress, 1933–1939* (Lexington: University Press of Kentucky, 1967); Christopher

L. Tomlins, *The State and the Unions: Labor Relations, Law, and the Organized Labor Movement in America, 1880–1960* (New York: Cambridge University Press, 1985).

22. Historians have also been slow to analyze the survival of proprietary individualism and a middle class grounded in ownership rather than white-collar employment. For glimpses, see Stuart M. Blumin, *The Emergence of the Middle Class: Social Experience in the American City, 1760–1900* (New York: Cambridge University Press, 1989); Philip Scranton, *Figured Tapestry: Production, Markets, and Power in Philadelphia Textiles, 1885–1941* (New York: Cambridge University Press, 1989); Scranton, *Endless Novelty: Specialty Production and American Industrialization, 1865–1925* (Princeton: Princeton University Press, 1997); and Martin J. Sklar, who, despite exaggerating this class's political decline, offers a fine portrait of it in *The Corporate Reconstruction of American Capitalism, 1890–1916: The Market, the Law, and Politics* (New York: Cambridge University Press, 1988). The proprietary middle class of the twentieth century awaits its historian.

23. On socialism's decline in these years, see James Weinstein, *The Decline of Socialism in America, 1912–1925* (1967; New Brunswick, N.J.: Monthly Review Press, 1984).

24. Nelson Lichtenstein, "Great Expectations: The Promise of Industrial Jurisprudence and Its Demise, 1930–1960," in *Industrial Democracy,* ed. Lichtenstein and Harris, p. 119.

25. Steven Fraser, "Dress Rehearsal for the New Deal: Shop-Floor Insurgents, Political Elites, and Industrial Democracy in the Amalgamated Clothing Workers," in *Working-Class America: Essays on Labor, Community, and American Society,* ed. Michael H. Frisch and Daniel J. Walkowitz (Urbana: University of Illinois Press, 1983), pp. 212–55; see also Fraser, *Labor Will Rule,* and David Brody, "Workplace Contractualism in Comparative Perspective," in *Industrial Democracy,* ed. Lichtenstein and Harris, pp. 176–205.

The constitutional order that Hillman and others wished to introduce to the workplace represented a bold modification of the democratic principles that undergirded nineteenth-century republicanism. Gone was the vision of a proprietary democracy, of a republic built on the civic-mindedness of independent producers. Labor activists now frankly recognized large corporations and the corresponding wage-earner status of the vast majority of American workers as accomplished facts. The republic would no longer depend on the virtue and morals of individual citizens—or on a widespread distribution of the means of production—but on complex group interactions among employers, workers, trade unions, and the state.

26. Lizabeth Cohen, *Making a New Deal: Industrial Workers in Chicago, 1919–1939* (New York: Cambridge University Press, 1990); Sanford M. Jacoby, *Employing Bureaucracy: Managers, Unions, and the Transformation of Work in American Industry, 1900–1945* (New York: Columbia University Press, 1985).

27. Lichtenstein, "Great Expectations."

28. On passage of NLRA, see James A. Gross, *The Making of the National Labor Relations Board: A Study in Economics, Politics, and Law,* 2 vols. (Albany: State University of New York Press, 1974–81); and Tomlins, *The State and the Unions;* Gerstle, *Working-Class Americanism,* 207–29.

29. Nelson Lichtenstein, *Labor's War at Home: The CIO in World War II* (New York: Cambridge University Press, 1982); Lichtenstein, *The Most Dangerous Man in Detroit:*

*Walter Reuther and the Fate of American Labor* (New York: Cambridge University Press, 1995); Howell John Harris, *The Right to Manage: Industrial Relations Policies of American Business in the 1940s* (Madison: University of Wisconsin Press, 1982).

30. Lichtenstein, "From Corporatism to Collective Bargaining: Organized Labor and the Eclipse of Social Democracy in the Postwar Era," in *The Rise and Fall of the New Deal Order, 1930–1980,* ed. Steve Fraser and Gary Gerstle (Princeton: Princeton University Press, 1989), pp. 22–52; Fraser, "The 'Labor Question,'" in *The Rise and Fall of the New Deal Order,* ed. Fraser and Gerstle, pp. 55–84; Ronald W. Schatz, "Philip Murray and the Subordination of the Industrial Unions to the United States Government," in *Labor Leaders in America,* ed. Dubofsky and Van Tine, pp. 234–57; Philip Murray and Morris Cooke, *Organized Labor and Production* (New York: Harper and Brothers, 1940); Clinton Golden and Harold Ruttenberg, *The Dynamics of Industrial Democracy* (New York: Harper and Brothers, 1942); Gerstle, *Working-Class Americanism,* pp. 177–87, 266–67.

31. See, for example, *The Public Papers and Addresses of Franklin D. Roosevelt* (New York: Random House, 1938; 1976 reprint), 5:230–36.

32. Fraser, "The 'Labor Question.'"

33. Ibid.; Lichtenstein, "From Corporatism to Collective Bargaining"; Alan Brinkley, *The End of Reform: The New Deal in Recession and War* (New York: Alfred A. Knopf, 1995); Melvyn Dubofsky, *The State and Labor in Modern America* (Chapel Hill: University of North Carolina Press, 1994).

34. George Lipsitz, *Rainbow at Midnight: Labor and Culture in the 1940s* (Urbana: University of Illinois Press, 1994); Robert H. Zieger, *The CIO, 1935–1955* (Chapel Hill: University of North Carolina Press, 1995); Bert Cochran, *Labor and Communism: The Conflict that Shaped American Unions* (Princeton: Princeton University Press, 1977); Steve Rosswurm, ed., *The CIO's Left-Led Unions* (New Brunswick, N.J.: Rutgers University Press, 1992).

35. Elizabeth Fones-Wolf, *Selling Free Enterprise: The Business Assault on Labor and Liberalism, 1945–1960* (Urbana: University of Illinois Press, 1994).

## From Child Labor to Child Work

This paper adapts and condenses materials from my book *Pricing the Priceless Child: The Changing Social Value of Children* (New York: Basic Books, 1985; reprint, Princeton: Princeton University Press, 1994). For further discussion of payments within families see my *The Social Meaning of Money* (Princeton: Princeton University Press, 1997) and "The Creation of Domestic Currencies," *American Economic Review Papers and Proceedings* 84 (May 1994): 138–42.

1. For child labor statistics, see *Children in Gainful Occupations at the Fourteenth Census of the United States* (Washington, D.C.: Government Printing Office, 1924); Grace Abbott, *The Child and the State* (Chicago: University of Chicago Press, 1938), 1:259–69; Raymond G. Fuller, "Child Labor," *International Encyclopedia of the Social Sciences* (1930), pp. 412–24.

2. A. J. McKelway, "The Awakening of the South against Child Labor," *Proceedings of the Third Annual Conference on Child Labor* (New York, 1907), p. 17.

3. Josephine J. Eschenbrenner, "What Is a Child Worth?" *National Child Labor Committee,* no. 236, 2.

4. Representative Sumners, cited in the *American Child* 6 (July 1924): 3.

5. Michael P. Haines, "Poverty, Economic Stress, and the Family in a Late Nineteenth-Century American City: Whites in Philadelphia, 1880," in *Philadelphia,* ed. Theodore Hershberg (New York: Oxford University Press, 1981), p. 265; Claudia Goldin, "Family Strategies and the Family Economy in the Late Nineteenth Century: The Role of Secondary Workers," in *Philadelphia,* ed. Theodore Hershberg, p. 284.

6. John Demos, *A Little Commonwealth* (New York: Oxford University Press, 1972), pp. 140–41. See also Edmund S. Morgan, *The Puritan Family* (New York: Harper and Row, 1966), p. 66; and Edith Abbott, "A Study of the Early History of Child Labor in America," *American Journal of Sociology* 14 (July 1908): 15–37.

7. On the effect of rising real income on the reduction of child labor, see Claudia Goldin, "Household and Market Production of Families in a Late Nineteenth-Century American City," *Explorations in Economic History* 16 (1979): 129. On the development of child labor and compulsory school legislation, see Forest Chester Ensign, "Compulsory School Attendance and Child Labor" (Ph.D. diss., Columbia University, 1921); and Miriam E. Loughran, *The Historical Development of Child-Labor Legislation in the United States* (Washington, D.C.: Catholic University of America Press, 1921).

8. Paul Osterman, *Getting Started: The Youth Labor Market* (Cambridge, Mass.: MIT Press, 1980). For Osterman, compulsory school legislation was the result, not the cause, of a changing youth labor market: "Since firms no longer required the labor of children and adolescents, those pressing for longer compulsory schooling were able to succeed. . . . On balance, as in so many other aspects of school-economy linkages, the schools were probably followers, not leaders" (pp. 60–61, 71). For additional economic explanations of the decline in child labor both in the United States and in nineteenth-century England, see Allen R. Sanderson, "Child Labor Legislation and the Labor Force Participation of Children," *Journal of Economic History* 34 (March 1974): 298–99; and Clark Nardinelli, "Child Labor and the Factory Acts," *Journal of Economic History* 40 (December 1980): 739–53.

9. *Niles' Register,* June 7, 1817, p. 226; Joan Huber, "Toward a Sociotechnological Theory of the Women's Movement," *Social Problems* 23 (April 1976): 371–88.

10. Osterman, *Getting Started,* pp. 56–59; Selwyn K. Troen, "The Discovery of the Adolescent by American Educational Reformers, 1900–1920," in *Schooling and Society,* ed. Lawrence Stone (Baltimore: Johns Hopkins University Press, 1976), pp. 239–51.

11. Elizabeth Fraser, "Children and Work," *Saturday Evening Post,* April 4, 1925, p. 145.

12. Letter to the *New York Chamber of Commerce Bulletin,* 16, no.5 (December 1924): 50, cited in Anne Kruesi Brown, "Opposition to the Child Labor Amendment Found in Trade Journals, Industrial Bulletins, and Other Publications for and by Business Men" (M.A. thesis, University of Chicago, 1937), pp. 35–36. See also "The Argument for Child Labor," *Literary Digest,* March 23, 1912, p. 595.

13. *Report on Condition of Woman and Child Wage-Earners in the United States,* (Washington, D.C.: Government Printing Office, 1910) 7:43; Mary Skinner, *Child Labor in New Jersey,* U.S. Department of Labor, Children's Bureau Publication 185 (Washington, D.C., 1928).

14. Viola I. Paradise, *Child Labor and the Work of Mothers in Oyster and Shrimp Canning Communities on the Gulf Coast,* U.S. Department of Labor, Children's Bureau Publication 98 (Washington, D.C., 1922), pp. 11, 17.

15. *Industrial Homework of Children,* U.S. Department of Labor, Children's Bureau Publication 100 (Washington, D.C., 1924), p. 23.

16. Marion Delcomyn, "Why Children Work," *Forum* 57 (March 1917): 324–25.

17. The Cost of Child Labor," *National Child Labor Committee* 5 (New York: 1905), 35.

18. Edward T. Devine, "The New View of the Child," *Annals of the American Academy* (July 1908): 9. Reformers, however, recognized the need to subsidize non-working children in families that could prove their financial need. In 1905, Child labor committees instituted a scholarship system in several cities to compensate needy families who kept a child in school with a weekly payment equivalent to the child's foregone income. Apparently, most scholarships went to the children of widowed or deserted women.

19. Raymond G. Fuller, "The Truth about Child Labor," *Good Housekeeping,* September 1922, p. 50.

20. Raymond G. Fuller, "Child Labor versus Children's Work," *American Child* 3 (February 1922): 281.

21. Fraser, "Children and Work," p. 145.

22. Raymond G. Fuller, *Child Labor and the Constitution* (New York: Thomas Y. Crowell, 1923), p. 76.

23. Edward N. Clopper, *Child Labor in City Streets* (New York: Garrett Press, 1970; reprint of 1912 ed. with new introduction), pp. 6–7.

24. "Children in Gainful Occupations," p. 16.

25. Fred Hall, *Forty Years, 1902–1942: The Work of the New York Child Labor Committee* (New York: New York Child Labor Committee, 1942), p. 89. No precise figures of the number of child homeworkers exist.

26. Jessie P. Rich, "Ideal Child Labor in the Home," *Child Labor Bulletin* 3 (May 1914): 8.

27. Arthur Hornblow, "The Children of the Stage," *Mumsey's Magazine,* October 1894, p. 33.

28. Francis Wilson, "The Child on the Stage," *Collier's,* May 21, 1910. Wilson (1854–1935) began his acting career at age seven. In 1913, he was named president of the newly formed Actor's Equity Association.

29. *Stage Children of America* (New York: Alliance for the Protection of Stage Children, 1911), p. 16.

30. F. Zeta Youmans, "Childhood, Inc.," *Survey,* July 25,1924, p. 462. The specific appeal of childhood meant that unlike other forms of labor, child acting did not replace adult work. Not surprisingly, while other labor unions opposed child labor, the Theatrical Stage Employees supported child acting. See "Stage Children of America," 20; and *Use of Children in Theatrical Productions,* 72d Congress, Hearing, Senate Committee on District of Columbia, United States Senate, March 15, 1932, pp.18–23.

31. McGill, *Child Workers on City Streets,* U.S. Department of Labor, Children's Bureau Publication 188 (Washington, D.C.,1928), p. 37; "The Lightning-Rod Agent," *American Child* 6 (October 1924): 7.

32. Lillian Davidson, "Idle Children," *Home Progress* 6 (June 1917): 474.

33. Ethel Packard Cook. "All Hands Help," *Parents' Magazine,* July 1934, p. 19.

34. Editorial, *Journal of Home Economics* 7 (August 1915): 372.

35. Gertrude E. Palmer, "Earnings, Spendings and Savings of School Children," *Commons* 8 (June 1903): 3–6. See also "The Child's Idea of Money," *New York Times,* February 10, 1899, p. 8. Benedict Burrell, "The Child and Money," *Harper's Bazaar,* November 3, 1900, p. 1721; "How Children Spend Their Money," *Harper's Bazaar,* July 1903, p. 682; and Edwin A. Kirkpatrick, *The Use of Money* (Indianapolis: Bobbs-Merrill, 1915).

36. Helen B. Seymour, "Money Matters with Young People," *Outlook,* September 23, 1893, p. 553.

37. Ibid.; Palmer, "Earnings, Spendings and Savings," p. 3.

38. Frances F. O'Donnell, "Every Child Needs an Allowance," *Parents' Magazine,* March 1930, p. 18.

39. Burrell, "The Child and Money," p. 1721.

40. Elliot, "Money and the Child's Own Standards of Living," p. 4.

41. Felix Adler, "Child Labor in the United States." Annual Meeting of the National Child Labor Committee, 1905, cited by Robert H. Bremner, *Children and Youth in America* (Cambridge: Harvard University Press, 1971), 2:653.

## The Rights of the Elderly as a Social Movement in the United States

This brief sketch draws heavily on the original researches of many scholars, some of whom are listed below.

1. Brian Gratton, "The New History of the Aged: A Critique," in *Old Age in a Bureaucratic Society: The Elderly, the Experts, and the State in American History,* ed. David Van Tassel and Peter N. Stearns (New York: Greenwood Press, 1986), pp. 6–14 and passim.

2. William Graebner, *A History of Retirement: The Meaning and Function of an American Institution, 1885–1978* (New Haven: Yale University Press, 1980), pp. 4–5, 10–17.

3. Gratton, "New History of the Aged," p. 10; Graebner, *History of Retirement,* p. 11.

4. Gratton, "New History of the Aged," p. 14 and passim.

5. Jill Quadagno, *The Transformation of Old Age Security: Class and Politics in the American Welfare State* (Chicago: University of Chicago Press, 1988), pp. 23–29; Gerald N. Grob, "Explaining Old Age History: The Need for Empiricism," in *Old Age,* ed. Van Tassel and Stearns, pp. 34–42.

6. Jill Quadagno, "The Transformation of Old Age Security," in *Old Age,* ed. Van Tassel and Stearns, pp. 138–39. Also see Theda Skocpol, *Protecting Soldiers and Mothers: The Political Origins of Social Policy in the United States* (Cambridge: Belknap Press of Harvard University Press, 1992).

7. Henry J. Pratt, *The Gray Lobby* (Chicago: University of Chicago Press, 1976), p. 11.

8. Quadagno, "Transformation of Old Age Security," pp. 142–44; Graebner, *History of Retirement,* p. 77; W. Andrew Achenbaum, "The Elderly's Social Security Entitlements as a Measure of Modern Life," in *Old Age,* ed. Van Tassel and Stearns, p. 162.

9. Pratt, *Gray Lobby,* p. 5.

10. Quadagno, "Transformation of Old Age Security," pp. 144–45.

11. The foregoing discussion draws heavily on Pratt, *Gray Lobby,* pp. 11–17.

12. Quadgano, "The Transformation of Old Age Security," p. 146.

13. Pratt, *Gray Lobby,* p. 17.

14. William Graebner, "A Comment: The Social Security Crisis in Perspective," in *Old Age,* ed. Van Tassel and Stearns, p. 219.

15. The foregoing discussion draws heavily on Pratt, *Gray Lobby,* especially pp. 15, 18–28, 42–47.

16. Quoted in Pratt, *Gray Lobby,* pp. 50, 53.

17. Quoted in Pratt, *Gray Lobby,* p. 50.

18. The foregoing discussion is particularly indebted to Pratt, *Gray Lobby,* especially pp. 56–92; Henry J. Pratt, "National Interest Groups among the Elderly: Consolidation and Constraint," in *Aging and Public Policy,* eds. William Browne and Laura K. Olson (Westport, Conn.: Greenwood Press, 1983), 157.

19. Henry J. Pratt, *Gray Agendas: Interest Groups and Public Pensions in Canada, Britain, and the United States* (Ann Arbor: University of Michigan Press, 1993), pp. 183–84; Christine L. Day, *What Older Americans Think: Interest Groups and Aging Policy* (Princeton: Princeton University Press, 1990), p. 27.

20. Pratt, *Gray Lobby,* pp. 87, 92–93.

21. Pratt, *Gray Lobby,* pp. 94–96.

22. Pratt, *Gray Lobby,* pp. 96–97.

23. Achenbaum, "The Elderly's Social Security Entitlements," pp. 163, 170–75.

24. Day, *What Older Americans Think,* pp. 35, 107–9; Pratt, *Gray Lobby,* p. 214.

# Why Become a Citizen?

1. Edward George Hartmann, *The Movement to Americanize the Immigrant* (New York: Columbia University Press, 1967), pp. 73, 102–4; John Higham, *Strangers in the Land: Patterns of American Nativism, 1860–1925* (New Brunswick, N.J.: Rutgers University Press, 1955); Elliot R. Barkan, "Whom Shall We Integrate? A Comparative Analysis of the Immigration and Naturalization Trends of Asians before and after the 1965 Immigration Act (1951–1978)," *Journal of American Ethnic History* 3 (1983): 30.

2. Dino Cinel, *From Italy to San Francisco: The Immigrant Experience* (Stanford: Stanford University Press, 1982), p. 248; Virginia Yans-McLaughlin, *Family and Community: Italian Immigrants in Buffalo, 1880–1930* (Ithaca, N.Y.: Cornell University Press, 1977), pp. 48–49. Support for naturalization by Italian American leaders is discussed in John W. Briggs, *An Italian Passage: Immigrants in Three American Cities, 1890–1930* (New Haven: Yale University Press, 1978), pp. 133–34.

3. Eva Morawska, *For Bread with Butter: The Life-Worlds of East Central Europeans in Johnstown, Pennsylvania, 1890–1940* (Cambridge: Cambridge University Press, 1985), pp. 170–71; Richard D. Alba, *Italian Americans: Into the Twilight of Ethnicity* (Englewood Cliffs, N.J.: Prentice-Hall, 1985), p. 54.

4. Judith E. Smith, *Family Connections: A History of Italian and Jewish Immigrant Lives in Providence, Rhode Island, 1900–1940* (Albany: State University of New York Press, 1985), p. 95.

5. William S. Bernard, "The Cultural Determinants of Naturalization," *American Sociological Review* 1 (1936): 943–53, demonstrated that naturalized citizens were those who had enjoyed social mobility and higher levels of schooling. Also see comments on this article in Alejandro Portes and Ruben Rumbaut, *Immigrant America: A Portrait* (Berkeley: University of California Press, 1990), p. 123.

6. The United States First District Court of Boston possessed a continuous series of naturalization applications for the first half of the twentieth century. The first district court was the principal clearinghouse for naturalization applications in the Boston metropolitan area. A sample of 1,230 successful applications from male and female immigrants arriving as adults (at least eighteen years old at arrival) was drawn from the series of petitions reviewed by the court from March 10, 1930, to June 30, 1930.

7. Those designated as "South Italians," under this system of classification of "peoples or races," were labeled in this study as "Italians," those designated "Hebrews" were labeled as "Jews," those designated "Irish" were labeled as "Irish," and those designated "English," "Scots," and "Welsh" were labeled as "British."

8. United States, *Statutes-at-Large*, vol. 34, chap. 3592, pp. 596–607.

9. Stephan Thernstrom, *The Other Bostonians: Poverty and Progress in the American Metropolis, 1880–1970* (Cambridge: Harvard University Press, 1973), chaps. 6–7.

10. Robert Mirak, *Torn between Two Lands* (Cambridge, Mass.: Distributed for the Department of Near Eastern Languages and Civilizations, Harvard University, by Harvard University Press, 1983), chap. 7; Theodore Saloutos, "Albanians" and "Greeks," in *Harvard Encyclopedia of American Ethnic Groups*, ed. Stephan Thernstrom (Cambridge: Harvard University Press, 1980), pp. 25, 432–33.

11. Bernard, "The Cultural Determinants of Naturalization"; Yans-McLaughlin, *Family and Community*, p. 49.

12. William S. Bernard, *American Immigration Policy* (New York: Harper, 1950), pp. 115–16; John Palmer Gavit, *Americans by Choice*, (Montclair, N.J.: Patterson Smith, 1971) pp. 253–54.

13. Milton Konvitz, *The Alien and the Asiatic in American Law* (Ithaca, N.Y.: Cornell University Press, 1946), chap. 6; Yans-McLaughlin, *Family and Community*, p. 49.

14. Thernstrom, *The Other Bostonians*, chaps. 6–7.

15. Yans-McLaughlin, *Family and Community*, pp. 95–100.

16. Joseph J. Barton, *Peasants and Strangers: Italians, Rumanians, and Slovaks in an American City* (Cambridge: Harvard University Press, 1975), pp. 53–54; Briggs, *An Italian Passage*, chap. 5; Cinel, *From Italy to San Francisco*, pp. 168–72; Donna R. Gabaccia, *From Sicily to Elizabeth Street: Housing and Social Change among Italian Immigrants, 1880–1930* (New York: State University of New York Press, 1984), pp. 58–59.

17. Dino Cinel, *The National Integration of Italian Return Migration, 1870–1929* (Cambridge: Cambridge University Press, 1991), p. 228.

18. Arthur Goren, "Jews," in *Harvard Encyclopedia of American Ethnic Groups*, ed. Thernstrom, p. 581; Stephen Steinberg, *The Ethnic Myth: Race, Ethnicity, and Class in America* (New York: Atheneum, 1981), p. 161.

19. Steinberg, *The Ethnic Myth,* pp. 163–64.
20. Cinel, *The National Integration of Italian Return Migration,* p. 228.
21. Smith, *Family Connections,* p. 196.

## The International Human Rights Movement and the Human Rights Idea

The following works have been useful in preparing this study: Jack Donnelly, *International Human Rights* (Boulder, Colo.: Westview Press, 1993); Ronald Dworkin, *Taking Rights Seriously* (Cambridge: Harvard University Press, 1977); Louis Henkin, *The Rights of Man Today* (Boulder, Colorado: Westview Press, 1978; rep., New York: Columbia University Center for the Study of Human Rights, 1988); Louis Henkin, *The Age of Rights* (New York: Columbia University Press, 1990); Myres S. McDougal, Harold D. Lasswell, and Lung-chu Chen, *Human Rights and World Public Order* (New Haven: Yale University Press, 1980); A. H. Robertson and J. G. Merrills, eds., *Human Rights in the World,* 4th ed. (Manchester and New York: Manchester University Press, 1996); R. J. Vincent, *Human Rights and International Relations* (Cambridge: Cambridge University Press, 1986); Morton Winston, ed. *The Philosophy of Human Rights* (Belmont, Calif.: Wadsworth, 1989).

## The Role of Ideas in the African-American Civil Rights Movement

1. Charles A. Lofgren, *The Plessy Case* (New York: Oxford University Press, 1987); Andrew Kull, *The Color-Blind Constitution* (Cambridge: Harvard University Press, 1992).
2. Albert P. Blaustein and Clarence Clyde Ferguson, Jr., *Desegregation and the Law,* 2d ed. (New York: Random House, 1962), pp. 158–79.
3. Hugh Davis Graham, "On Riots and Riot Commissions: Civil Disorders in the 1960s," *Public Historian* 2 (Summer 1980): 7–27.
4. Neil J. Smelser, *Theory of Collective Behavior* (New York: Free Press, 1963).
5. See Emil Lederer, *The State of the Masses* (New York: Norton, 1940); Karl Mannheim, *Man and Society in an Age of Reconstruction* (New York: Harcourt, Brace, 1940); Hannah Arendt, *Origins of Totalitarianism* (New York: Harcourt, Brace, 1951); William Kornhauser, *The Politics of Mass Society* (Glencoe: Free Press, 1959). A precursor was Ortega y Gasset, *The Revolt of the Masses* (New York: Norton, 1932), whose tradition was continued in the United States by longshoreman-philosopher Eric Hoffer in *The True Believer: Thoughts on the Nature of Mass Movements* (New York: Harper, 1951).
6. Anthony Oberschall, "Theories of Social Conflict," *Annual Review of Sociology* 4 (1978): 291–315.
7. J. Craig Jenkins, "Resource Mobilization Theory and the Study of Social Movements," *Annual Review of Sociology* 9 (1983): 527–53. See also Anthony Oberschall, *Social Conflict and Social Movements* (Englewood Cliffs, N.J.: Prentice-Hall, 1973); John D. McCarthy and Mayer N. Zald, "Resource Mobilization and

Social Movements: A Partial Theory," *American Journal of Sociology* 82 (1977) pp. 1212–41; and Francis Fox Piven and Richard A. Cloward, *Poor People's Movements: Why They Succeed, How They Fail* (New York: Vintage, 1979).

8. Mancur Olson, Jr., *The Logic of Collective Action* (New York: Schocken, 1968).

9. See generally Hugh Davis Graham, *The Civil Rights Era: Origins and Development of National Policy 1960–1972* (New York: Oxford University Press, 1990).

10. Morroe Berger, *Equality by Statute* (Garden City, N.Y.: Doubleday, 1952); Jack Greenberg, *Race Relations and American Law* (New York: Columbia University Press, 1952); Michael I. Sovern, *Legal Restraints on Racial Discrimination in Employment* (New York: Twentieth Century Fund, 1966).

11. Elizabeth Jacoway and David R. Colburn, eds., *Southern Businessmen and Desegregation* (Baton Rouge: Louisiana State University Press, 1982).

12. Numan Bartley and Hugh D. Graham, *Southern Politics and the Second Reconstruction* (Baltimore: Johns Hopkins University Press, 1975); Alexander P. Lamis, *The Two-Party South* (New York: Oxford University Press, 1984).

13. *Green v. County Board of New Kent County,* 391 U.S. 430 (1968); *Swann v. Charlotte-Mecklenburg Board of Education,* 402 U.S. 1 (1971); J. Harvie Wilkinson III, *From Brown to Bakke: The Supreme Court and School Integration 1954–1978* (New York: Oxford University Press, 1979).

14. Graham, *Civil Rights Era,* pp. 258–77. Significant enforcement authority was denied to the Department of Housing and Urban Development until the 1988 Fair Housing Amendments.

15. James W. Button, *Black Violence: Political Impact of the 1960s Riots* (Princeton: Princeton University Press, 1978).

16. *Report of the National Advisory Commission on Civil Disorders* (New York: Praeger, 1968).

17. In 1971 John Rawls provided a philosophical treatise to justify contractarian obligations for compensating benefits to society's least advantaged members in *A Theory of Justice* (Cambridge, Mass.: Belknap Press, 1971). On the eve of the *Bakke* decision, Ronald Dworkin published a defense of preferential treatment in *Taking Rights Seriously* (Cambridge: Harvard University Press, 1977), pp. 223–39.

18. *Public Papers of the Presidents: Lyndon B. Johnson, 1965* (Washington, D.C.: Government Printing Office, 1966), 2:636.

19. Louis L. Knowles and Kenneth Pruitt, eds., *Institutional Racism in America* (Englewood Cliffs, N.J.: Prentice-Hall, 1969); Joe R. Feagin and Clairece B. Feagin, *Discrimination American Style: Institutional Racism and Sexism* (Englewood Cliffs, N.J.: Prentice-Hall, 1978).

20. Wilkinson, *From Brown to Bakke,* pp. 108–18.

21. *Griggs v. Duke Power Company,* 401 U.S. 424 (1971); Donald L. Horowitz, *The Courts and Social Policy* (Washington, D.C.: Brookings Institution, 1977); Cass R. Sunstein, *After the Rights Revolution* (Cambridge: Harvard University Press, 1990).

22. John David Skrentny, *The Ironies of Affirmative Action* (Chicago: University of Chicago Press, 1996).

23. Nixon's reasons for backing the Labor Department's Philadelphia Plan not surprisingly included partisan motives, chiefly a desire to drive a wedge between organized labor and the black rights organizations, and to accelerate controversial

racial policies that would be associated in the public eye with the Great Society legislation of Lyndon Johnson and the Democratic left associated with George McGovern. More positively, Nixon also wished to force the inclusion of African Americans in the nation's skilled labor pool, and by fostering "black capitalism," to increase the stake of the black middle class in a stable social order. See Hugh Davis Graham, "Richard Nixon and Civil Rights: Exploring an Enigma," *Presidential Studies Quarterly* 26 (Winter 1996): 93–106.

24. *University of California Regents v. Bakke* 438 U.S. 265 (1978); *Kaiser Aluminum & Chemical Corp. v. Weber* 443 U.S. 193 (1979); *Fullilove v. Klutznick* 448 U.S. 448 (1980).

25. George H. Gallup, *The Gallup Poll: Public Opinion 1972–1977* (Wilmington, Del.: Scholarly Resources, 1978), 2:1059; Seymour Martin Lipset, "Equal Chances versus Equal Results," *Annals* 523 (September 1992): 66–69.

26. Jennifer L. Hochschild, *Facing Up to the American Dream: Race, Class, and the Soul of the Nation* (Princeton: Princeton University Press, 1995).

27. Press release, Latino National Political Survey, Washington, D.C., December 15, 1992.

28. Paul M. Sniderman and Thomas Piazza, *The Scar of Race* (Cambridge: Harvard University Press, 1993).

29. Most notably in racial classifications privileging minorities in contract set-aside programs: *City of Richmond v. J. A. Croson Co.,* 488 U.S. 469 (1989), and *Adarand Constructors v. Pena,* 115 S.Ct. 2097 (1995). In these rulings the conservative majority applied strict scrutiny to racial classifications, a standard developed by the Warren Court to invalidate segregation laws, but abandoned during the 1970s and 1980s in order to accommodate affirmative-action programs.

30. A prime example is housing, where federal regulators of mortgage finance since the New Deal fostered residential segregation and depressed values for African-American housing. These institutionalized racist policies, operating over the decades in a decentralized and racially hypersensitive housing market, effectively robbed African-American families of the prime nest egg available to most Americans: appreciation of the market value of their homes. The denial of home equity helps explain why the median family wealth of white Americans in 1990 was *eleven times* higher than that of black families. Douglas S. Massey and Nancy A. Denton, *American Apartheid: Segregation and the Making of the Underclass* (Cambridge: Harvard University Press, 1993); Gerald David Jaynes and Robin M. Williams, Jr., eds., *A Common Destiny: Blacks and American Society* (Washington, D.C.: National Academy Press, 1989), pp. 269–328.

31. Seymour Martin Lipset, *American Exceptionalism: A Double-Edged Sword* (New York: Norton, 1996), pp. 125–31.

32. Thomas Byrne Edsall, with Mary Edsall, *Chain Reaction: The Impact of Race, Rights, and Taxes on American Politics* (New York: Norton, 1992).

33. Byron E. Shafer and William J. M. Claggett, *The Two Majorities: The Issue Context of Modern American Politics* (Baltimore: Johns Hopkins University Press, 1995).

34. Paul M. Sniderman and Edward G. Carmines, *Reaching beyond Race* (Cambridge: Harvard University Press, 1997).

## Sentiments, Ideas, and Animals

1. For further details on animal protection movements in the United States, see James M. Jasper and Dorothy Nelkin, *The Animal Rights Crusade* (New York: Free Press, 1992).

2. The major traditions of recent social scientific explanations of social movements all tend to overlook the motivating power of ideas. Rational choice approaches such as Mancur Olson, Jr., *The Logic of Collective Action* (Cambridge: Harvard University Press, 1965), and Russell Hardin, *Collective Action* (Baltimore: Johns Hopkins University Press for Resources for the Future, 1982), tend to reduce human motivations to simple material interests and dismiss many others as "extrarational." Resource mobilization approaches such as Anthony Oberschall, *Social Conflict and Social Movements* (Englewood Cliffs, N.J., Prentice-Hall, 1973), and John McCarthy and Mayer Zald, "Resource Mobilization and Social Movements: A Partial Theory," *American Journal of Sociology* 82 (1977) pp. 1212–41, sometimes do the same, adding an analysis of the organizations that protectors form to pursue their interests. Political process approaches add the insight that groups must first fight to participate in the system: Charles Tilly, *From Mobilization to Revolution* (Reading, Mass.: Addison-Wesley, 1978), and Doug McAdam, *Political Process and the Development of Black Insurgency, 1930–1970* (Chicago: University of Chicago Press, 1982). In all these works, there is little recognition of the collective construction of interests and goals. For a critique, as well as an effort to bring in culture and emotions, see James M. Jasper, *The Art of Moral Protest: Culture, Biography, and Creativity in Social Movements* (Chicago: University of Chicago Press, 1998).

3. Norbert Elias, *The Civilizing Process* (New York: Pantheon, 1978). Increased awareness of individual feelings led both to more refined table manners and to a greater need for privacy. Servants who once had slept in the same room with their masters were now put in another wing or floor of the house; children were given their own rooms.

4. See Edward Shorter, *The Making of the Modern Family* (New York: Basic Books, 1975), and Viviana Zelizer, *Pricing the Priceless Child* (New York: Basic Books, 1985; Princeton: Princeton University Press, 1994).

5. Several historical works on uses of and attitudes toward domesticated animals in Western Europe include James Turner, *Reckoning with the Beast: Animals, Pain, and Humanity in the Victorian Mind* (Baltimore: Johns Hopkins University Press, 1980); Keith Thomas, *Man and the Natural World* (New York: Pantheon, 1983); Yi-Fu Tuan, *Dominance and Affection: The Making of Pets* (New Haven: Yale University Press, 1984); James Serpell, *In the Company of Animals* (New York: Basil Blackwell, 1986); and Harriet Ritvo, *The Animal Estate* (Cambridge: Harvard University Press, 1987).

6. Charles Darwin, *The Descent of Man and Selection in Relation to Sex* (1871; Princeton: Princeton University Press, 1981); Darwin, *The Expression of the Emotions in Man and Animals* (New York: D. Appleton, 1896); and George Louis Leclerc, comte de Buffon, *Natural History: General and Particular* (London: T. Cadell and W. Davies, 1812).

7. These are the official words of the Royal Society for the Prevention of Cruelty to Animals, quoted in Turner, *Reckoning with the Beast,* p. 55.

8. Popular works include Dorothy L. Cheney and Robert M. Seyfarth, *How Monkeys See the World* (Chicago: University of Chicago Press, 1990); Donald R. Griffin, *Animal Thinking* (Cambridge: Harvard University Press, 1984); Griffin, *Animal Minds* (Chicago: University of Chicago Press, 1992); R. J. Hoage and Larry Goldman, eds., *Animal Intelligence: Insights into the Animal Mind* (Washington, D.C.: Smithsonian Institution Press, 1986); Eugene Linden, *Apes, Men, and Language* (New York: Saturday Review Press, 1974); Linden, *Silent Partners: The Legacy of the Ape Language Experiments* (New York: Times Books, 1986); and Stephen F. Walker, *Animal Thought* (London: Routledge and Kegan Paul, 1983).

9. Peter Singer, *Animal Liberation* (New York: New York Review of Books Press, 1975). He had worked out many of these ideas in "Animal Liberation," *New York Review of Books,* April 5, 1973, and "All Animals Are Equal," *Philosophical Exchange* 1 (Summer 1974): 103–16.

10. Tom Regan, *The Case for Animal Rights* (Berkeley: University of California Press, 1983), p. 280. Also see Regan, "The Moral Basis of Vegetarianism," *Canadian Journal of Philosophy* 5 (1975): 181–214; and *All That Dwell Therein: Animal Rights and Environmental Ethics* (Berkeley: University of California Press, 1982).

11. For critiques of pet ownership, see George Cave, "Up from the Roots," *Between the Species* 4 (Summer 1988): 221–29; and Jim Mason, "For the Pleasure of Their Company," *The Animals' Voice* 3 (1990): 25–27.

12. Mary Anne Warren, "Difficulties with the Strong Animal Rights Position," *Between the Species* 2 (Fall 1986): 160–79; and Josephine Donovan, "Animal Rights and Feminist Theory," *Signs* 15 (1990): 350–75.

13. Alan Wolfe compares the mental capacities of human and nonhuman species in "Social Theory and the Second Biological Revolution," *Social Research* 57 (Fall 1990), concluding, "To a surprising degree, other animal species can communicate, choose between alternatives, manipulate signs, recognize themselves in mirrors, and follow rules that allow other species besides their own to live alongside them." But they lack "the capacity . . . to define for oneself what a rule might mean" (p. 631).

14. Mary Midgley, *Animals and Why They Matter* (Athens: University of Georgia Press, 1983).

15. See J. E. Lovelock, *Gaia: A New Look at Life on Earth* (New York: Oxford University Press, 1979).

16. See Christopher Stone, *Should Trees Have Standing?* (Los Altos, Calif.: William Kaufman, 1974), on the rights of trees. For similar arguments, see Christopher Stone, *Earth and Other Ethics* (New York: Harper and Row, 1987); Bill Devall and George Sessions, *Deep Ecology: Living As If Nature Mattered* (Salt Lake City: Gibbs M. Smith, 1985); Paul W. Taylor, *Respect for Nature* (Princeton: Princeton University Press, 1986); Mark Sagoff, *The Economy of the Earth* (Cambridge: Cambridge University Press, 1988); and J. Baird Callicott, *In Defense of the Land Ethic* (Albany: State University of New York Press, 1989).

17. Efforts by *The Animals' Agenda,* which changed its subtitle to "Helping Animals and the Earth," and by many individuals within the animal rights movement to build bridges to environmentalism have not succeeded.

## Fear and Redemption in the Environment Movement

1. Recent surveys of the environmental movement in the United States include Robert Gottlieb, *Forcing the Spring: The Transformation of the American Environment Movement* (Covelo, Calif.: Island Press, 1993); Samuel P. Hays, *Beauty, Health, and Permanence: Environmental Politics in the United States, 1955–1985* (New York: Cambridge University Press, 1987); Hal K. Rothman, *The Greening of a Nation? Environmentalism in the United States since 1945* (Fort Worth, Tex.: Harcourt, Brace, 1998); and Kirkpatrick Sale, *The Green Revolution: The American Environmental Movement, 1962–1992* (New York: Hill and Wang, 1993).

2. Robert Jungk, *Brighter than a Thousand Suns* (New York: Harcourt, Brace, 1958), pp. 196–202; Alice Kimball Smith, *A Peril and a Hope: The Scientists' Movement in America, 1945–47* (Chicago: University of Chicago Press, 1965). See also Donald Worster, *Nature's Economy: A History of Ecological Ideas,* 2d ed. (New York: Cambridge University Press, 1994), pt. 6.

3. Neal Hines, "Bikini Report," *Scientific Monthly* 72 (February 1951): 102–13; Richard Miller, *Under the Cloud: The Decades of Nuclear Testing* (New York: Free Press, 1986), pp. 75–79. The first shot, called Able, occurred on July 1, and the second, Baker, on July 25.

4. Philip L. Fradkin, *Fallout: An American Nuclear Tragedy* (Tucson: University of Arizona Press, 1989), chaps. 6–7.

5. "Biological Effects of Atomic Radiations," *Science* 123 (June 22, 1956): 1110–11. Representative of the popular press coverage of the issues are "Atomic Aftermath," *Newsweek,* June 25, 1956, p. 70; and "Atomic Radiation: The rs are coming," *Time,* June 25, 1956, pp. 64–65.

6. According to Donald Fleming, the catalyzing factor in Commoner's political involvement was a request by presidential candidate Adlai Stevenson in 1956 for information on fallout from atmospheric testing—"the first time a scientific issue had been introduced into a presidential campaign." See Fleming, "Roots of the New Conservation Movement," *Perspectives in American History* 6 (1972): 42.

7. Rachel Carson, *The Sea around Us* (New York: Oxford University Press, 1961; reprint, 1989), p. xi.

8. Rachel Carson, *Silent Spring* (Boston: Houghton Mifflin, 1962), pp. 8, 297.

9. For excellent discussions of Carson as a feminist, consult Vera Norwood, *Made from This Earth: American Women and Nature* (Chapel Hill: University of North Carolina Press, 1993), pp. 143–71; and H. Patricia Hynes, *The Recurring Silent Spring* (New York: Pergamon Press, 1989), pp. 180–215. For a general account of Carson's life and work, see Linda Lear, *Rachel Carson: Witness for Nature* (New York: Henry Holt and Co., 1997); and Paul Brooks, *The House of Life: Rachel Carson at Work* (Boston: Houghton Mifflin, 1972).

10. In 1967, a group of American scientists founded the Environmental Defense Fund, which, inspired by Carson, succeeded in getting DDT banned in 1972 as a threat to both human life and natural ecosystems. See Thomas R. Dunlap, *DDT: Scientists, Citizens, and Public Policy* (Princeton: Princeton University Press, 1981); and John Perkins, *Insects, Experts, and the Insecticide Crisis: The Quest for New Pest Management Strategies* (New York: Plenum Press, 1982), pp. 86–87.

11. "Environmentalism," *Encyclopaedia of the Social Sciences* (New York, 1931), 5:561.

12. Samuel Hays identifies the period after 1965 as a new phase in American environmental politics when pollution took its place alongside the older conservation concerns. See Hays, *Beauty, Health, and Permanence*, p. 55.

13. The Russian scientist Vladimir Vernadsky, a student of the relation of living organisms to geochemical cycles, was the first to develop the biosphere concept scientifically. He defined it as "that part of the atmosphere and surface of the earth where life exists." Kendall E. Bailes, *Science and Russian Culture in an Age of Revolutions: V. I. Vernadsky and His Scientific School, 1863–1945* (Bloomington: Indiana University Press, 1990), pp. 123–24.

14. Betty J. Meggers, "Environmental Limitation on the Development of Culture," *American Anthropologist* 56 (October 1954): 801–24; Julian H. Steward, *The Theory of Cultural Change* (Urbana: University of Illinois Press, 1955); Carl Ortwin Sauer, *Land and Life,* ed. John Leighly (Berkeley: University of California Press, 1963); Fairfield Osborn, *Our Plundered Planet* (Boston: Little, Brown, 1948); William Vogt, *Road to Survival* (New York: W. Sloane Associates, 1948); William L. Thomas, ed., *Man's Role in Changing the Face of the Earth* (Chicago: University of Chicago Press, 1956).

15. Paul B. Sears, "The Processes of Environmental Change by Man," in *Changing the Face of the Earth,* ed. Thomas, p. 471.

16. Frank Fraser Darling, *Wilderness and Plenty* (Boston: Houghton Mifflin, 1970), p. 54.

17. Paul R. Ehrlich, *The Population Bomb* (New York: Ballantine Books, 1968); Donella H. Meadows et al., The *Limits to Growth* (New York: Signet, 1972); Edward Goldsmith et al., *Blueprint for Survival* (New York: New American Library, 1972); and E. F. Schumacher, *Small Is Beautiful* (London: Blond & Briggs, 1973).

18. Barry Commoner, *The Closing Circle: Nature, Man, and Technology* (New York: Alfred A. Knopf, 1971), pp. 94, 200, 268. Commoner identified four basic laws of ecology, which became widely cited as the popular essence of the science: (1) Everything is connected to everything else; (2) Everything must go somewhere; (3) Nature knows best; and (4) There is no such thing as a free lunch (pp. 33–46).

19. U.S. public expenditures for pollution control rose from about $800 million in 1969 to $4.2 billion in 1975. *Environmental Quality: The Sixth Annual Report of the Council on Environmental Quality* (Washington, D.C., 1975), p. 527. Great Britain likewise increased its expenditures, and the results were notable: output of smoke fell from over 2 million metric tons in 1953 to 0.5 million in 1976. The mileage of unpolluted rivers went up from 14,603 in 1958 to 17,279 in 1972, an increase of 18 percent. See Eric Ashby, *Reconciling Man with the Environment* (Stanford, Calif.: Stanford University Press, 1978), pp. 6–7.

20. Michael McClosky, in *Ecotactics: The Sierra Club Handbook for Environmental Activists,* ed. John Mitchell and Constance Stallings (New York: Simon & Schuster, 1970), p. 11. William Ophuls, *Ecology and Politics of Scarcity Revisited: The Unravelling of the American Dream* (San Francisco: W. H. Freeman, 1977; 2d ed., New York: W. H. Freeman, 1992), p. 3.

21. "A Giant Step—or a Springtime Skip?" *Newsweek,* May 4, 1970, pp. 26–28. For other coverage see "The Dawning of Earth Day," *Time,* April 27, 1970, p. 46.

## The Future of the Global Environment

1. Fyodor M. Dostoyevsky, *Notes from Underground,* trans. C. Garnett (New York: Dell, 1960), p. 43.

2. As is true of all such generalizations there are exceptions, e.g., assuming no change in celestial mechanics, we can predict eclipses, the return of comets, the location of planetary bodies, etc., far into the future.

3. Our technological capability is approaching the point where we are able to prevent catastrophic collisions with other objects in space, e.g., asteroids, comets, etc. Whether we will have the political will to invest in this kind of planetary fire insurance remains an open question. Earthquake prediction is also moving forward with increasing possibilities for more accurate forecasts of time of occurrence.

4. For a readable account of this new hypothesis, see Steven Jay Gould, *Wonderful Life* (New York: Norton, 1989). Much of this discussion on human evolution is drawn from Gould. For greater detail, see Ernst Mayr, *Populations, Species and Evolution* [an abridgment of *Animal Species and Evolution*] (Cambridge: Belknap Press of Harvard University Press, 1970).

5. "A geological episode of unimaginable proportions, the formation of the rift played a vital role in the evolution of our species. In fact, it is possible that had the Gregory Rift not formed when and where it did, the human species might not have evolved at all ever." Richard Leakey and Roger Lewin, *Origins Reconsidered* (New York: Doubleday, 1992), p. 9. For an in-depth exploration of these linkages, see Steven Pinker, *How the Mind Works* (New York: W. W. Norton, 1997). To gain a hint of the controversy surrounding evolutionary psychology, see the exchange of letters between Gould and Pinker in the *New York Review of Books,* October 9, 1997, pp. 35–38.

6.The scientific uncertainty and complexity surrounding these global issues is illustrated by Anne M. Thompson, "The Oxidizing Capacity of the Earth's Atmosphere: Probable Past and Future Changes," *Science* 256 (May 22, 1992): 1157–63.

7. Forecasts of the rate of population growth have in the past been subject to substantial error. Today it appears that growth is slowing. The question is, Is the reduction fast enough?

8. For a readable account of the sustainability problem, see Robert Solow, *An Almost Practical Step toward Sustainability,* Fortieth Anniversary Lecture (Washington, D.C.: Resources for the Future, 1992).

9. This paper was written before the December 1997 meetings in Kyoto, Japan, on global warming. However, the key issue to be raised at that meeting involves a worldwide reduction of "greenhouse gases." The attempt to limit and/or reduce emissions into the atmosphere has caused heated political debate in the United States over "environmental drag." As noted in this paper, the inability to specify costs and benefits of actions taken to protect the environment contributes to the sound and fury of the debate, rather than to the clarification of the issues. Accordingly the Kyoto meetings will be just one step in a long political process. For a model of these negotiations recall the extended debate over the Law of the Sea Convention.

10. See Partha Dasgupta, "The Population Problem: Theory and Evidence," *Journal of Economic Literature* 33 (December 1995): 1879–902. The reader who is

interested in the population problem is urged to consult Dasgupta. This discussion of the determinants of human fertility draws on his contribution. For an exhaustive enumeration of alternative estimates of population growth, see Joel E. Cohen, *How Many People Can the Earth Support?* (New York: W. W. Norton, 1995). The rate of and kind of technological change that takes place influence the impact of population and income on resource use. Today technological change indicates an environmentally friendly bias. However, there is no adequate measure of the gain from this bias.

11. Any specific economic calculus of the benefit of a reduction in the number of births is subject to questions about the methodology employed and the scope of the study. However, while no one study can be definitive, collectively they indicate significant economic benefits from birth control, e.g., Enke and Zind estimate that the value of preventing the birth of a marginal infant is about twice an LDC's annual income per head. See S. Enke and R. Zind, "Effects of Fewer Births on Average Income," *Journal of Biosocial Science* 1 (1969): 41–55.

12. Two more technical papers the reader may wish to refer to are W. D. Nordhaus, "An Optimal Transition Path for Controlling Greenhouse Gases," *Science* 228 (November 1992): 1315–19; and C. Rosenzweig and M. L. Parry, "Potential Impact of Climate Change on World Food Supply," *Nature* 367 (1994): 133–38.

13. Greenhouse gases are carbon dioxide, methane, chlorofluorocarbons, nitrous oxide, and ozone. If these are emitted into or formed in the atmosphere in higher concentrations, they act to increase radiative forcing, increasing the heat budget of the planet. Note that some of the gases are long lived in the atmosphere so that even if emissions were reduced to zero today, the effects of previous emissions would continue well into the next century. Since what we can hope for is gradual reduction in emissions, the heat buildup will continue at least into the last half of the next century.

14. Scientific evidence is building that climatic change may be sudden and catastrophic, not incremental. This also applies to the behavior of ocean currents. If this current evidence is correct, it will cause us to rethink the whole climate change scenario on which the argument of this paper is based.

15. The key issue in moving from command and control regulation to market incentives is to have the market price reflect the full social cost of production. For a lucid explanation of why currently markets fail to do so, see Allen V. Kneese, "Industrial Ecology and 'Getting the Prices Right,'" *Resources*, Issue 130 (Winter 1998): 10–13. In the same issue, Jesse H. Ausubel, "Industrial Ecology: A Coming-of-Age Story," *Resources*, Issue 130 (Winter 1998): 14–16, provides a brief overview of the new field of industrial ecology.

16. Thomas Crocker, "The Structuring of an Atmospheric Pollution Control System," in *The Economics of Air Pollution*, ed. Harold Wolozin (New York: W. W. Norton, 1966); and J. H. Dales, *Pollution, Property, and Prices* (Toronto: University of Toronto Press, 1968).

17. For a general equilibrium approach that allows for technological change and population growth, and estimates an optimal path for emission reduction, see Nordhaus, "An Optimal Transition Path for Controlling Greenhouse Gases."

18. Most scientists assume an equilibrium four-degree Centigrade increase in average temperature with a range of two to four degrees.

19. See Rosenzweig and Parry, "Potential Impact of Climate Change on World Food Supply."

20. Note the changes in U.S. government policy on birth control from 1970 to 1993.

# Contributors

**Eleanor Bruchey** holds a Ph.D. in history from the Johns Hopkins University and a law degree from Columbia University. A former member of the New York Bar, she has served the last thirteen years providing legal services for the Eastern Agency on Aging in Bangor, Maine.

**Stuart Bruchey** is Allan Nevins Professor of History Emeritus at Columbia University and Libra Professor of History Emeritus at the University of Maine.

**Peter A. Coclanis** is George and Alice Welsh Professor of History at the University of North Carolina, Chapel Hill.

**Lacy K. Ford, Jr.** is a professor of history at the University of South Carolina.

**Gary Gerstle** is a member of the history department at the University of Maryland.

**Hugh Davis Graham** is Holland McTyeire Professor of History at Vanderbilt University.

**Thomas L. Haskell** is a professor of history at Rice University.

**Louis Henkin** is an emeritus professor at the Columbia University School of Law.

**James M. Jasper** writes about politics and culture. He lives in New York City.

**Ruth Nadelhaft** is an emeritus professor of English at the University of Maine.

**Mark A. Noll** is a professor of history at Wheaton College.

Contributors

**Giulio Pontecorvo** is an emeritus professor of economics at the Columbia Business School.

**Reed Ueda** is an associate professor of history at Tufts University.

**Donald Worster** is Hall Distinguished Professor of History at the University of Kansas.

**Viviana A. Zelizer** is a professor of sociology at Princeton University.

# Index